CHAPTER ONE

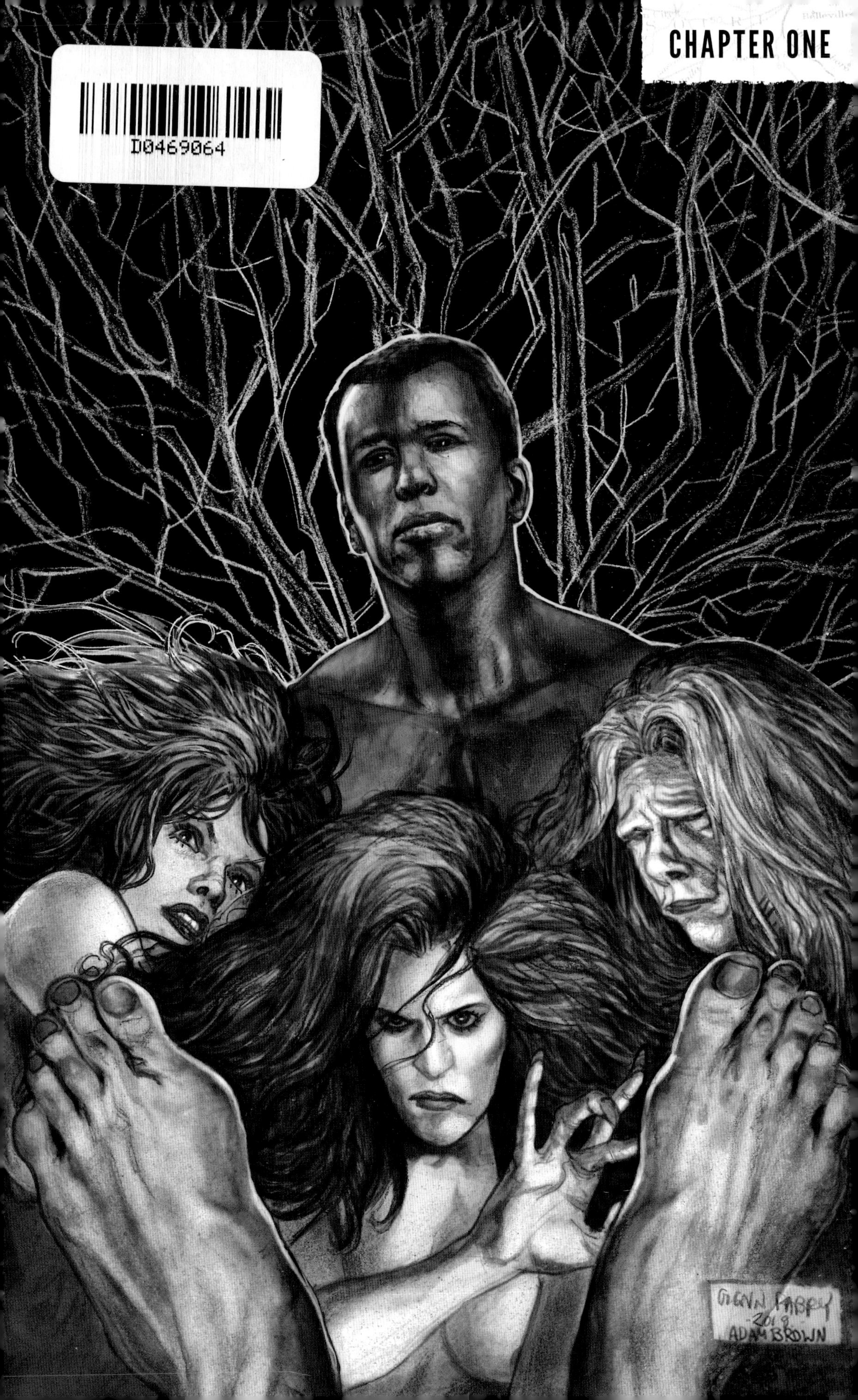
GLENN FABRY
-2018-
ADAM BROWN

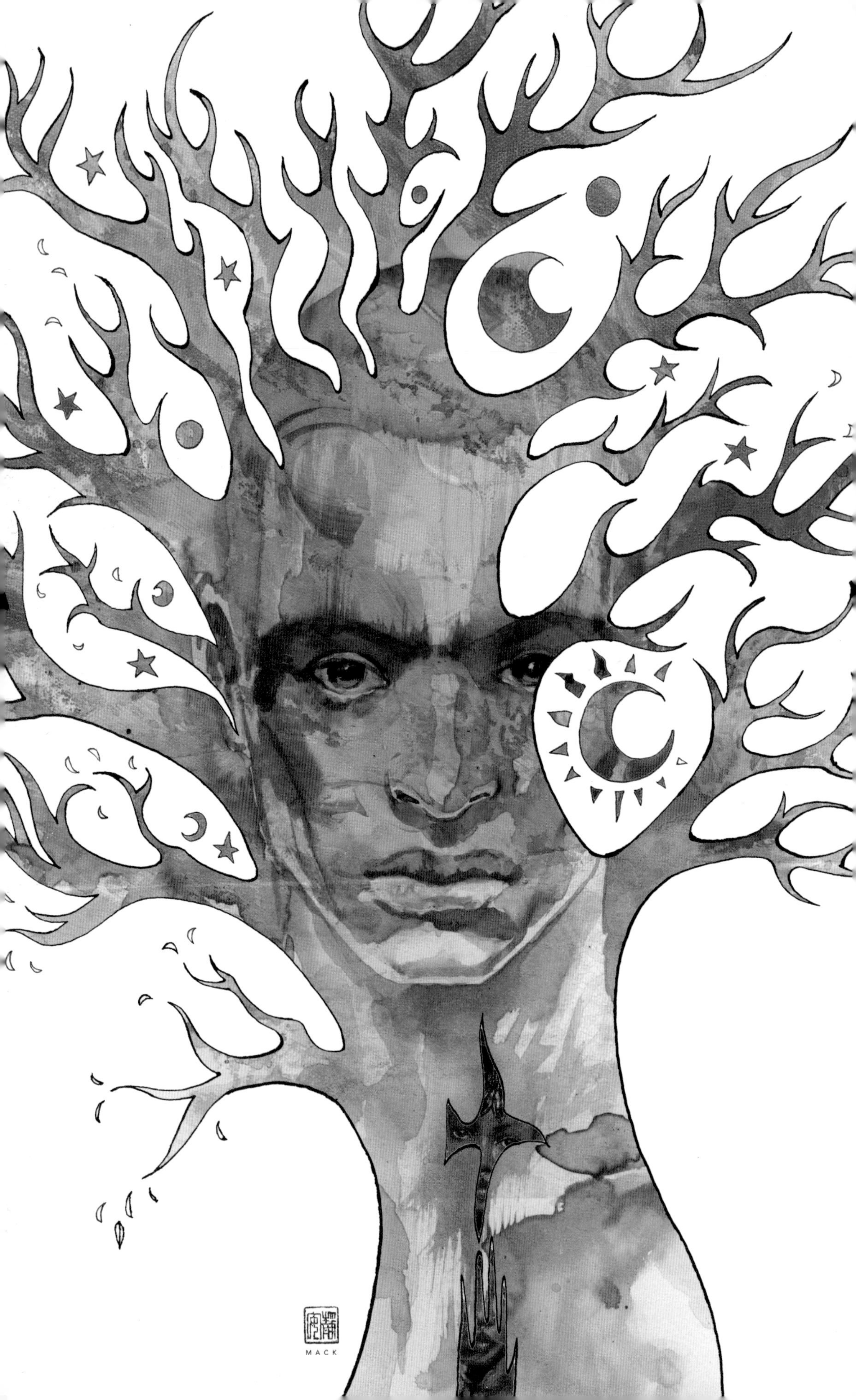
MACK

MINNEAPOLIS. AS THEY WAITED TO CHANGE CARS IN THE AIRPORT'S PARKING LOT, THEY WERE APPROACHED BY THE BARREL-CHESTED YOUNG MAN WHO HAD HUMMED SO DEEPLY AS THEY DROVE AWAY FROM THE *HOUSE ON THE ROCK* THAT THE CAR HAD VIBRATED.

I HEARD OF THE ALL-FATHER'S DEATH. THEY WILL PAY, AND THEY WILL PAY DEARLY.

WEDNESDAY WAS YOUR FATHER?

HE WAS THE ALL-FATHER. YOU TELL THEM, TELL THEM ALL, THAT WHEN WE ARE NEEDED, MY PEOPLE WILL BE THERE.

AND HOW MANY OF YOU IS THAT? TEN? TWENTY?

AND AREN'T TEN OF US WORTH A HUNDRED OF THEM? BUT THERE ARE MORE OF US THAN THAT AT THE EDGES OF THE CITIES. SOME IN THE CATSKILLS, A FEW IN THE CARNY TOWNS IN FLORIDA. THEY KEEP THEIR AXES SHARP. THEY WILL COME IF I CALL THEM.

YOU DO THAT, ELVIS. YOU CALL THEM. IT'S WHAT THE OLD BASTARD WOULD HAVE WANTED.

ELVIS?

THEY BETRAYED HIM. I LAUGHED AT WEDNESDAY, BUT I WAS WRONG. NONE OF US ARE SAFE ANY LONGER. YOU CAN RELY ON US.

YOU WILL PARDON ME ASKING, BUT OUR NEW VEHICLE IS WHICH?

THERE.

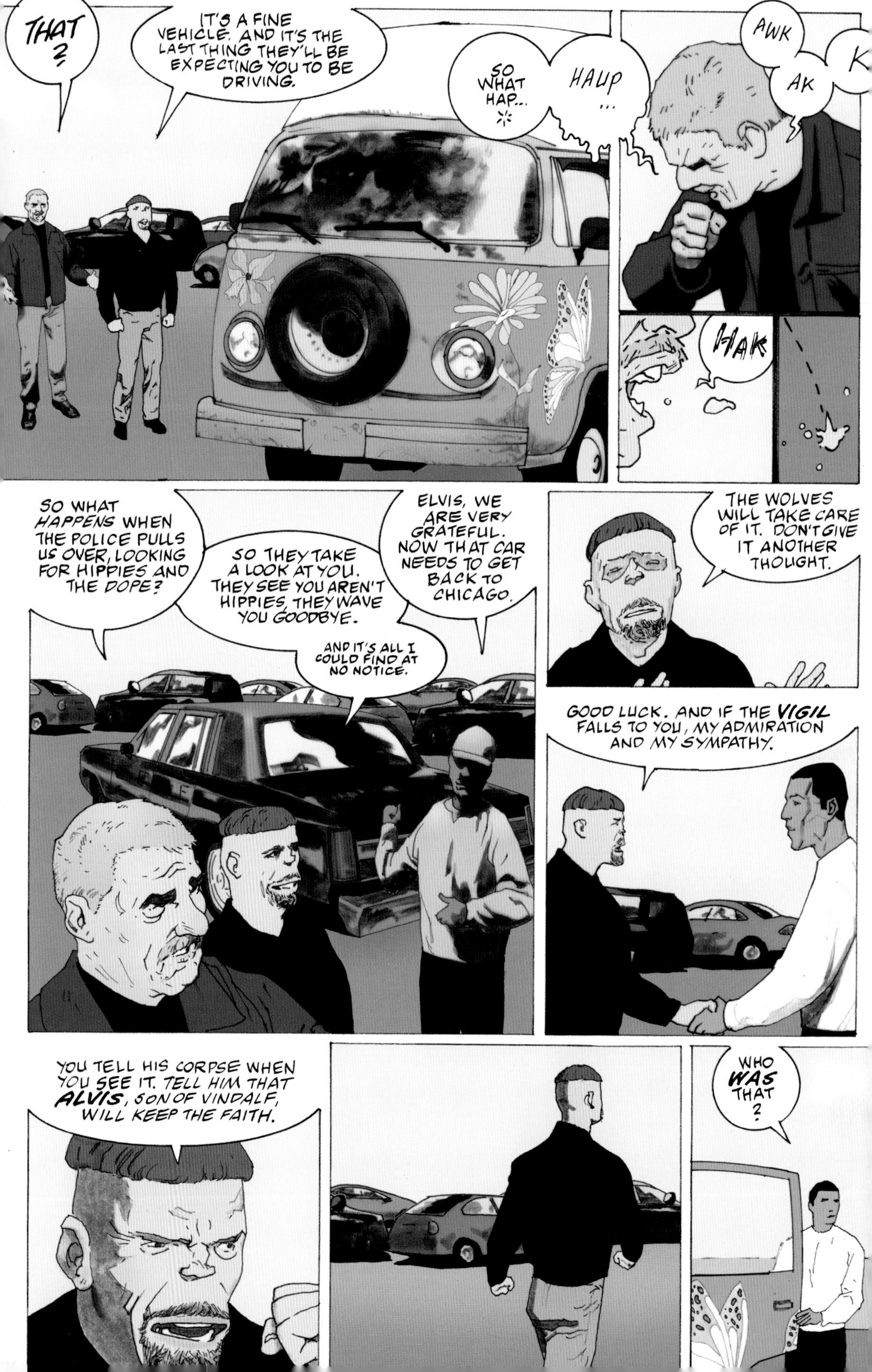
THAT ?
IT'S A FINE VEHICLE. AND IT'S THE LAST THING THEY'LL BE EXPECTING YOU TO BE DRIVING.
SO WHAT HAP...
HAUP ...
AWK
AK
K
HAK
SO WHAT HAPPENS WHEN THE POLICE PULLS US OVER, LOOKING FOR HIPPIES AND THE DOPE?
SO THEY TAKE A LOOK AT YOU. THEY SEE YOU AREN'T HIPPIES, THEY WAVE YOU GOODBYE.
AND IT'S ALL I COULD FIND AT NO NOTICE.
ELVIS, WE ARE VERY GRATEFUL. NOW THAT CAR NEEDS TO GET BACK TO CHICAGO.
THE WOLVES WILL TAKE CARE OF IT. DON'T GIVE IT ANOTHER THOUGHT.
GOOD LUCK. AND IF THE VIGIL FALLS TO YOU, MY ADMIRATION AND MY SYMPATHY.
YOU TELL HIS CORPSE WHEN YOU SEE IT. TELL HIM THAT ALVIS, SON OF VINDALF, WILL KEEP THE FAITH.
WHO WAS THAT ?

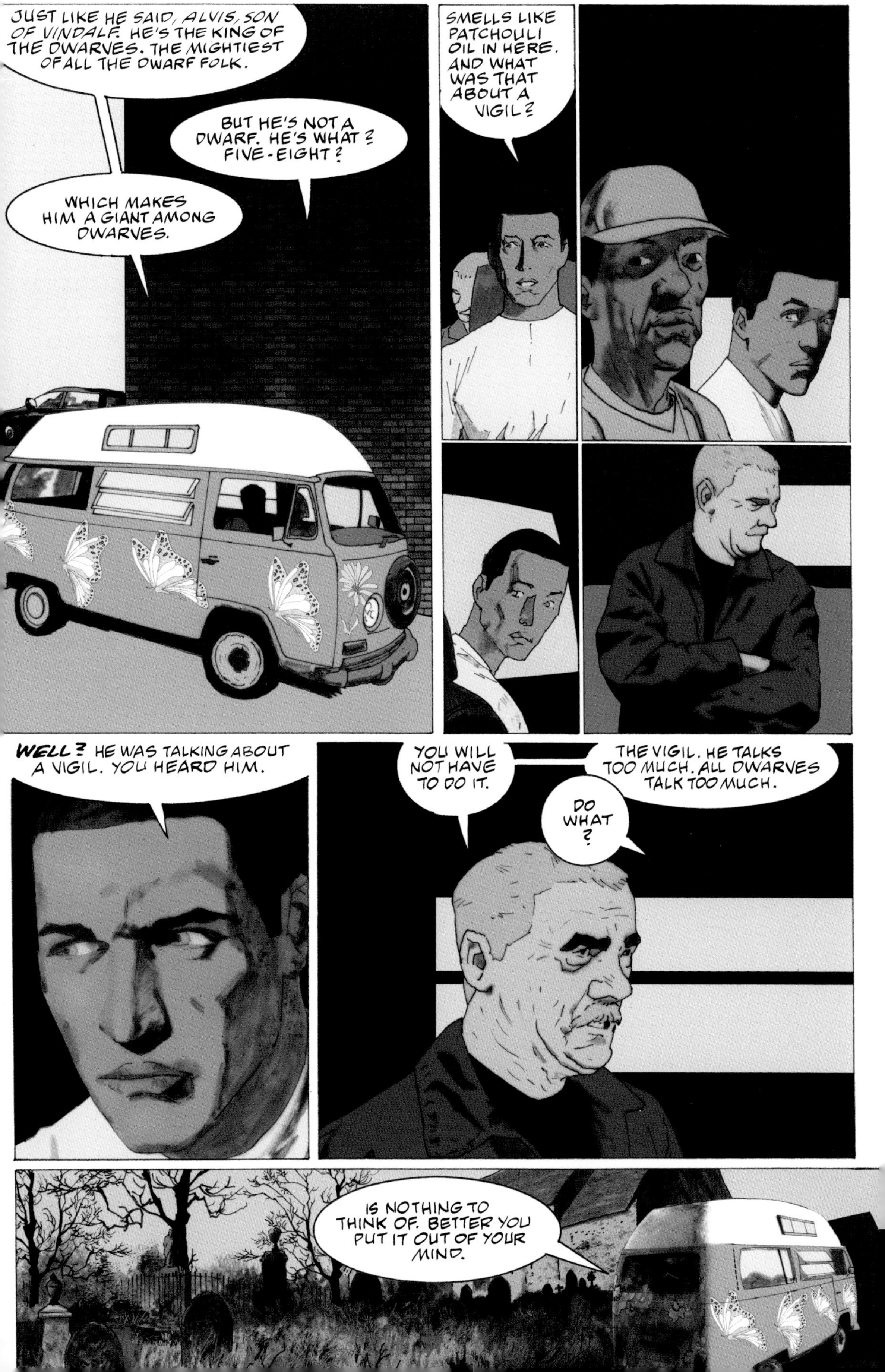
JUST LIKE HE SAID, ALVIS, SON OF VINDALF. HE'S THE KING OF THE DWARVES. THE MIGHTIEST OF ALL THE DWARF FOLK.
BUT HE'S NOT A DWARF. HE'S WHAT? FIVE-EIGHT?
WHICH MAKES HIM A GIANT AMONG DWARVES.
SMELLS LIKE PATCHOULI OIL IN HERE. AND WHAT WAS THAT ABOUT A VIGIL?
WELL? HE WAS TALKING ABOUT A VIGIL. YOU HEARD HIM.
YOU WILL NOT HAVE TO DO IT.
THE VIGIL. HE TALKS TOO MUCH. ALL DWARVES TALK TOO MUCH.
DO WHAT?
IS NOTHING TO THINK OF. BETTER YOU PUT IT OUT OF YOUR MIND.

KENTUCKY.

I DREAMED A STRANGE DREAM.

I DREAMED THAT I AM TRULY BIELEBOG.

THAT FOREVER THE WORLD IMAGINES THAT THERE ARE TWO OF US, THE LIGHT GOD AND THE DARK, BUT NOW THAT WE ARE BOTH OLD, I FIND IT WAS ONLY ME ALL THE TIME...

GIVING THEM GIFTS. TAKING MY GIFTS AWAY.

AREN'T YOU WORRIED ABOUT LUNG CANCER?

I *AM* LUNG CANCER. I DO NOT FRIGHTEN MYSELF.

FOLKS LIKE US DON'T GET CANCER. WE'RE KIND OF HARD TO KILL.

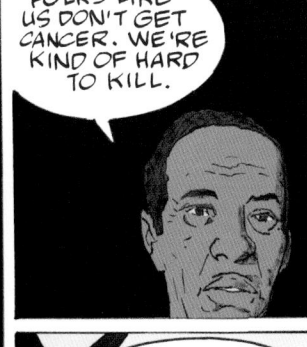

THEY KILLED WEDNESDAY.

MELROY'S

Phone

Phone

NOW, MA'AM -- YOU MAKE SURE THOSE FRIES ARE REAL *CRISP* NOW.

THINK BURNT.

Phone

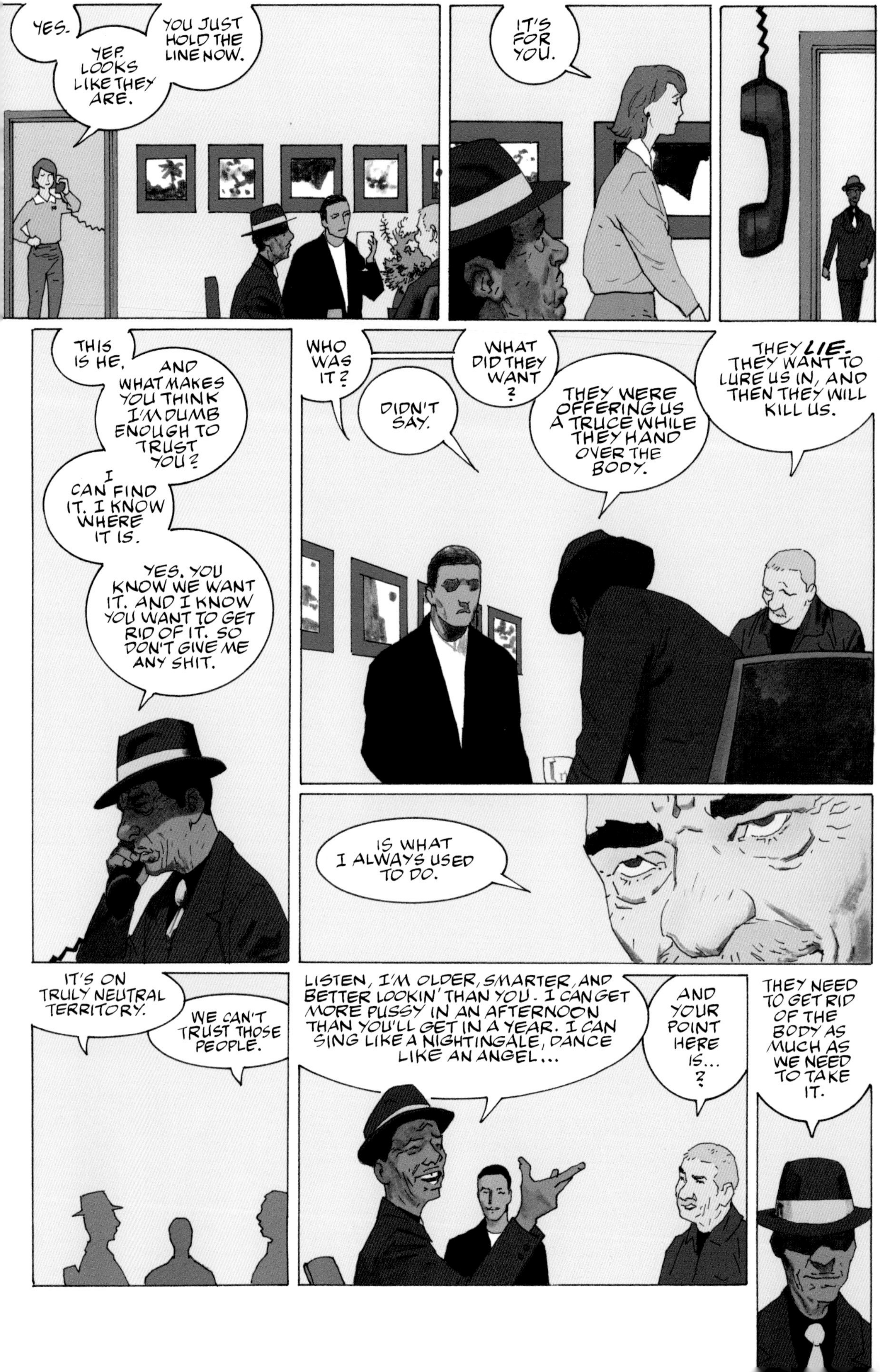
YES.
YEP. LOOKS LIKE THEY ARE.
YOU JUST HOLD THE LINE NOW.
IT'S FOR YOU.
THIS IS HE.
AND WHAT MAKES YOU THINK I'M DUMB ENOUGH TO TRUST YOU?
I CAN FIND IT. I KNOW WHERE IT IS.
YES. YOU KNOW WE WANT IT. AND I KNOW YOU WANT TO GET RID OF IT. SO DON'T GIVE ME ANY SHIT.
WHO WAS IT?
DIDN'T SAY.
WHAT DID THEY WANT?
THEY WERE OFFERING US A TRUCE WHILE THEY HAND OVER THE BODY.
THEY LIE. THEY WANT TO LURE US IN, AND THEN THEY WILL KILL US.
IS WHAT I ALWAYS USED TO DO.
IT'S ON TRULY NEUTRAL TERRITORY.
WE CAN'T TRUST THOSE PEOPLE.
LISTEN, I'M OLDER, SMARTER, AND BETTER LOOKIN' THAN YOU. I CAN GET MORE PUSSY IN AN AFTERNOON THAN YOU'LL GET IN A YEAR. I CAN SING LIKE A NIGHTINGALE, DANCE LIKE AN ANGEL...
AND YOUR POINT HERE IS...?
THEY NEED TO GET RID OF THE BODY AS MUCH AS WE NEED TO TAKE IT.

THERE IS NO SUCH NEUTRAL PLACE.

THERE'S ONE. IT'S THE CENTER.

NO. THEY WOULD NOT MEET US THERE. IT IS A BAD PLACE FOR ALL OF US.

THAT'S JUST WHY THEY'VE PROPOSED TO MAKE THE HANDOVER AT THE CENTER.

PERHAPS.

"DETERMINING THE EXACT CENTER OF ANYTHING CAN BE PROBLEMATIC AT BEST. NEAR AS ANYONE COULD FIGURE IT OUT, THE EXACT CENTER OF THE CONTINENTAL UNITED STATES WAS SEVERAL MILES FROM LEBANON, KANSAS, ON JOHNNY GRIBBS'S HOG FARM. BY THE 1930S, THE PEOPLE OF LEBANON WERE READY TO PUT UP A MONUMENT ON THE HOG FARM.

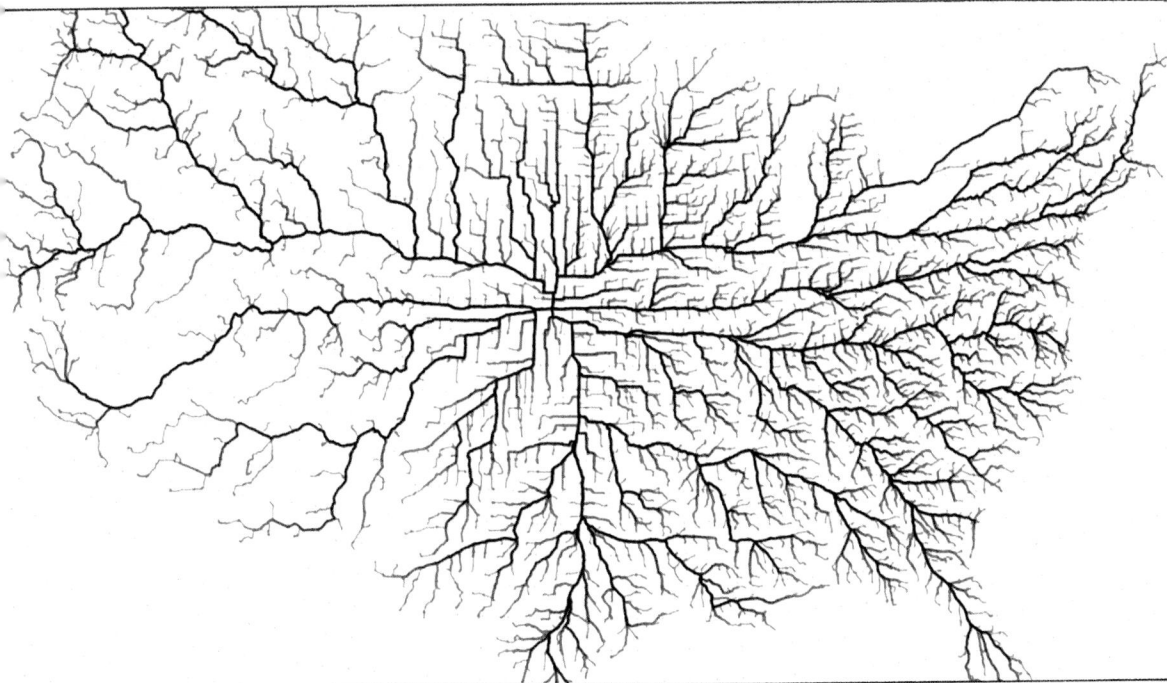

"BUT JOHNNY DIDN'T WANT TOURISTS UPSETTING THE HOGS, SO THEY PUT THE MONUMENT TWO MILES NORTH OF THE TOWN. THEY BUILT A PARK, A MOTEL, AND A LITTLE MOBILE CHAPEL BY THE MONUMENT, AND WAITED FOR THE TOURISTS.

"THE TOURISTS DID NOT COME. NOBODY CAME."

WHICH IS WHY THE EXACT CENTER OF AMERICA IS A TINY RUN-DOWN PARK, AN EMPTY CHURCH, A PILE OF STONES AND A DERELICT MOTEL.

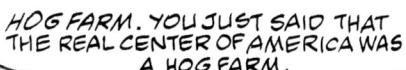
HOG FARM. YOU JUST SAID THAT THE REAL CENTER OF AMERICA WAS A HOG FARM.

THIS ISN'T ABOUT WHAT IT IS. IT'S ABOUT WHAT PEOPLE *THINK* IT IS. THAT'S WHY IT'S IMPORTANT. PEOPLE ONLY FIGHT OVER IMAGINARY THINGS.

MY KIND OF PEOPLE? OR *YOUR* KIND OF PEOPLE?

SNRK

SHADOW HAD SLEPT A LITTLE, BUT ONLY A LITTLE. HE HAD A BAD FEELING IN THE PIT OF HIS STOMACH. THIS WAS BAD. HE FELT SICK, AND SEVERAL TIMES, IN WAVES, HE FELT SCARED.

HUMANSVILLE, MISSOURI (POP. 1,084)

HEY.

HEY.

IT'S TRUE ISN'T IT? THEY *KILLED* HIM.

YES. THEY KILLED HIM...

THEY THINK THEY CAN CRUSH US LIKE COCKROACHES. WE DON'T CRUSH THAT *EASY*, DO WE?

NO. WE DON'T.

I'LL BE THERE, SIR.

I KNOW YOU WILL, GWYDION.

HE'S A *GOOD* BOY. CAME OVER IN THE SEVENTH CENTURY. WELSH.

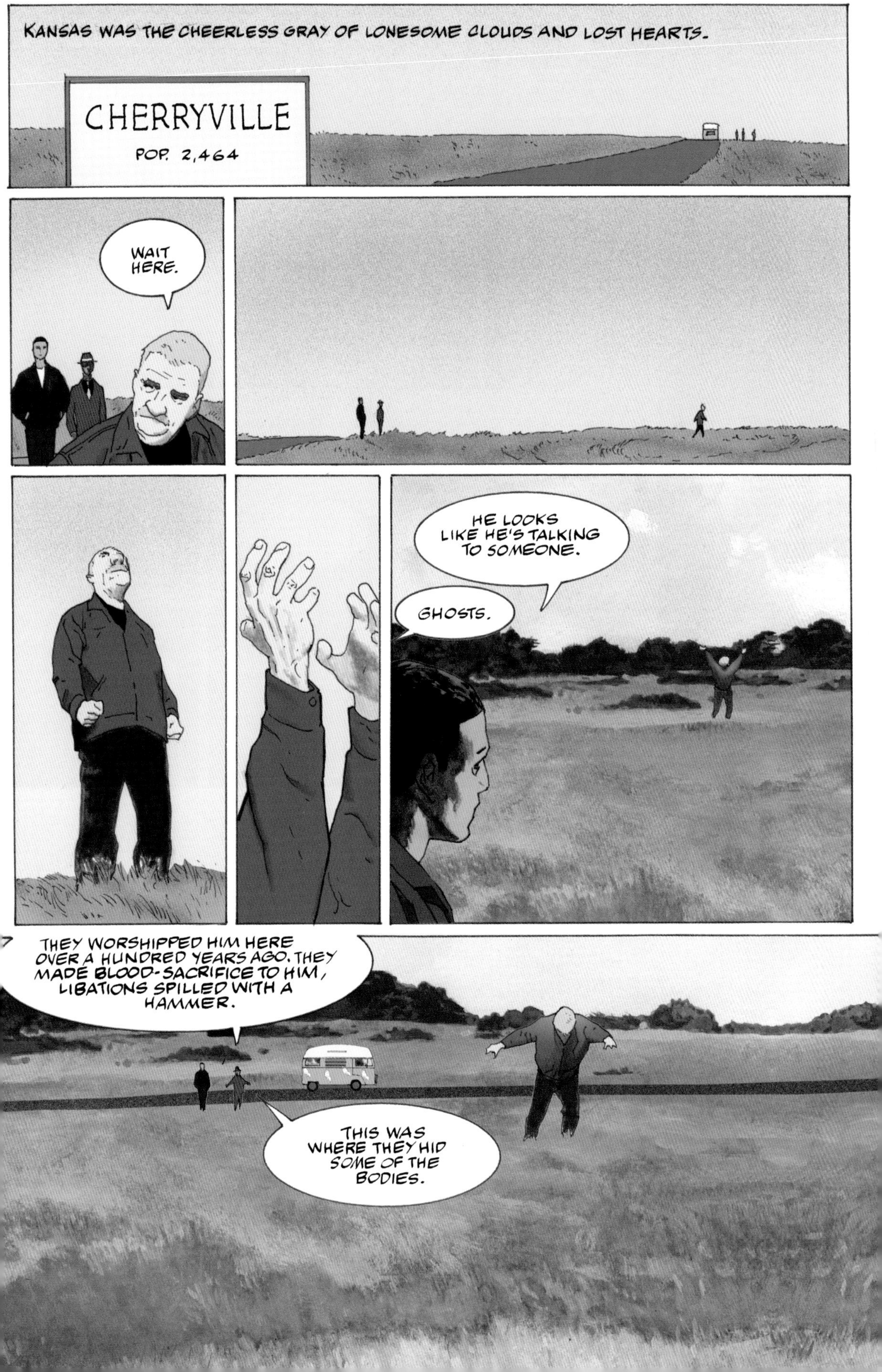

KANSAS WAS THE CHEERLESS GRAY OF LONESOME CLOUDS AND LOST HEARTS.
CHERRYVILLE
POP. 2,464
WAIT HERE.
HE LOOKS LIKE HE'S TALKING TO SOMEONE.
GHOSTS.
THEY WORSHIPPED HIM HERE OVER A HUNDRED YEARS AGO. THEY MADE BLOOD-SACRIFICE TO HIM, LIBATIONS SPILLED WITH A HAMMER.
THIS WAS WHERE THEY HID SOME OF THE BODIES.

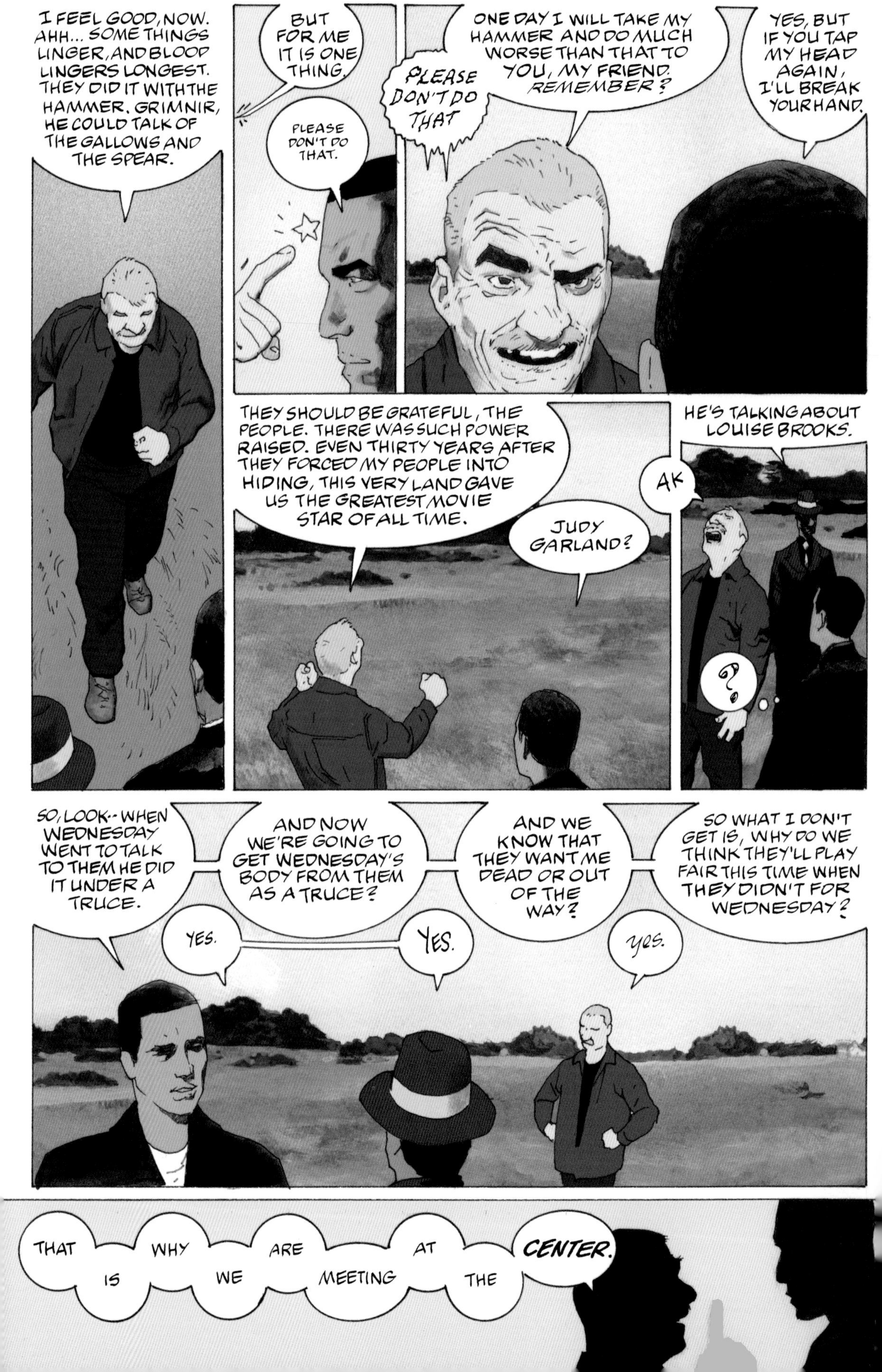
I FEEL GOOD, NOW. AHH... SOME THINGS LINGER, AND BLOOD LINGERS LONGEST. THEY DID IT WITH THE HAMMER. GRIMNIR, HE COULD TALK OF THE GALLOWS AND THE SPEAR.
BUT FOR ME IT IS ONE THING.
PLEASE DON'T DO THAT.
PLEASE DON'T DO THAT
ONE DAY I WILL TAKE MY HAMMER AND DO MUCH WORSE THAN THAT TO YOU, MY FRIEND. REMEMBER?
YES, BUT IF YOU TAP MY HEAD AGAIN, I'LL BREAK YOUR HAND.
THEY SHOULD BE GRATEFUL, THE PEOPLE. THERE WAS SUCH POWER RAISED. EVEN THIRTY YEARS AFTER THEY FORCED MY PEOPLE INTO HIDING, THIS VERY LAND GAVE US THE GREATEST MOVIE STAR OF ALL TIME.
JUDY GARLAND?
HE'S TALKING ABOUT LOUISE BROOKS.
AK
?
SO, LOOK-- WHEN WEDNESDAY WENT TO TALK TO THEM HE DID IT UNDER A TRUCE.
YES.
AND NOW WE'RE GOING TO GET WEDNESDAY'S BODY FROM THEM AS A TRUCE?
YES.
AND WE KNOW THAT THEY WANT ME DEAD OR OUT OF THE WAY?
yes.
SO WHAT I DON'T GET IS, WHY DO WE THINK THEY'LL PLAY FAIR THIS TIME WHEN THEY DIDN'T FOR WEDNESDAY?
THAT IS WHY WE ARE MEETING AT THE CENTER.

THE CENTER IS... WHAT IS THE WORD FOR IT? THE OPPOSITE OF SACRED?

PROFANE?

NO. I MEAN A PLACE OF NEGATIVE SACREDNESS, WHERE THEY CAN BUILD NO TEMPLES. PLACES WHERE GODS ONLY WALK IF THEY ARE FORCED TO.

I DON'T KNOW. I DON'T THINK THERE IS A WORD FOR IT.

ALL OF AMERICA HAS IT A LITTLE. THAT IS WHY WE ARE NOT WELCOME HERE.

WE ALL TREAD TOO CAREFULLY THERE TO DARE BREAK THE TRUCE.

BUT THE CENTER IS WORST. IS LIKE A MINEFIELD.

I TOLD YOU ALL THIS ALREADY.

YOU DON'T WORRY...

WHATEVER...

NOBODY ELSE IS GOING TO KILL YOU.

NO-BODY BUT ME.

SHADOW FOUND THE CENTER OF AMERICA AT EVENING THAT SAME DAY BEFORE IT WAS FULLY DARK. IT WAS ON A SLIGHT HILL TO THE NORTHWEST OF LEBANON.

DO YOU THINK THEY'LL EVEN HAVE BEDS HERE? THIS PLACE LOOKS LIKE IT'S JUST WAITING TO BE DEMOLISHED.

THE WOMAN WAITING FOR THEM WAS PERFECTLY MADE UP, PERFECTLY COIFFED. SHE REMINDED SHADOW OF EVERY NEWSCASTER HE'D EVER SEEN.

LOVELY TO SEE YOU.

NOW, *YOU* MUST BE CZERNOBOG. I'VE HEARD A LOT ABOUT YOU.

AND *YOU'RE* ANANSI. ALWAYS UP TO MISCHIEF, EH? YOU JOLLY OLD MAN.

AND *YOU* MUST BE SHADOW. YOU'VE CERTAINLY LED US A MERRY CHASE, HAVEN'T YOU?

I'M MEDIA. GOOD TO MEET YOU. I HOPE WE CAN GET THIS EVENING'S BUSINESS DONE AS *PLEASANTLY AS POSSIBLE.*

SOMEHOW, TOTO, I DON'T BELIEVE WE'RE IN KANSAS ANYMORE.

WE'RE IN KANSAS, ALL RIGHT. DAMN, BUT THIS COUNTRY IS FLAT.

THIS PLACE HAS NO LIGHTS, NO POWER, AND NO HOT WATER -- AND NO OFFENSE, YOU PEOPLE REALLY *NEED* THE HOT WATER. *YOU SMELL.*

I DON'T THINK THERE'S *ANY* NEED TO GO THERE. WE'RE ALL FRIENDS HERE. COME ON IN. WE'LL SHOW YOU TO YOUR ROOMS.

WE TOOK THE FIRST FOUR ROOMS. YOUR LATE FRIEND IS IN THE FIFTH. ALL THE ONES BEYOND ROOM FIVE ARE EMPTY. YOU CAN TAKE YOUR PICK.

I'M AFRAID IT'S NOT THE *FOUR SEASONS*, BUT THEN, WHAT *IS* ?

YOU PEOPLE HUNGRY ?

I CAN ALWAYS EAT.

DRIVER'S GONE OUT FOR A SACK OF HAMBURGERS. HE'LL BE BACK SOON.

BIG GUY. YOU'RE SHADOW, HUH? THE ASSHOLE WHO KILLED WOODY AND STONE ?

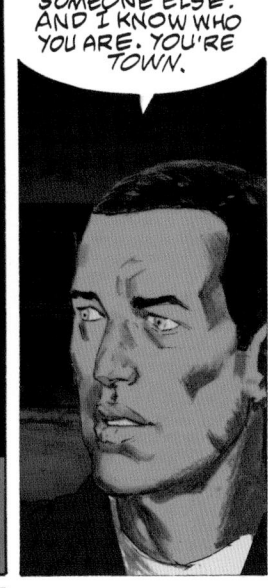

NO. THAT WAS SOMEONE ELSE. AND I KNOW WHO YOU ARE. YOU'RE TOWN.

HAVE YOU SLEPT WITH WOOD'S WIDOW YET ?

CAREFUL. DON'T START ANYTHING YOU'RE NOT PREPARED TO FINISH.

TRUCE, REMEMBER? WE'RE AT THE *CENTER.*

YOU'RE DOWN AT THE END OF THE HALL.

HERE.

IS THERE A FLASHLIGHT ON THE BUS?

NO. BUT IT'S JUST THE DARK. YOU MUSN'T BE AFRAID OF THE DARK.

I'M NOT. I'M AFRAID OF THE *PEOPLE* IN THE DARK.

DARK IS GOOD.

MEDIA. I THINK I HAVE HEARD OF HER. ISN'T SHE THE ONE WHO KILLED HER CHILDREN?

DIFFERENT WOMAN. SAME DEAL.

SHADOW'S ROOM SMELLED DAMP, AND DUSTY, AND DESERTED. HE SAT DOWN ON THE BED, PULLED OFF HIS SHOES, AND STRETCHED OUT. HE HAD DRIVEN TOO MUCH IN THE LAST FEW DAYS.

PERHAPS HE SLEPT.

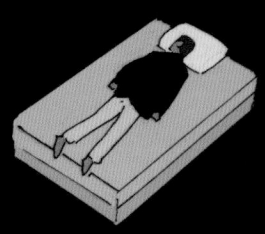

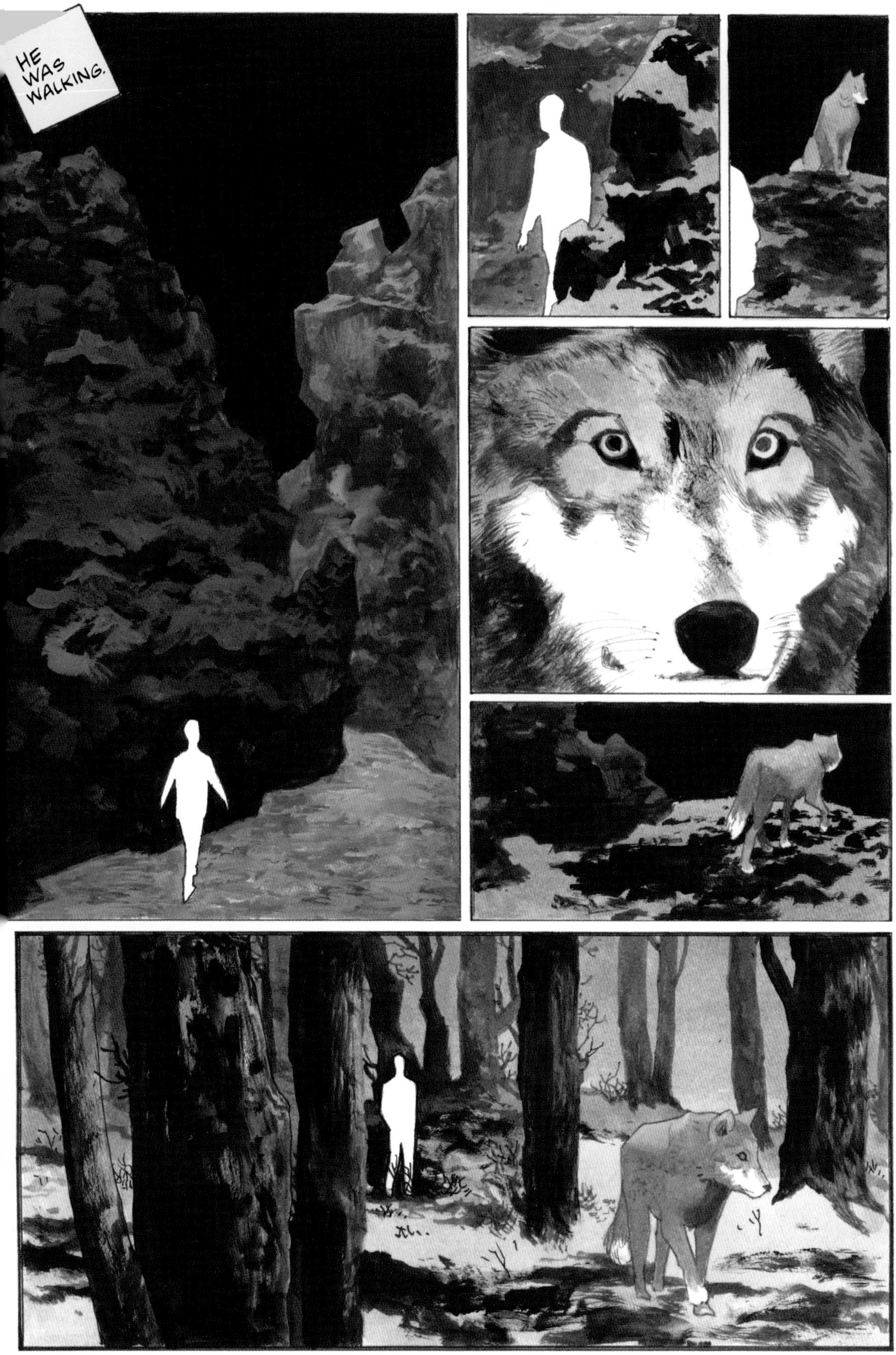
HE WAS WALKING.

BEYOND THE FOREST WAS A BONFIRE, AND BEYOND THAT WAS A BUILDING THAT LOOKED A LITTLE LIKE AN OVERTURNED BOAT.

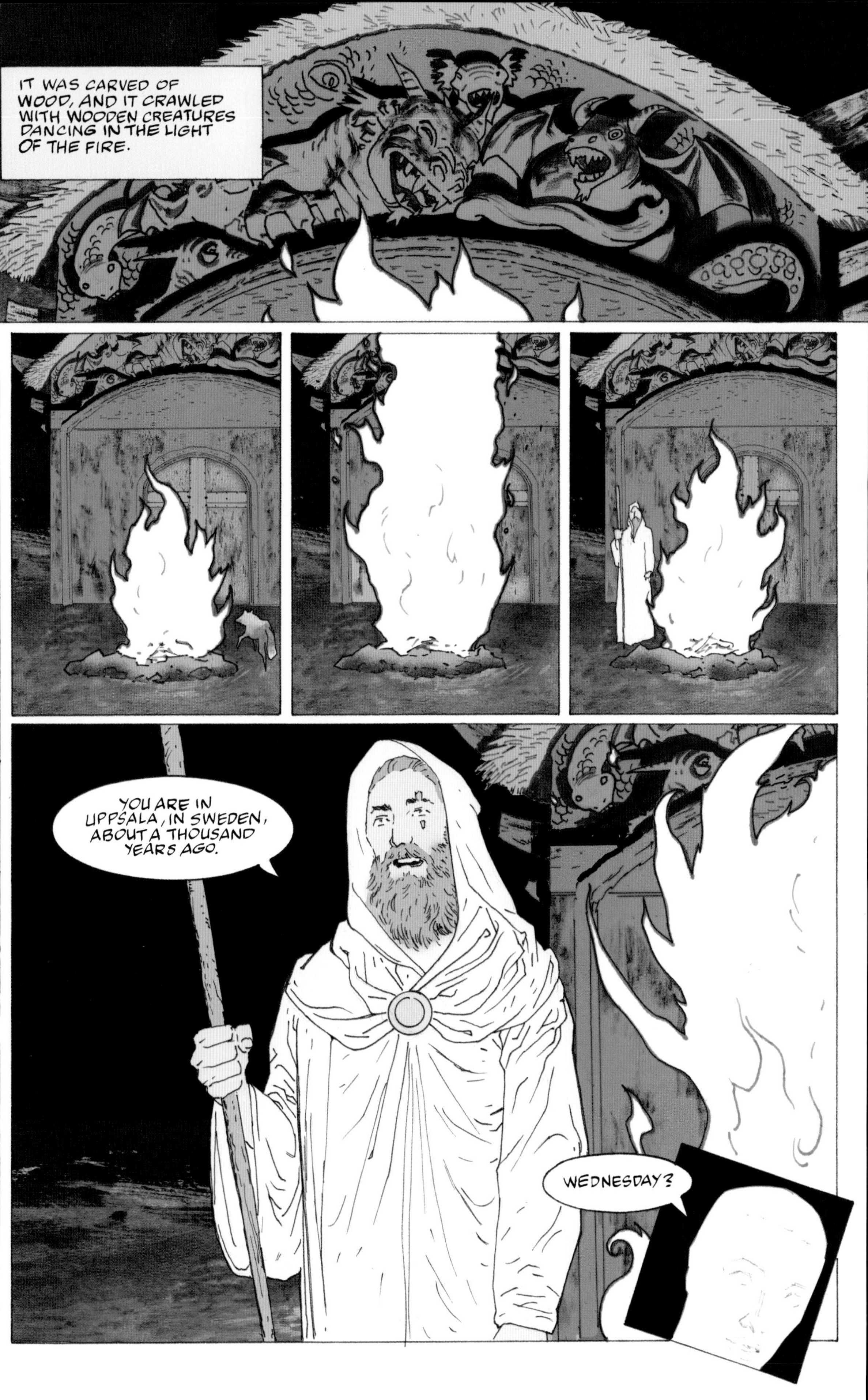
IT WAS CARVED OF WOOD, AND IT CRAWLED WITH WOODEN CREATURES DANCING IN THE LIGHT OF THE FIRE.
YOU ARE IN UPPSALA, IN SWEDEN, ABOUT A THOUSAND YEARS AGO.
WEDNESDAY?

FIRST, EVERY YEAR. THEN WHEN THE ROT SET IN, AND THEY BECAME LAX, EVERY NINE YEARS, THEY WOULD SACRIFICE HERE A SACRIFICE OF NINES. EACH DAY FOR NINE DAYS, THEY WOULD HANG NINE ANIMALS FROM TREES IN THE GROVE.

ONE OF THESE ANIMALS WAS ALWAYS A MAN.

YIP

YIP

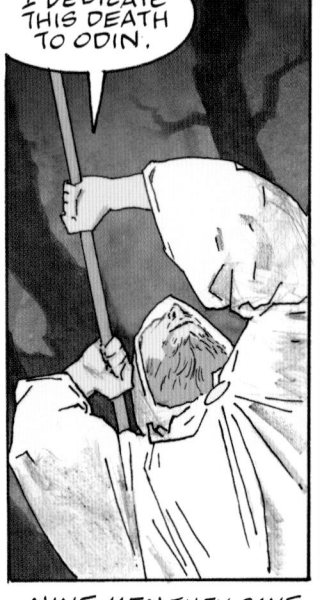

I DEDICATE THIS DEATH TO ODIN.

YIP

IT IS ONLY A GESTURE BUT GESTURES MEAN EVERYTHING. THE DEATH OF ONE DOG SYMBOLIZES THE DEATH OF ALL DOGS.

NINE MEN THEY GAVE TO ME, BUT THEY STOOD FOR ALL MEN, ALL THE BLOOD, ALL THE POWER, IT JUST WASN'T ENOUGH. ONE DAY THE BLOOD STOPPED FLOWING. BELIEF WITHOUT BLOOD ONLY TAKES US SO FAR. THE BLOOD MUST FLOW.

I SAW YOU DIE.

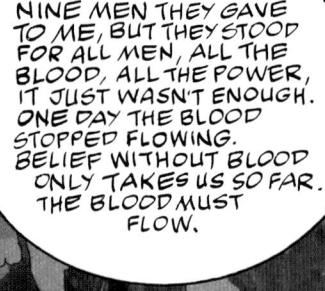

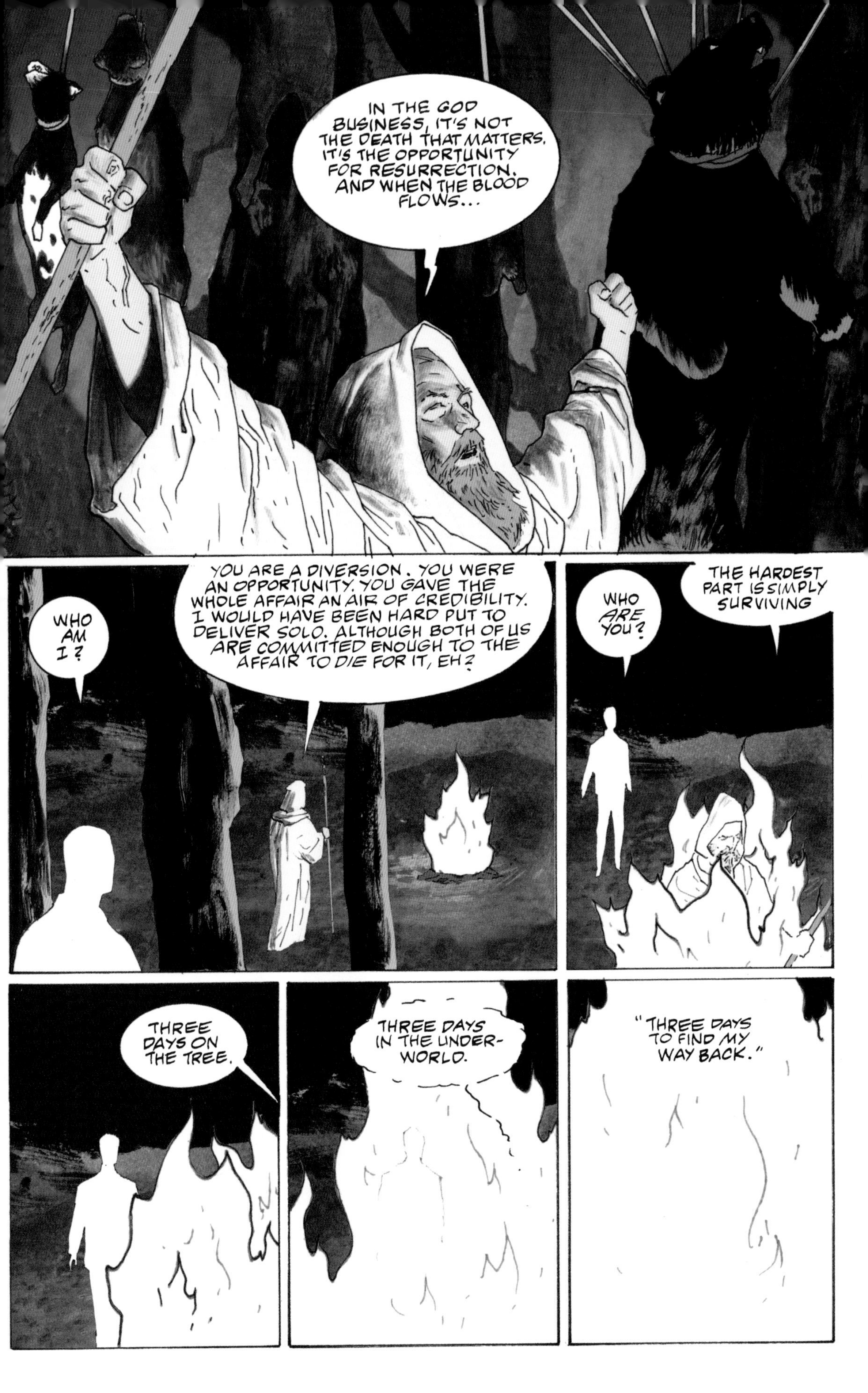
IN THE GOD BUSINESS, IT'S NOT THE DEATH THAT MATTERS. IT'S THE OPPORTUNITY FOR RESURRECTION. AND WHEN THE BLOOD FLOWS...
WHO AM I?
YOU ARE A DIVERSION. YOU WERE AN OPPORTUNITY. YOU GAVE THE WHOLE AFFAIR AN AIR OF CREDIBILITY. I WOULD HAVE BEEN HARD PUT TO DELIVER SOLO. ALTHOUGH BOTH OF US ARE COMMITTED ENOUGH TO THE AFFAIR TO DIE FOR IT, EH?
WHO ARE YOU?
THE HARDEST PART IS SIMPLY SURVIVING
THREE DAYS ON THE TREE.
THREE DAYS IN THE UNDER-WORLD.
"THREE DAYS TO FIND MY WAY BACK."

!

DINNER'S SERVED.

SORRY ABOUT THE DELAY. I GOT EVERYBODY THE SAME: BURGERS, FRIES, LARGE COKE, APPLE PIE.

OH, GREAT. THESE BURGERS ARE NEARLY COLD.

SORRY ABOUT THAT. THE GUY HAD TO DRIVE A WAY TO FIND THEM. THE NEAREST McDONALDS IS IN NEBRASKA.

OW!

THAT STUFF *BURNS*.

THOSE PIES ARE A CLASS ACTION SUIT WAITING TO FUCKING HAPPEN.

SHADOW REALIZED HE WANTED TO HIT THE KID. NOT A WISE THING TO BE THINKING, NOT *HERE*, NOT *NOW*.

CAN'T WE JUST TAKE WEDNESDAY'S BODY AND GET OUT OF HERE **?**

MIDNIGHT.

THESE THINGS MUST BE DONE ACCORDING TO THE RULES.

YEAH, BUT NOBODY TELLS ME WHAT THEY ARE...YOU KEEP TALKING ABOUT THE GODDAMN RULES, I DON'T EVEN KNOW WHAT GAME YOU PEOPLE ARE PLAYING.

IT'S LIKE BREAKING THE STREET DATE. YOU KNOW, WHEN THINGS ARE ALLOWED TO BE ON SALE.

I THINK THE WHOLE THING'S A CROCK OF SHIT. BUT IF THEIR RULES MAKE THEM HAPPY, THEN MY AGENCY IS HAPPY. YOU TAKE THE BODY. WE'RE ALL LOVEY-DOVEY. THEN WE CAN GET ON HUNTING YOU DOWN LIKE THE RATS YOU ARE.

HEY! REMINDS ME... DID YOU EVER TELL YOUR BOSS I SAID HE WAS HISTORY?

I TOLD HIM. AND YOU KNOW WHAT HE SAID TO ME?

HE SAID TO TELL THE LITTLE SNOT, IF EVER I SAW HIM AGAIN, TO REMEMBER THAT TODAY'S FUTURE IS TOMORROW'S YESTERDAY.

WEDNESDAY HAD NEVER SAID ANY SUCH THING.

THIS PLACE IS SUCH A FUCKING DUMP.

I'M GOING TO SEE THE CENTER OF AMERICA.

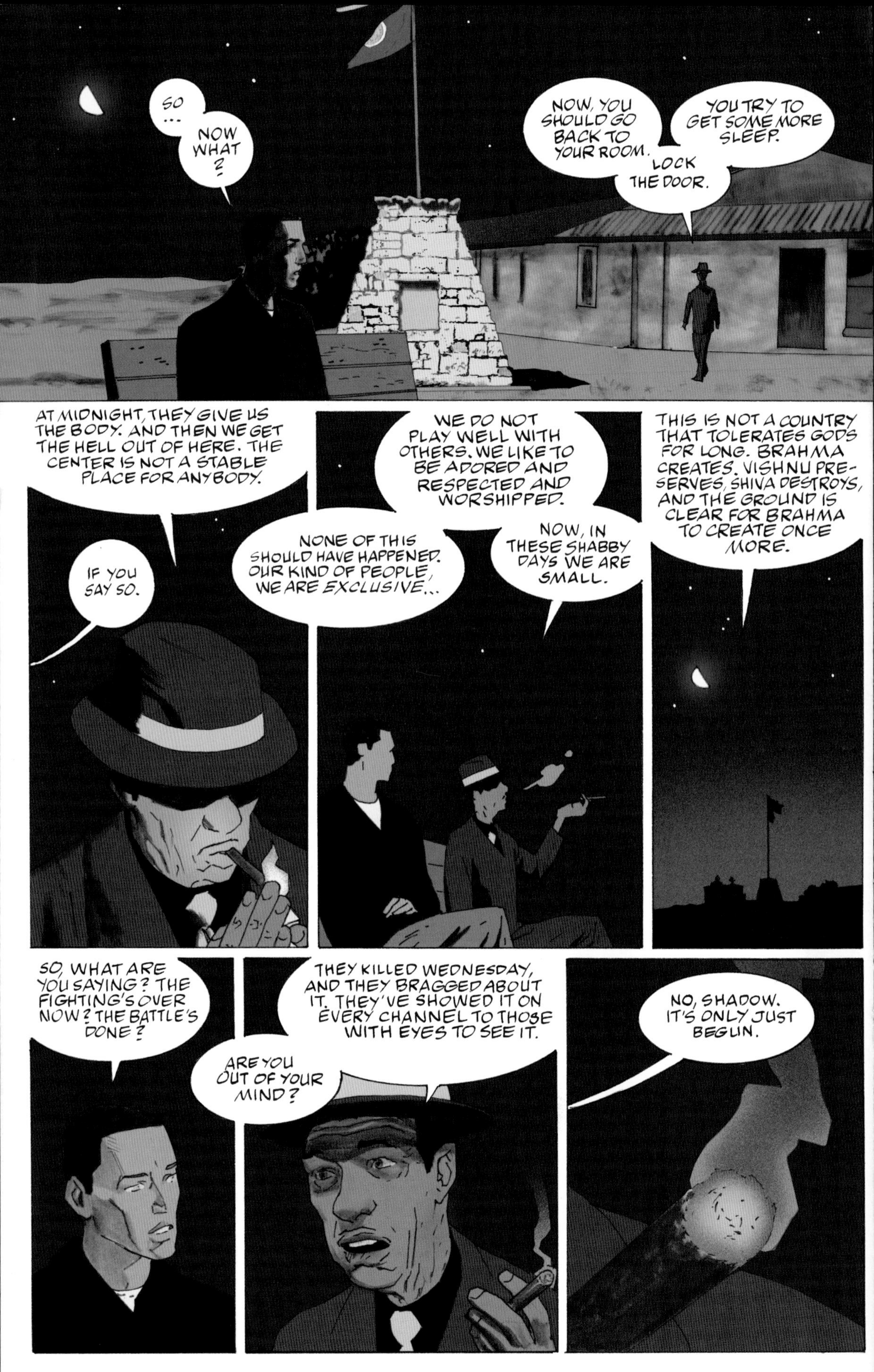

SO ... NOW WHAT?
NOW, YOU SHOULD GO BACK TO YOUR ROOM. LOCK THE DOOR.
YOU TRY TO GET SOME MORE SLEEP.
AT MIDNIGHT, THEY GIVE US THE BODY. AND THEN WE GET THE HELL OUT OF HERE. THE CENTER IS NOT A STABLE PLACE FOR ANYBODY.
IF YOU SAY SO.
NONE OF THIS SHOULD HAVE HAPPENED. OUR KIND OF PEOPLE, WE ARE *EXCLUSIVE*...
WE DO NOT PLAY WELL WITH OTHERS. WE LIKE TO BE ADORED AND RESPECTED AND WORSHIPPED.
NOW, IN THESE SHABBY DAYS WE ARE SMALL.
THIS IS NOT A COUNTRY THAT TOLERATES GODS FOR LONG. BRAHMA CREATES. VISHNU PRESERVES, SHIVA DESTROYS, AND THE GROUND IS CLEAR FOR BRAHMA TO CREATE ONCE MORE.
SO, WHAT ARE YOU SAYING? THE FIGHTING'S OVER NOW? THE BATTLE'S DONE?
ARE YOU OUT OF YOUR MIND?
THEY KILLED WEDNESDAY, AND THEY BRAGGED ABOUT IT. THEY'VE SHOWED IT ON EVERY CHANNEL TO THOSE WITH EYES TO SEE IT.
NO, SHADOW. IT'S ONLY JUST BEGUN.

CHAPTER TWO

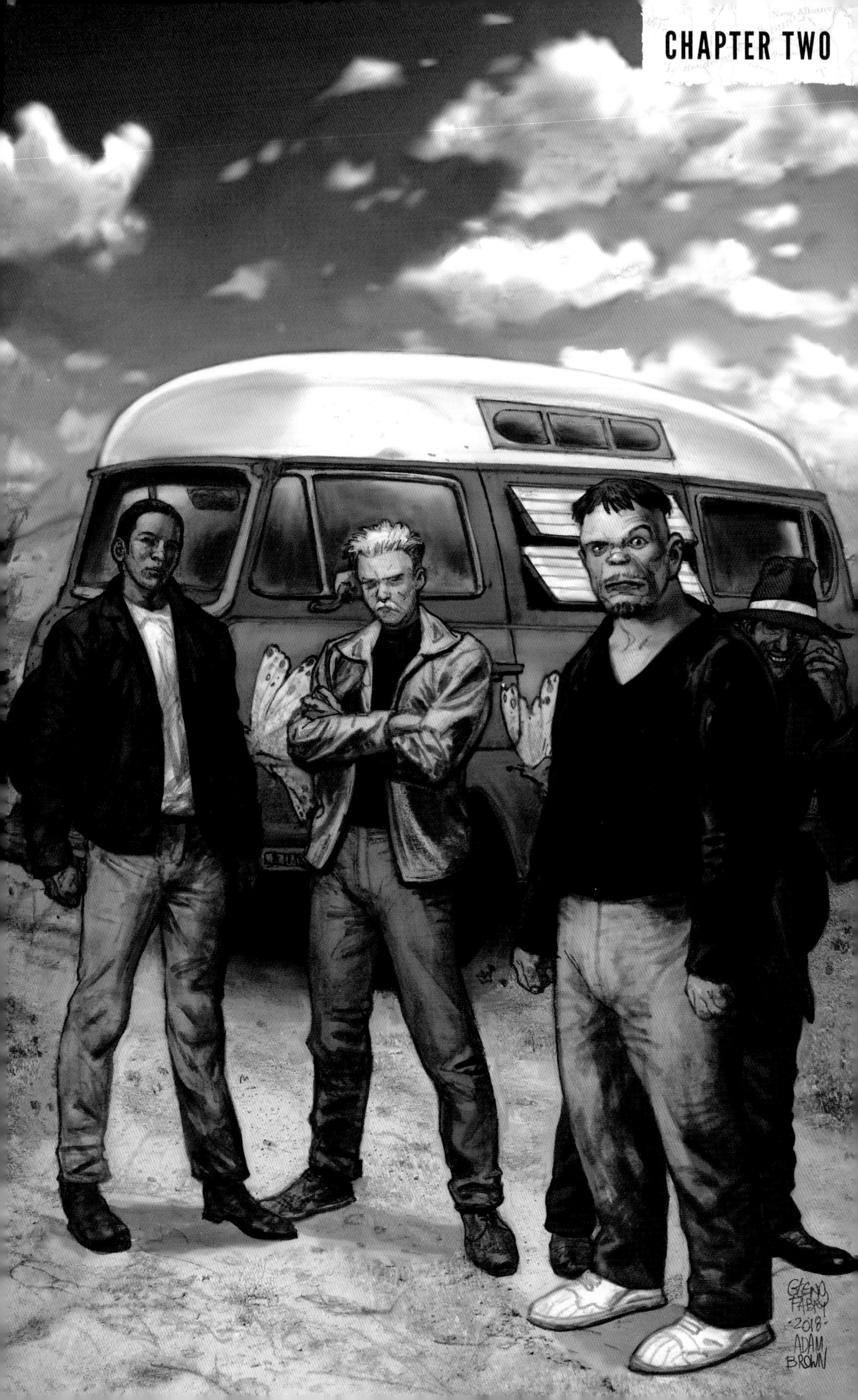
GLENN FABRY
-2018-
ADAM BROWN

WHO WILL MOURN and HOLD VigiL for the All-FatHer?

SHadOW Nods.

MACK

YOU USED TO MAKE JOKES. YOU DON'T ANYMORE.

IT'S HARD TO FIND THE JOKES THESE DAYS.

WEDNESDAY'S DEAD.

ARE YOU COMIN' INSIDE?

SOON.

YOU GOING TO SHOOT ME?

JESUS-- I WISH.

IT'S ONLY FOR SELF-DEFENSE.

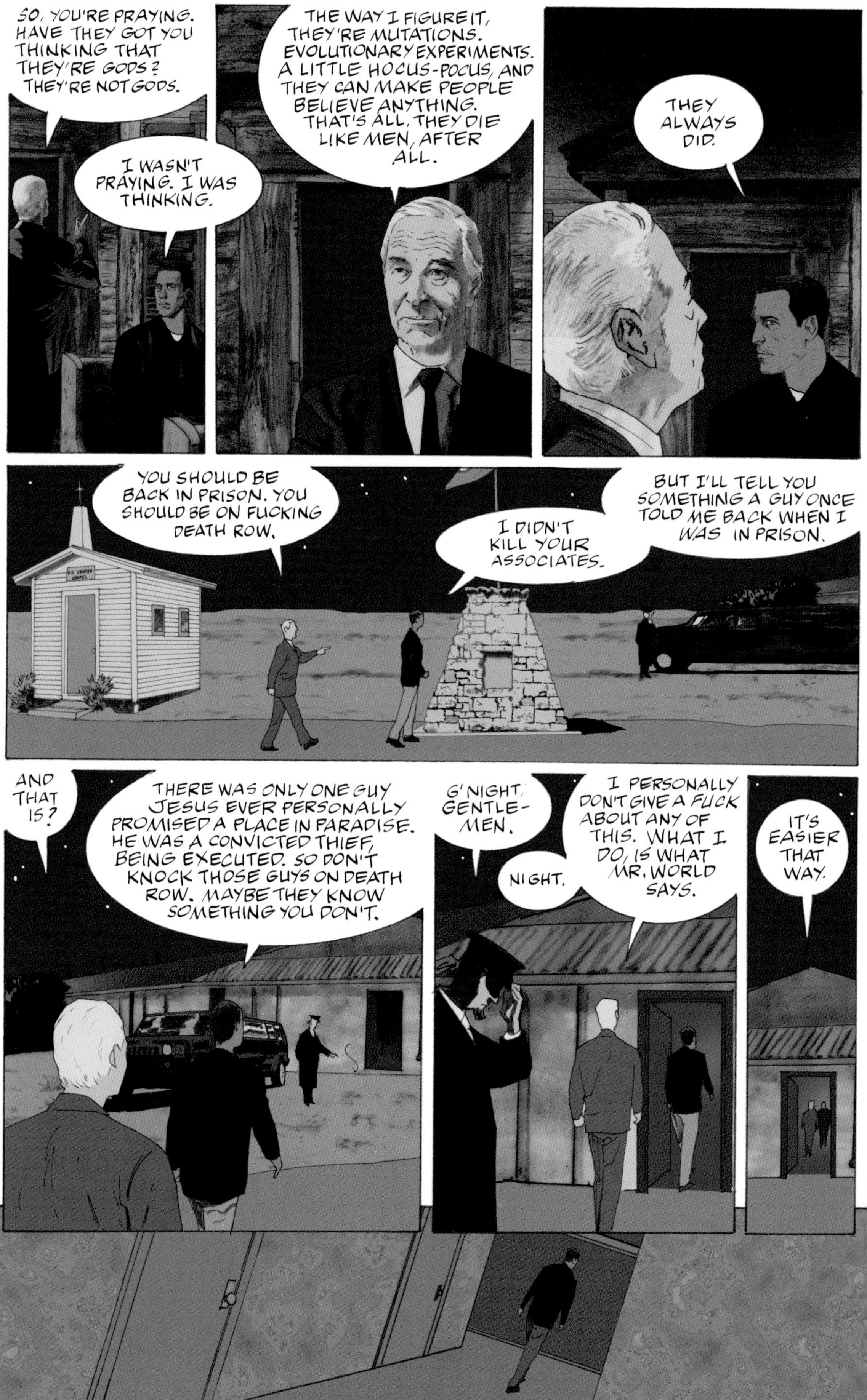
SO, YOU'RE PRAYING. HAVE THEY GOT YOU THINKING THAT THEY'RE GODS? THEY'RE NOT GODS.
I WASN'T PRAYING. I WAS THINKING.
THE WAY I FIGURE IT, THEY'RE MUTATIONS. EVOLUTIONARY EXPERIMENTS. A LITTLE HOCUS-POCUS, AND THEY CAN MAKE PEOPLE BELIEVE ANYTHING. THAT'S ALL. THEY DIE LIKE MEN, AFTER ALL.
THEY ALWAYS DID.
YOU SHOULD BE BACK IN PRISON. YOU SHOULD BE ON FUCKING DEATH ROW.
I DIDN'T KILL YOUR ASSOCIATES.
BUT I'LL TELL YOU SOMETHING A GUY ONCE TOLD ME BACK WHEN I WAS IN PRISON.
AND THAT IS?
THERE WAS ONLY ONE GUY JESUS EVER PERSONALLY PROMISED A PLACE IN PARADISE. HE WAS A CONVICTED THIEF, BEING EXECUTED. SO DON'T KNOCK THOSE GUYS ON DEATH ROW. MAYBE THEY KNOW SOMETHING YOU DON'T.
G'NIGHT, GENTLEMEN.
NIGHT.
I PERSONALLY DON'T GIVE A FUCK ABOUT ANY OF THIS. WHAT I DO, IS WHAT MR. WORLD SAYS.
IT'S EASIER THAT WAY.

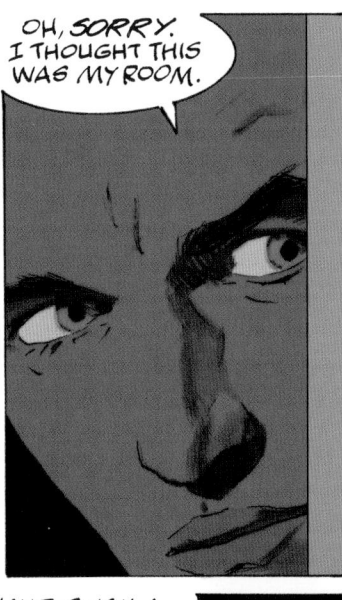

OH, *SORRY.* I THOUGHT THIS WAS MY ROOM.

IT IS. I WAS WAITING FOR YOU. I WON'T BE HERE FOR LONG. I JUST THOUGHT IT MIGHT BE AN APPROPRIATE TIME TO MAKE YOU AN OFFER.

OKAY. MAKE THE OFFER.

CLICK

RELAX. YOU HAVE *SUCH A* STICK UP YOUR BUTT. LOOK, WEDNESDAY'S DEAD. TIME TO COME OVER TO THE WINNING TEAM.

WE CAN MAKE YOU *FAMOUS,* SHADOW. WE CAN GIVE YOU *POWER* OVER WHAT PEOPLE BELIEVE AND SAY AND DREAM. YOU WANT TO BE THE NEXT CARY GRANT? WE CAN MAKE THAT HAPPEN.

I THINK I PREFERRED IT WHEN YOU WERE OFFERING TO SHOW ME LUCY'S TITS.

AND THEN OF COURSE WE CAN TURN IT ALL AROUND. WE *CAN* MAKE IT *BAD* FOR YOU. YOU COULD BE REMEMBERED FOREVER AS A MONSTER: A MANSON OR A HITLER. HOW WOULD YOU *LIKE* THAT?

I'M KIND OF TIRED. I NEED MY ROOM BACK. GOOD NIGHT.

I OFFERED YOU THE *WORLD.* WHEN YOU'RE DYING IN A GUTTER, YOU REMEMBER THAT.

I'LL MAKE A POINT OF IT.

AFTER SHE HAD GONE, HER PERFUME LINGERED.

LYING ON THE BARE MATTRESS HE THOUGHT ABOUT...

LAURA GIGGLING. LAURA PLAYING FRISBEE, LAURA EATING A ROOT BEER FLOAT WITHOUT A SPOON.

BUT WHAT-EVER HE THOUGHT ABOUT...

IT ALWAYS MORPHED, IN HIS MIND, INTO LAURA SUCKING ROBBIE'S COCK...

AND A TRUCK SLAMMING THEM OFF THE ROAD AND INTO OBLIVION.

AND THEN HE HEARD HER WORDS AND THEY HURT EVERY TIME...

YOU'RE NOT DEAD. BUT I'M NOT SURE THAT YOU'RE ALIVE EITHER.

THIS PLACE IS TURNING INTO GRAND CENTRAL STATION.

THOSE HAMBURGERS, THEY WERE JUST ICKY. CAN YOU BELIEVE IT? FIFTY MILES FROM A McDONALDS. I DIDN'T THINK *ANYPLACE* WAS FIFTY MILES FROM A McDONALDS.

OKAY, SO I GUESS YOU ARE HERE TO OFFER ME THE FREEDOM OF THE INTERNET IF I COME OVER TO YOUR SIDE OF THE FENCE, RIGHT?

NO. YOU'RE ALREADY DEAD MEAT.

YOU-- YOU'RE A FUCKING ILLUMINATED GOTHIC, BLACK-LETTER MANUSCRIPT. YOU COULD NOT BE *HYPERTEXT* IF YOU TRIED.

I'M ...

I'M SYNAPTIC ...

WHILE ...

WHILE YOU'RE SYNOPTIC ...

ARE YOU HERE FOR A REASON?

JUST WANTED TO TALK. IT'S CREEPY IN MY ROOM, THAT'S ALL. IT'S *CREEPY* IN THERE.

MAYBE I COULD STAY IN HERE WITH YOU.

WHAT ABOUT YOUR FRIENDS FROM THE LIMO? SHOULDN'T YOU ASK THEM TO STAY WITH YOU?

THE CHILDREN WOULDN'T OPERATE OUT HERE. IT'S A DEAD ZONE.

I THINK MAYBE YOU NEED REST. I KNOW I DO.

CLICK
KA-THUNK

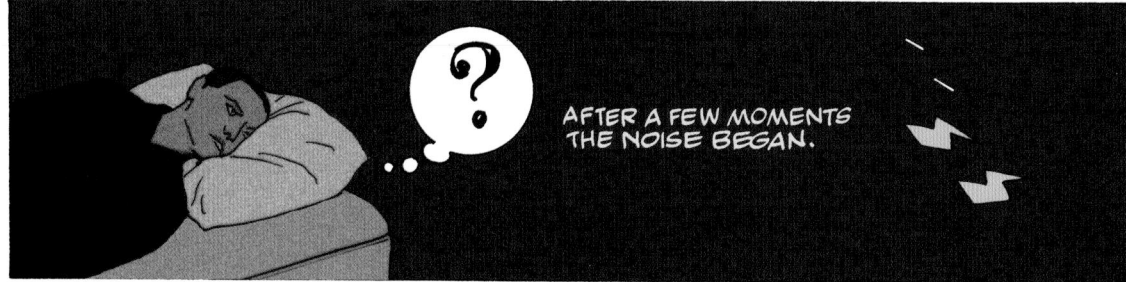
? AFTER A FEW MOMENTS THE NOISE BEGAN.

IT WAS THE FAT KID. FROM THE SOUNDS, SHADOW GUESSED THAT HE WAS THROWING HIMSELF AGAINST THE WALLS OF HIS ROOM.

HE WAS SOBBING ...

IT'S JUST ME.

OR PERHAPS ...

IT'S JUST MEAT.

CZERNABOG.

QUIET!

COULDN'T SLEEP, SIR?

NO.

CIGARETTE, SIR?

NO, THANK YOU.

YOU DON'T MIND IF I DO?

GO RIGHT AHEAD.

YOU'RE LOOKING GOOD, BIG GUY.

!

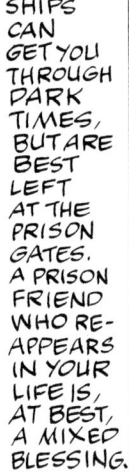

PRISON FRIENDSHIPS CAN GET YOU THROUGH DARK TIMES, BUT ARE BEST LEFT AT THE PRISON GATES. A PRISON FRIEND WHO REAPPEARS IN YOUR LIFE IS, AT BEST, A MIXED BLESSING.

LOW KEY?

JESUS. LOW KEY LYESMITH.

LOKI LIE-SMITH.

LOKI.

YOU'RE SLOW... BUT YOU GET THERE IN THE END.

YOU LIED TO ME.

WHY WERE YOU IN MY CELL?

AND NOW YOU'RE A DRIVER FOR THE OPPOSITION.

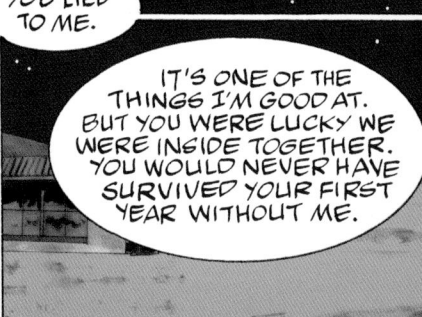

IT'S ONE OF THE THINGS I'M GOOD AT. BUT YOU WERE LUCKY WE WERE INSIDE TOGETHER. YOU WOULD NEVER HAVE SURVIVED YOUR FIRST YEAR WITHOUT ME.

COINCIDENCE. PURE AND SIMPLE. YOU DON'T BELIEVE ME? IT'S TRUE.

IT DEPENDS WHERE YOU'RE STANDING. THE WAY I FIGURE IT, I'M DRIVING FOR THE WINNING TEAM.

WITH WEDNESDAY GONE, THE REST OF THEM ARE GOING TO HAVE TO FACE FACTS: IT'S CHANGE OR DIE, EVOLVE OR PERISH.

HE'S DEAD. WAR'S OVER.

YOU AREN'T THAT STUPID. YOU WERE ALWAYS SO SHARP. HIS DEATH ISN'T GOING TO END ANYTHING. IT'S JUST PUSHED ALL OF THE ONES ON THE FENCE OVER THE EDGE. IT *UNITED* THEM.

PERHAPS. IT'S NOT ANY OF MY BUSINESS. I JUST DRIVE.

SO TELL ME. WHY DOES EVERYONE CARE ABOUT ME? THEY ACT LIKE I'M IMPORTANT.

YOU'RE AN INVESTMENT. YOU WERE IMPORTANT TO US BECAUSE YOU WERE IMPORTANT TO WEDNESDAY. AS FOR THE *WHY* OF IT,,, I DON'T THINK ANY OF US KNOW. HE *DID*. HE'S DEAD. JUST ANOTHER ONE OF LIFE'S LITTLE MYSTERIES.

I'M TIRED OF MYSTERIES.

YEAH? I THINK THEY ADD ZEST TO THE WORLD.

TIME TO LIGHT THE CANDLES FOR THIS. SAY A FEW WORDS ABOUT THE DEARLY DEPARTED. DO THE FORMALITIES.

FIVE TO MIDNIGHT. *TIME*.

YOU COMING?

DEEP BREATH.

I'M COMING.

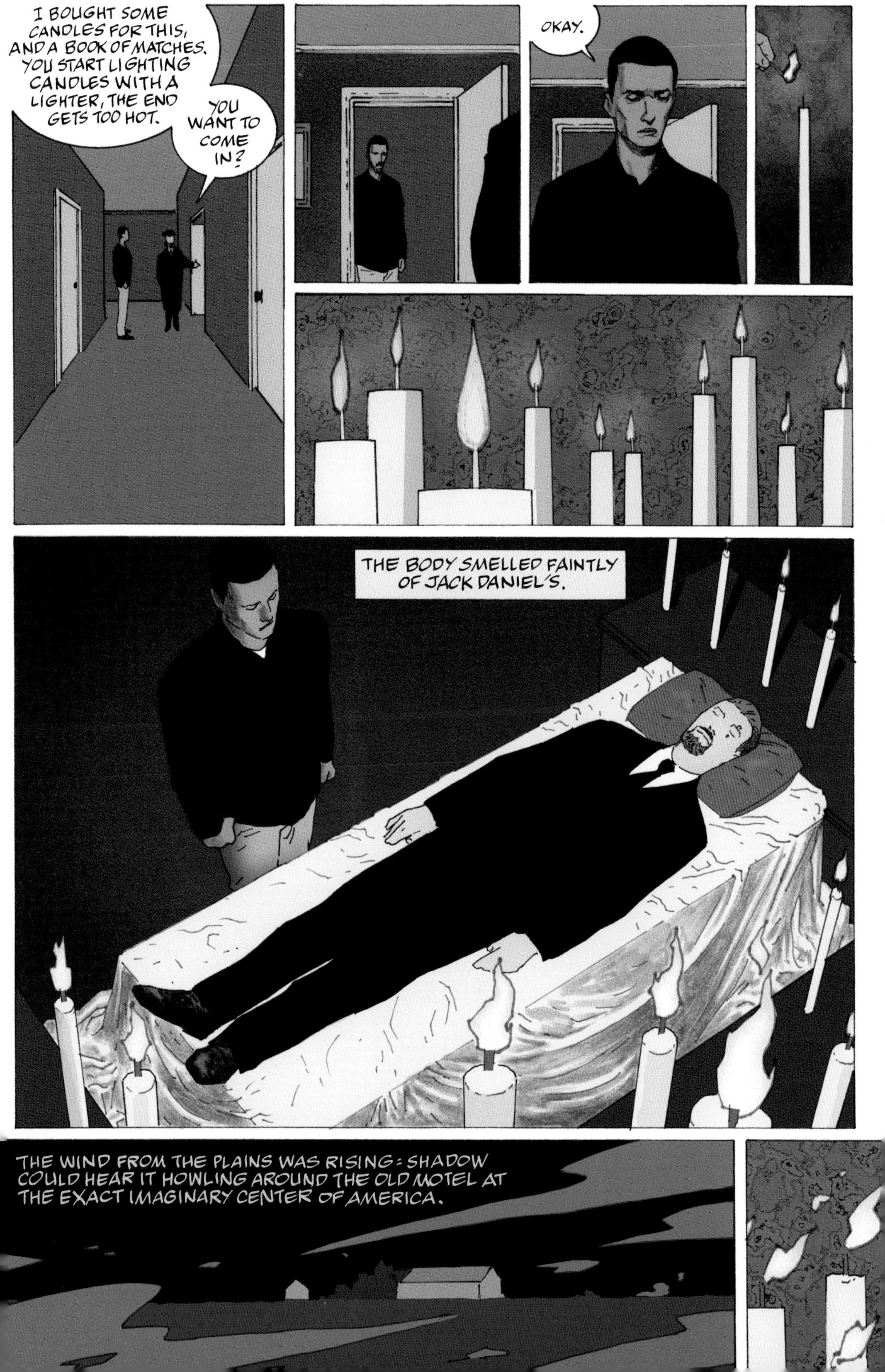

I BOUGHT SOME CANDLES FOR THIS, AND A BOOK OF MATCHES. YOU START LIGHTING CANDLES WITH A LIGHTER, THE END GETS TOO HOT.

YOU WANT TO COME IN?

OKAY.

THE BODY SMELLED FAINTLY OF JACK DANIEL'S.

THE WIND FROM THE PLAINS WAS RISING: SHADOW COULD HEAR IT HOWLING AROUND THE OLD MOTEL AT THE EXACT IMAGINARY CENTER OF AMERICA.

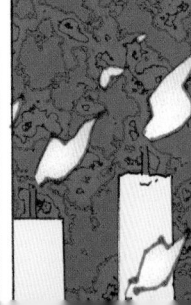

FOOTSTEPS IN THE HALLWAY.

HURRY UP, PLEASE. IT'S TIME.

THE LAST IN WAS THE FAT KID. HE HAD FRESH RED BRUISES ON HIS FACE, AND HIS LIPS WERE MOVING ALL THE TIME.

THE ATMOSPHERE IN THE ROOM WAS RELIGIOUS-- DEEPLY RELIGIOUS, IN A WAY THAT SHADOW HAD NEVER PREVIOUSLY EXPERIENCED.

WE ARE COME TOGETHER IN THIS GODLESS PLACE TO PASS ON THE BODY OF THIS INDIVIDUAL TO THOSE WHO WILL DISPOSE OF IT PROPERLY ACCORDING TO THE RITES. IF ANYONE WOULD LIKE TO SAY SOMETHING, SAY IT NOW.

NOT ME. I NEVER PROPERLY MET THE GUY.

THESE ACTIONS WILL HAVE CONSEQUENCES, YOU KNOW THAT? THIS CAN ONLY BE THE START OF IT ALL.

HEE

"TURNING AND TURNING IN THE WIDENING GYRE

OKAY. OKAY. I'VE GOT IT.

THE FALCON CANNOT HEAR THE FALCONER;

THINGS FALL APART; THE CENTER CANNOT HOLD..."

UM ...

SHIT. I USED TO KNOW THE WHOLE THING.

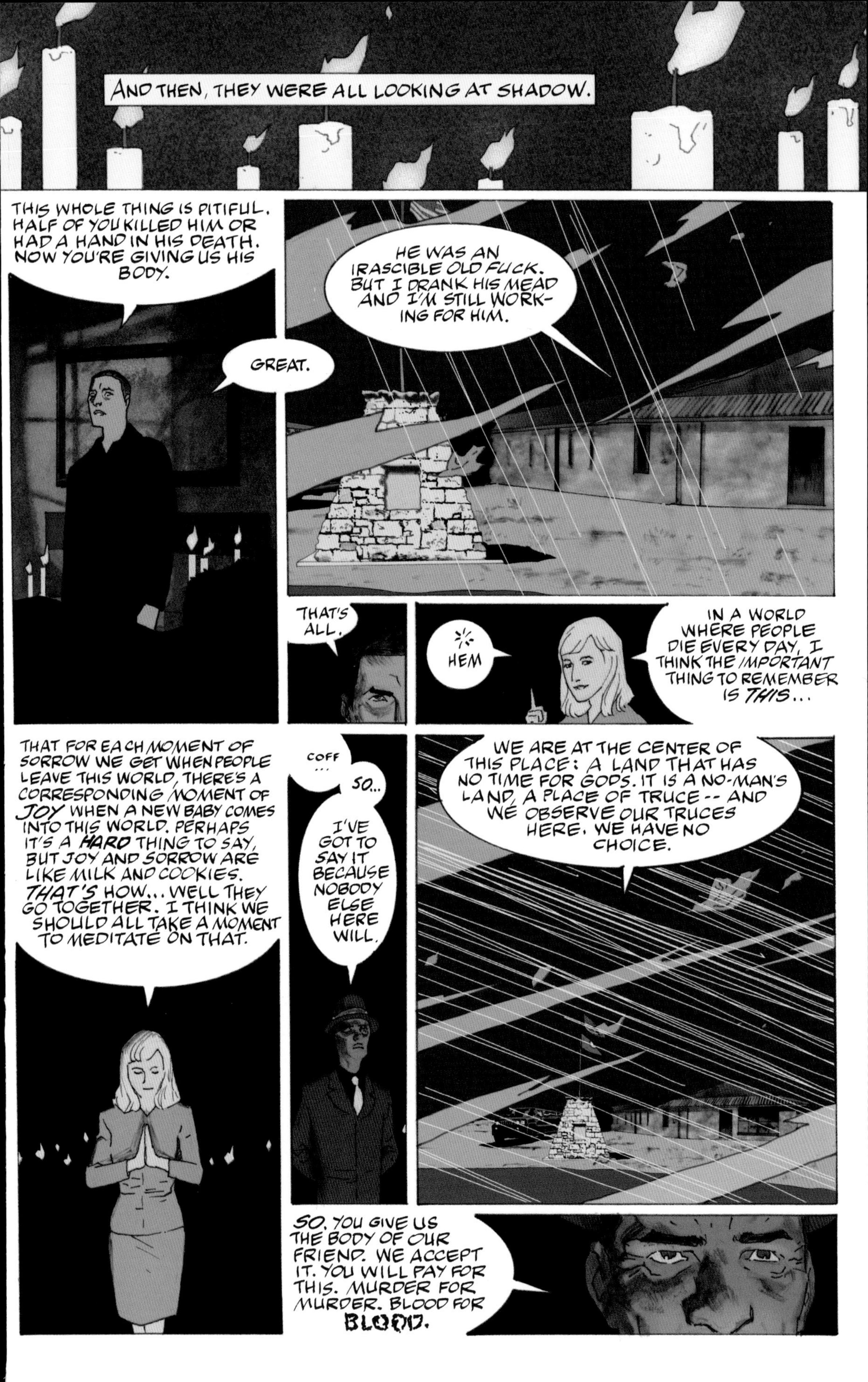
AND THEN, THEY WERE ALL LOOKING AT SHADOW.
THIS WHOLE THING IS PITIFUL. HALF OF YOU KILLED HIM OR HAD A HAND IN HIS DEATH. NOW YOU'RE GIVING US HIS BODY.
HE WAS AN IRASCIBLE OLD FUCK. BUT I DRANK HIS MEAD AND I'M STILL WORKING FOR HIM.
GREAT.
THAT'S ALL.
*HEM
IN A WORLD WHERE PEOPLE DIE EVERY DAY, I THINK THE IMPORTANT THING TO REMEMBER IS THIS...
THAT FOR EACH MOMENT OF SORROW WE GET WHEN PEOPLE LEAVE THIS WORLD, THERE'S A CORRESPONDING MOMENT OF JOY WHEN A NEW BABY COMES INTO THIS WORLD. PERHAPS IT'S A HARD THING TO SAY, BUT JOY AND SORROW ARE LIKE MILK AND COOKIES. THAT'S HOW... WELL THEY GO TOGETHER. I THINK WE SHOULD ALL TAKE A MOMENT TO MEDITATE ON THAT.
COFF...
SO...
I'VE GOT TO SAY IT BECAUSE NOBODY ELSE HERE WILL.
WE ARE AT THE CENTER OF THIS PLACE: A LAND THAT HAS NO TIME FOR GODS. IT IS A NO-MAN'S LAND, A PLACE OF TRUCE -- AND WE OBSERVE OUR TRUCES HERE. WE HAVE NO CHOICE.
SO. YOU GIVE US THE BODY OF OUR FRIEND. WE ACCEPT IT. YOU WILL PAY FOR THIS. MURDER FOR MURDER. BLOOD FOR BLOOD.

WHATEVER. YOU COULD SAVE YOURSELVES A LOT OF EFFORT BY SIMPLY SHOOTING YOURSELVES IN THE HEAD. CUT OUT THE MIDDLEMAN.

YOU WILL NOT EVEN DIE IN BATTLE. YOU WILL DIE A SOFT, POOR DEATH.

FUCK YOU! AND FUCK YOUR MOTHER AND THE FUCKING HORSE YOU FUCKING RODE IN ON.

THE BLOOD-DIMMED TIDE IS LOOSE.

I THINK THAT COMES NEXT.

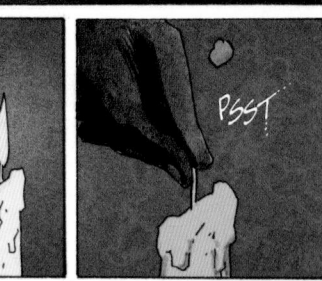

PSST

OKAY. HE'S YOURS. WE'RE DONE.

TAKE THE OLD BASTARD AWAY.

NOW WHAT HAPPENS?

NOW WE WRAP HIM UP AND TAKE HIM AWAY FROM HERE.

OKAY. I'VE GOT HIM. LET'S PUT HIM INTO THE BACK OF THE CAR.

WEDNESDAY'S WORDS WERE IN SHADOW'S HEAD WITH EVERY STEP HE TOOK, AND HE COULD TASTE THE SOUR-SWEETNESS OF MEAD IN THE BACK OF HIS THROAT.

I BROUGHT YOU MEAD TO DRINK BECAUSE IT'S TRADITIONAL AND RIGHT NOW WE NEED ALL THE TRADITION WE CAN GET. IT SEALS OUR BARGAIN.

IN AN EMERGENCY, YOU HURT PEOPLE WHO NEED TO BE HURT.

IN THE UNLIKELY EVENT OF MY DEATH, YOU WILL HOLD MY VIGIL.

WE HAVEN'T MADE A BARGAIN.

YOU INVESTIGATE, GO PLACES, AND ASK QUESTIONS FOR ME.

AND IN RETURN, I SHALL SEE THAT YOUR NEEDS ARE ADEQUATELY TAKEN CARE OF.

SURE WE HAVE. YOU WORK FOR ME. YOU PROTECT ME. YOU HELP ME. YOU TRANSPORT ME FROM PLACE TO PLACE.

HE PLACED WEDNESDAY DOWN AS GENTLY AS HE COULD IN THE BACK OF THE BUS.

" I BROUGHT YOU MEAD TO DRINK..."

HERE. MISTER WORLD WANTED YOU TO HAVE THIS. WE FOUND IT IN THE MASONIC HALL WHEN WE WERE CLEANING UP. KEEP IT FOR LUCK.

GOD KNOWS YOU'LL NEED IT.

SHADOW WISHED HE COULD COME BACK WITH SOMETHING SHARP AND CLEVER, BUT TOWN WAS ALREADY BACK AT THE LIMO AND SHADOW STILL COULDN'T THINK OF ANYTHING CLEVER TO SAY.

I SHOULD HAVE EATEN HIS HEART, NOT JUST CURSED HIS DEATH. HE NEEDS TO BE TAUGHT RESPECT.

YOU RIDE SHOTGUN. I'LL DRIVE A WHILE.

PRINCETON, MISSOURI.

ANYWHERE YOU WANT US TO DROP YOU? IF I WERE YOU, I'D RUSTLE UP SOME I.D. AND HEAD FOR CANADA OR MEXICO. YOU AREN'T WORKING FOR WEDNESDAY, ANYMORE. ONCE WE DROP HIS BODY OFF, YOU'RE FREE TO GO.

AND DO WHAT?

KEEP OUT OF THE WAY WHILE THE WAR IS ON. THEN, WHEN THIS IS OVER, YOU WILL COME BACK TO ME, AND I WILL FINISH THE WHOLE THING.

WITH MY HAMMER.

WHERE ARE WE TAKING THE BODY?

VIR-GINIA, THERE'S A TREE.

A WORLD TREE. WE HAD ONE IN MY PART OF THE WORLD. BUT OURS GREW UNDER THE WORLD, NOT ABOVE IT.

WE PUT HIM AT THE FRONT OF THE TREE. WE LEAVE HIM THERE AND LET YOU GO. WE DRIVE SOUTH. THERE'S A BATTLE, MANY DIE. THE WORLD CHANGES. A LITTLE.

MOST OF THIS BATTLE WILL BE FOUGHT IN A PLACE YOU CANNOT GO.

YOU MEAN BACKSTAGE LIKE THE DESERT, WITH ALL THE BONES IN IT.

BACKSTAGE. YES. EVERY TIME I FIGURE YOU DON'T HAVE ENOUGH SENSE TO BRING GUTS TO A BEAR, YOU SURPRISE ME.

THAT'S WHERE THE REAL BATTLE WILL HAPPEN. EVERYTHING ELSE WILL JUST BE FLASH AND THUNDER.

TELL ME ABOUT THE VIGIL.

IT'S A TRADITION. THE PERSON ON THE VIGIL GETS TIED TO THE TREE. JUST LIKE WEDNESDAY WAS, AND THEN THEY HANG THERE FOR NINE DAYS AND NINE NIGHTS, NO FOOD, NO WATER. AT THE END, THEY CUT THE PERSON DOWN, AND IF THEY LIVED... WELL, IT *COULD* HAPPEN, AND WEDNESDAY WILL HAVE HAD HIS VIGIL.

I'LL DO IT.

NO!

YES.

"WHY"?

BECAUSE IT'S THE KIND OF THING A LIVING PERSON WOULD DO.

THERE WAS ANOTHER PART OF HIM--MAYBE IT WAS *MIKE AINSEL*, HE OF THE LAKESIDE POLICE DEPARTMENT--WHO WAS STILL TRYING TO FIGURE IT ALL OUT, TRYING TO SEE THE BIG PICTURE.

HIDDEN INDIANS.

WHAT?

"THE PICTURES YOU'D GET TO COLOR AS KIDS. CAN YOU SEE THE HIDDEN INDIANS IN THIS PICTURE? AT FIRST GLANCE, YOU COULD ONLY SEE THE WATERFALL AND THE ROCKS AND THE TREES. THEN YOU SEE THAT SHADOW IS AN INDIAN."

THERE ARE NO INDIANS IN THE WATERFALL. SLEEP.

BUT THE BIG PICTURE...

THEN HE SLEPT AND DREAMED OF HIDDEN INDIANS.

SHADOW HAD LOST ALL SENSE OF TIME ON THE DRIVE FROM KANSAS. HAD THEY BEEN DRIVING FOR TWO DAYS? THREE DAYS? HE DID NOT KNOW.

THE BODY IN THE BACK OF THE BUS DID NOT SEEM TO BE ROTTING. HE COULD SMELL IT-- A FAINT ODOR OF JACK DANIEL'S AND SOUR HONEY.

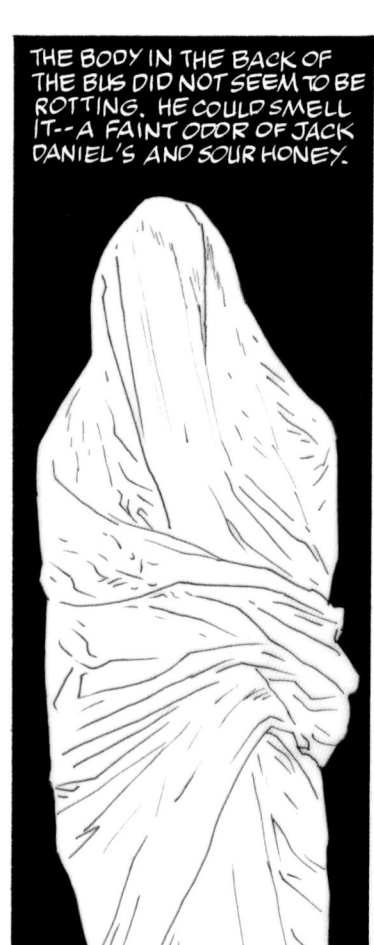

FROM TIME TO TIME, HE WOULD TAKE OUT THE GLASS EYE FROM HIS POCKET AND LOOK AT IT. IT WAS A GHASTLY SOUVENIR, BUT ODDLY COMFORTING: AND HE SUSPECTED THAT IT WOULD HAVE AMUSED WEDNESDAY TO KNOW THAT HIS EYE HAD WOUND UP IN SHADOW'S POCKET.

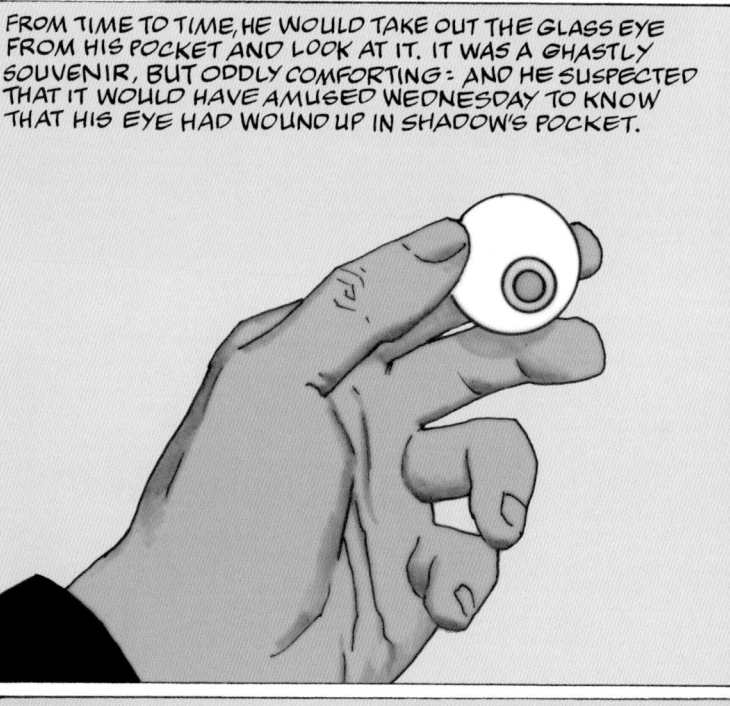

VIRGINIA

ASH

ASH

ASH

THEY JOLTED OVER A RIDGE AND SHADOW SAW THE TREE.

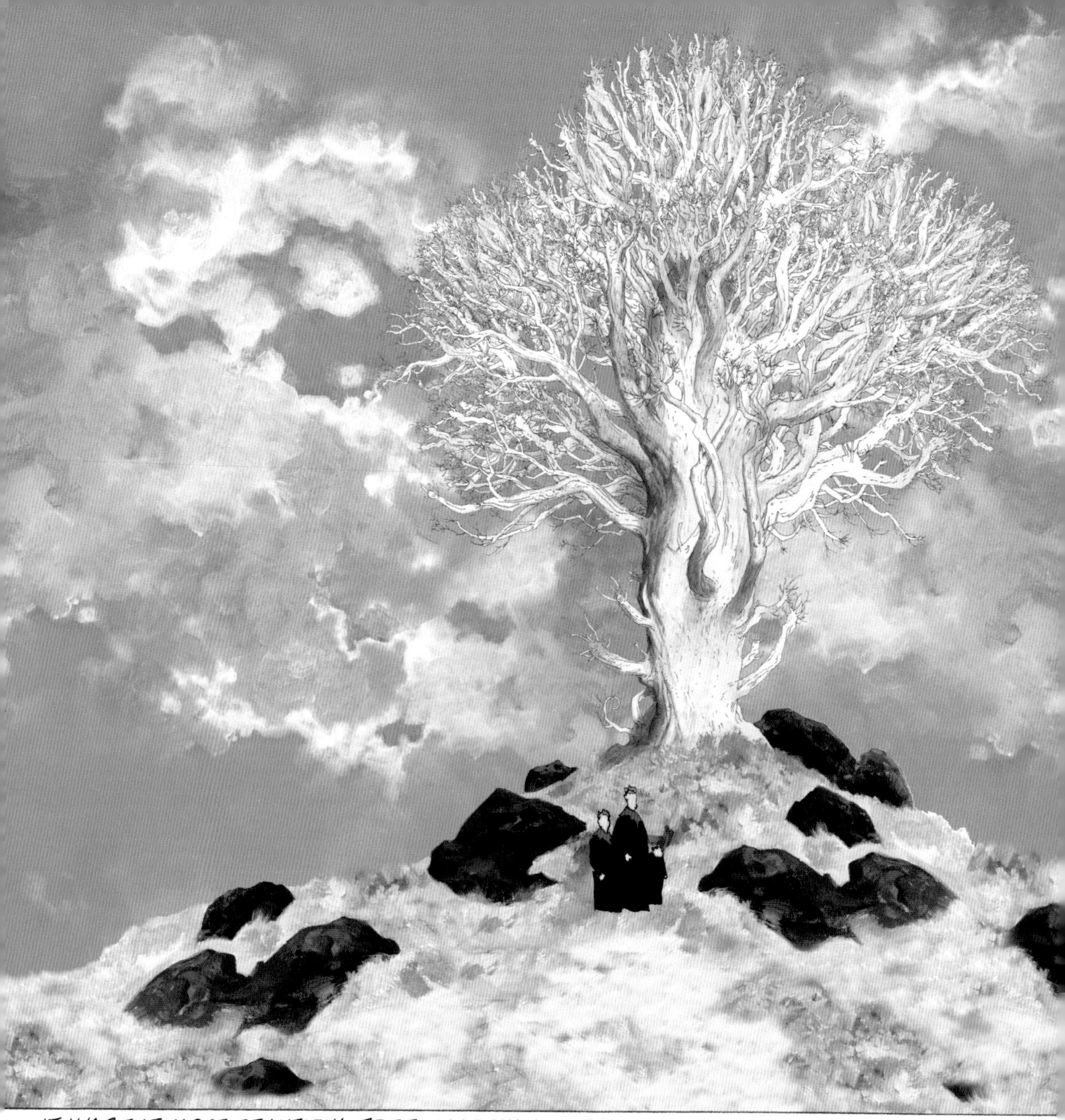

IT WAS THE MOST BEAUTIFUL TREE SHADOW HAD EVER SEEN. IT ALSO LOOKED INSTANTLY FAMILIAR. HE WONDERED IF HE HAD DREAMED IT, THEN REALIZED THAT, NO, HE HAD SEEN IT BEFORE, OR A REPRESENTATION OF IT MANY TIMES. IT WAS WEDNESDAY'S SILVER TIEPIN.

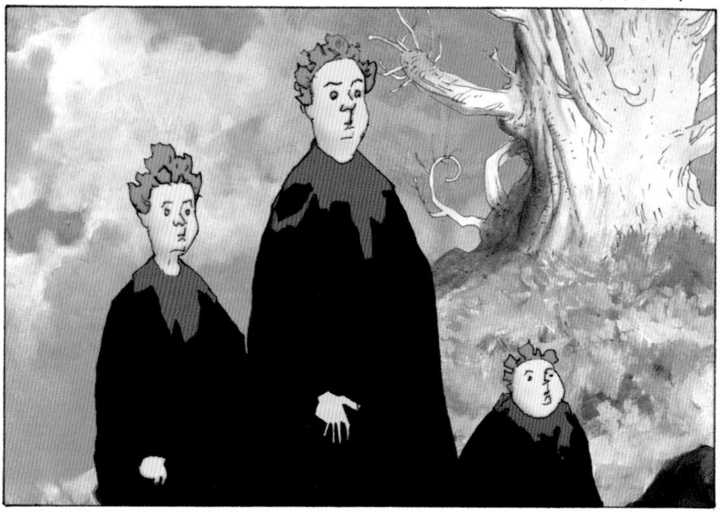

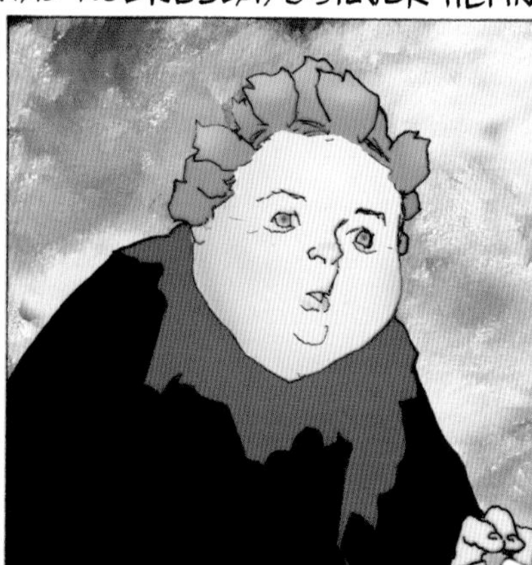

"THE ONE WHO WILL MOURN THE ALL-FATHER?"

"YOU ARE THE ONE?"

"YOU HAVE CHOSEN TO TAKE THE VIGIL?"

"YES."

SHADOW, YOU DON'T *HAVE* TO DO THIS. YOU AIN'T READY FOR IT.

I'M DOING IT.

YOU DON'T KNOW WHAT YOU'RE LETTING YOUR-SELF IN FOR.

IT DOESN'T MATTER.

THEN IT KILLS ME.

AND IF YOU DIE, IF IT KILLS YOU?

I *SAID* YOU HAVE *SHIT* FOR BRAINS, AND YOU STILL HAVE *SHIT* FOR BRAINS. CAN'T YOU SEE WHEN SOMEBODY'S TRYING TO HELP YOU OUT?

I'M SORRY.

YOU MUST COME THROUGH THIS ALIVE, COME THROUGH THIS SAFELY FOR ME.

BAM!

THE BIGGEST WOMAN, WHOSE NAME SEEMED TO BE URTHA OR URDER-- SHADOW COULD NOT REPEAT IT TO HER TO HER SATISFACTION, TOLD HIM, IN PANTOMINE TO TAKE OFF HIS CLOTHES.

ALL OF THEM ?

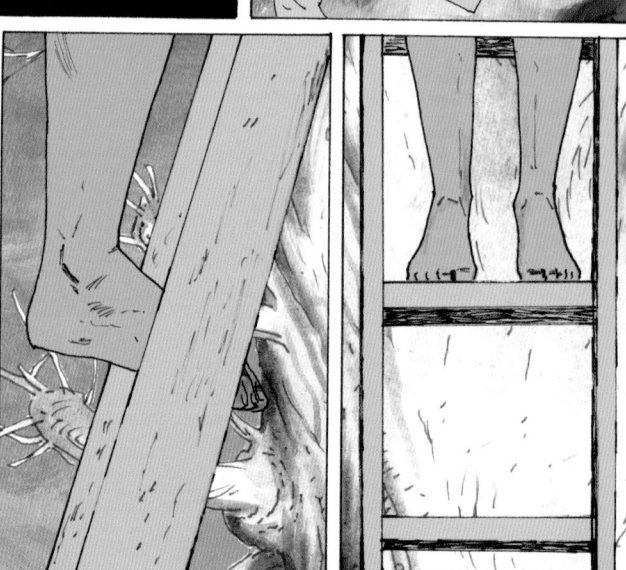

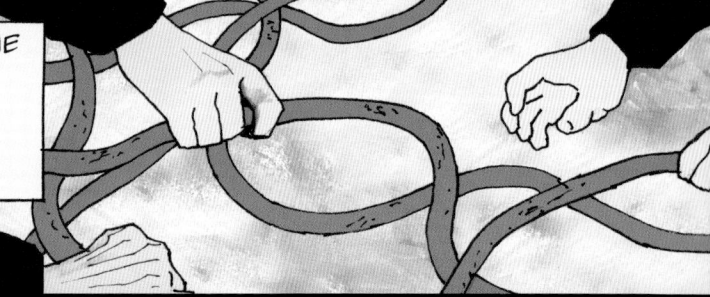

THE MIDDLE WOMAN TIPPED OUT THE CONTENTS OF THE SACK SHE WAS CARRYING. IT WAS FILLED WITH A TANGLE OF THIN ROPES, BROWN WITH AGE AND DIRT, AND THE WOMEN BEGAN TO SORT THEM OUT INTO LENGTHS.

THEY CLIMBED THEIR OWN LADDERS NOW, AND THEY BEGAN TO KNOT THE ROPES, INTRICATE AND ELEGANT KNOTS, AND THEY WRAPPED THE ROPES FIRST ABOUT THE TREE, AND THEN ABOUT SHADOW.

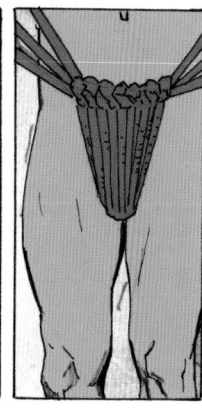

THE ROPES WENT UNDER HIS ARMS, BETWEEN HIS LEGS, AROUND HIS WAIST, HIS ANKLES, BINDING HIM TO THE TREE.

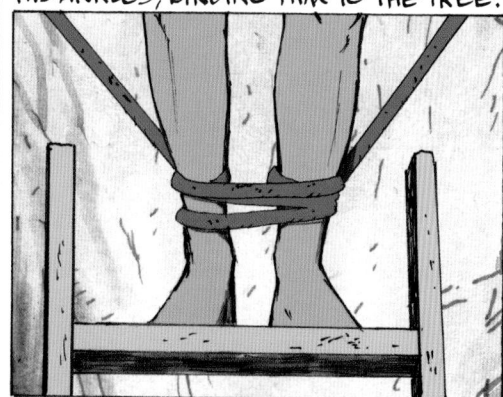

THE FINAL ROPE WAS TIED LOOSELY, ABOUT HIS NECK.

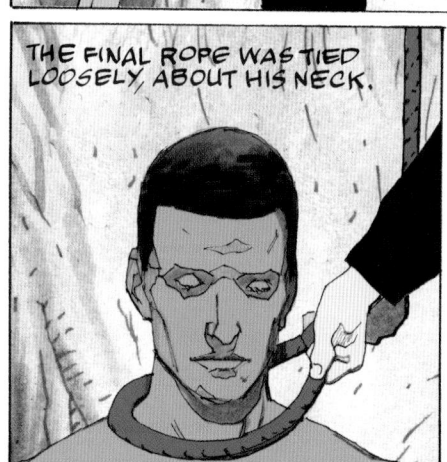

THEY TOOK THE LADDERS AWAY.

THERE WAS A MOMENT OF PANIC AS HE DROPPED A FEW INCHES, AS ALL HIS WEIGHT WAS TAKEN BY THE ROPES. HE MADE NO SOUND.

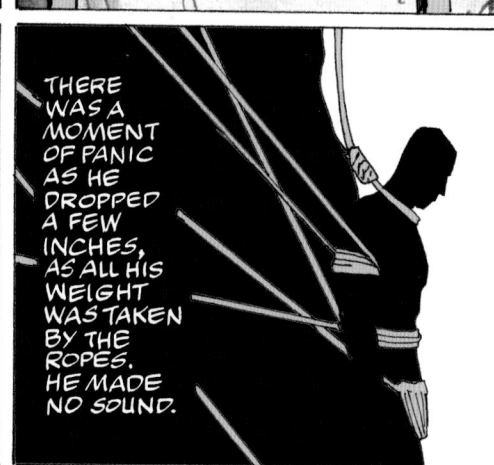

THE WOMEN PLACED WEDNESDAY'S BODY, WRAPPED IN ITS MOTEL-SHEET SHROUD AT THE FOOT OF THE TREE, AND THEY LEFT HIM THERE.

THEY LEFT HIM THERE ALONE.

CHAPTER THREE

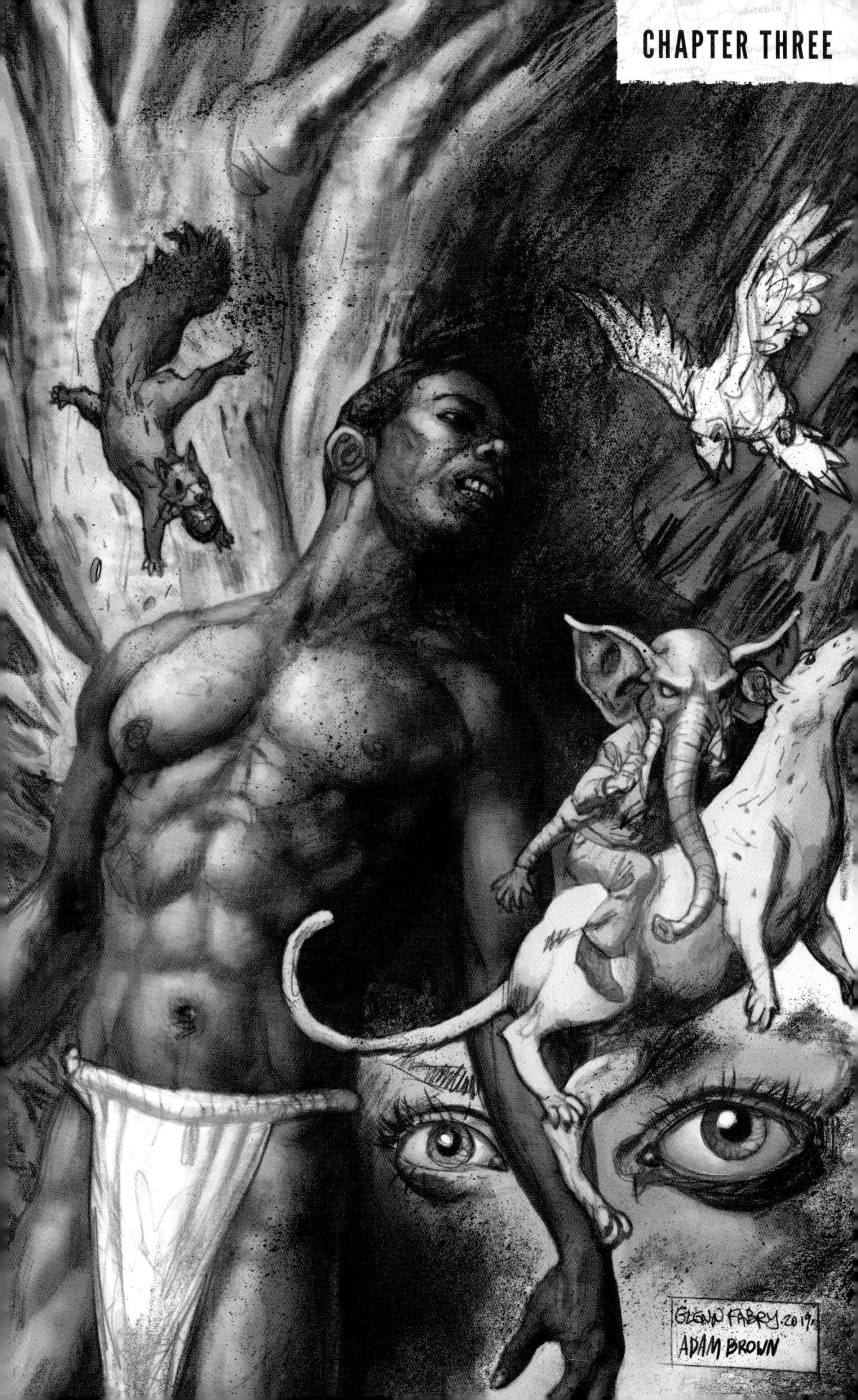
GLENN FABRY 2019
ADAM BROWN

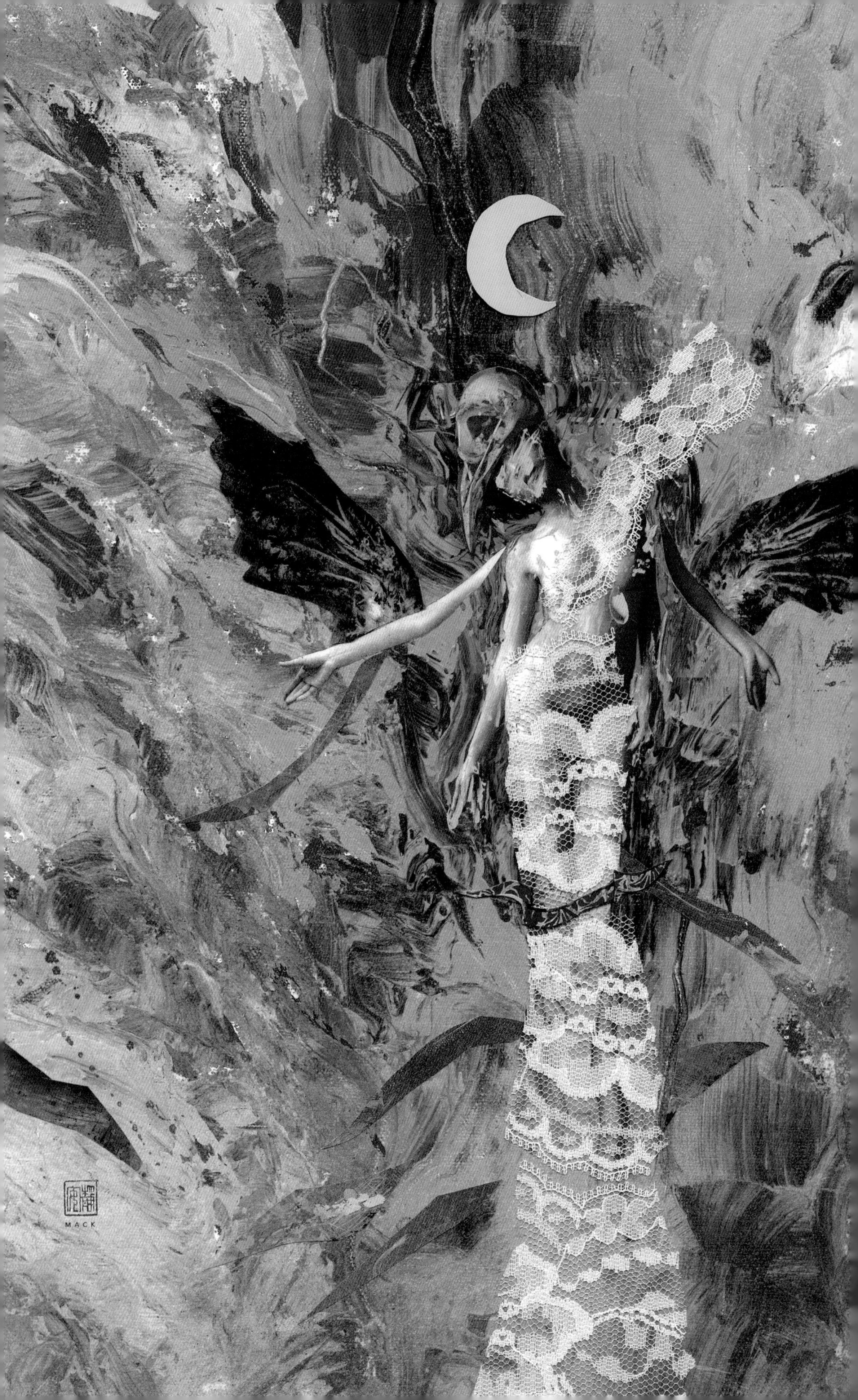
MACK

15

THE FIRST DAY THAT SHADOW HUNG FROM THE TREE, HE EXPERIENCED ONLY DISCOMFORT, THAT EDGED SLOWLY INTO PAIN, AND THEN, INTO ACCEPTANCE. HE HUNG. THE WIND WAS STILL.

THE PAIN IN HIS ARMS AND LEGS BECAME, BY DEGREES INTOLERABLE.

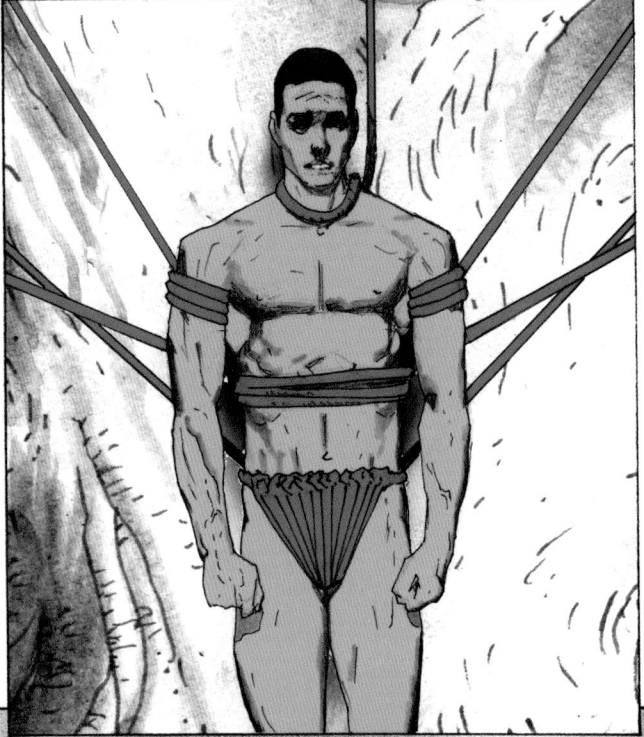

IF HE RELAXED THEM, THEN THE ROPE AROUND HIS NECK WOULD TAKE UP THE SLACK, AND THE WORLD WOULD SHIMMER AND SWIM.

HE COULD FEEL HIS HEART LABORING IN HIS CHEST, A POUNDING, ARRHYTHMIC TATTOO. HIS BREATH CAME IN SHALLOW GULPS.

AFTER SEVERAL HOURS, FLEETING BURSTS OF COLOR STARTED TO EXPLODE ACROSS HIS VISION, THROBBING AND PULSING WITH A LIFE OF THEIR OWN.

SHADOW'S TONGUE TURNED DRY AND SKIN-LIKE IN HIS MOUTH.

HE PUSHED HIMSELF UP AND AWAY FROM THE TREE IN SUCH A WAY THAT WOULD ALLOW HIM TO FILL HIS LUNGS.

HE BREATHED UNTIL HE COULD HOLD HIMSELF UP NO MORE.

THEN HE FELL BACK INTO THE BONDS AND HUNG FROM THE TREE.

WHEN THE ANGRY, LAUGHING CHATTERING STARTED, HE CLOSED HIS MOUTH, CONCERNED THAT IT WAS HE HIMSELF THAT WAS MAKING IT.

IT'S THE WORLD LAUGHING AT ME.

CHK CHK CHK CHK CHK CHK CHK

SOMETHING RAN DOWN THE TREE TRUNK BESIDE HIM.

RATATOSK.

HE SLEPT.

THE PAIN WOKE HIM SEVERAL TIMES IN THE NEXT FEW HOURS.

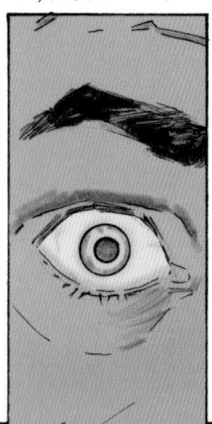

IT PULLED HIM FROM A DARK DREAM IN WHICH DEAD CHILDREN REPROACHED HIM FOR FAILING THEM.

AND IT PULLED HIM FROM ANOTHER DREAM IN WHICH A MAMMOTH LUMBERED OUT OF THE MIST.

AWAKE FOR A MOMENT, A SPIDER EDGING ACROSS HIS FACE, AND HE SHOOK HIS HEAD, DISLODGING IT, OR FRIGHTENING IT.

NOW THE MAMMOTH WAS AN ELEPHANT-HEADED MAN ON THE BACK OF A HUGE MOUSE.

IF YOU HAD INVOKED ME BEFORE YOU STARTED THIS JOURNEY, PERHAPS SOME OF YOUR TROUBLES COULD HAVE BEEN AVOIDED.

IT'S IN THE TRUNK.

YES. IN THE TRUNK.

YOU WILL FORGET MANY THINGS. YOU WILL GIVE MANY THINGS AWAY. YOU WILL LOSE MANY THINGS.

BUT DO NOT LOSE THIS.

HE OPENED HIS MOUTH TO CATCH THE RAIN AS IT FELL.

A FLASH OF LIGHTNING SO BRIGHT IT FELT LIKE A BLOW.

THEN A CRACK AND A BOOM, AND THE RAIN REDOUBLED.

THE WIND PULLED AT SHADOW, FLAYING HIS SKIN, CUTTING TO THE BONE, AND SHADOW KNEW THAT THE REAL STORM HAD BEGUN, THE TRUE STORM, AND THAT NOW THERE WAS NOTHING ANY OF THEM COULD DO BUT RIDE IT OUT: *NONE OF THEM, OLD GODS OR NEW, SPIRITS, POWERS, OR MEN.*

A STRANGE JOY ROSE WITHIN HIM, THEN AS THE RAIN LASHED HIS NAKED SKIN, AND HE EXHULTED, HE WAS ALIVE. HE HAD NEVER FELT LIKE THIS.

EVER.

AT THE FOOT OF THE TREE, THE RAIN HAD MADE THE SHEET PARTLY TRANSPARENT, AND HAD PUSHED IT FORWARD SO THAT SHADOW COULD SEE WEDNESDAY'S DEAD HAND, WAXY AND PAL—

BY THE FOLLOWING MORNING, THE PAIN WAS OMNIPRESENT. HE WAS HUNGRY, HIS HEAD WAS POUNDING, AND HE WAS FORCED TO SUCK AIR LIKE A DIVER SURFACING FROM THE DEPTHS.

HIS SKIN WAS ON FIRE, WITH PINS AND NEEDLES. THE SENSATION WAS INTOLERABLE.

HIS LIFE WAS LAID OUT BELOW HIM LIKE THE ITEMS AT SOME SURREALIST PICNIC: HE COULD SEE HIS MOTHER'S PUZZLED STARE, THE AMERICAN EMBASSY IN NORWAY, LAURA'S EYES ON THEIR WEDDING DAY.

OUR WEDDING DAY, YOU BRIBED THE ORGANIST TO PLAY THE THEME SONG TO *SCOOBY-DOO* AS YOU WALKED DOWN THE AISLE. DO YOU REMEMBER?

HEH

WHAT'S SO FUNNY, PUPPY?

OF COURSE I REMEMBER, DARLING. I WOULD HAVE MADE IT, TOO, IF IT WASN'T FOR THOSE MEDDLING KIDS.

I LOVED YOU SO MUCH.

HE COULD FEEL HER LIPS ON HIS, WARM AND WET, NOT COLD AND DEAD. SO HE KNEW THAT THIS WAS ANOTHER HALLUCINATION.

YOU AREN'T HERE, ARE YOU?

NO

BUT YOU ARE CALLING ME FOR THE LAST TIME. AND I AM COMING. SLEEP, PUPPY.

HE SLEPT.

SHADOW WAS COLD. HIS MOUTH AND THROAT BURNING, PAINFUL, AND CRACKED. BUT THE PART OF HIM THAT UNDERSTOOD THAT SEEMED VERY FAR AWAY FROM THE REST OF HIM.

SOMETIMES, IN THE DAYLIGHT, HE WOULD SEE STARS FALL.

OTHER TIMES, HE SAW HUGE BIRDS FLYING TOWARD HIM.

NOTHING REACHED HIM; NOTHING TOUCHED HIM.

RATATOSK.

THE SQUIRREL LANDED HEAVILY, WITH SHARP CLAWS, A WALNUT-SHELL IN ITS FRONT PAWS.

WATER

BY THE THIRD WALNUT-SHELL, HE WAS NO LONGER THIRSTY.

HE BEGAN TO STRUGGLE, PULLING AT THE ROPES, TRYING TO GET DOWN, TO GET FREE, TO GET AWAY.

BUT THE ROPES WERE STRONG AND SOON HE EXHAUSTED HIMSELF ONCE MORE.

IN HIS DELIRIUM, SHADOW BECAME THE TREE. ITS ROOTS WENT DEEP DOWN INTO TIME, INTO THE HIDDEN SPRINGS OF THE WOMAN CALLED *URD*, WHO GUARDED THE WATERS OF TIME. NOW, WHEN HE WAS THIRSTY, HE PULLED WATER FROM HIS ROOTS, PULLED THEM UP INTO THE BODY OF HIS BEING.

HE WAS THE TREE AND THE WIND AND THE DARK SKY; HE WAS RATATOSK THE SQUIRREL; HE WAS THE MAD-EYED HAWK WHO SAT AT THE TOP OF THE TREE; HE WAS THE WORM AT THE HEART OF THE TREE.

HE HAD A HUNDRED THOUSAND FINGERS. THE STARS WHEELED, AND HE PASSED HIS HANDS OVER THE GLITTERING STARS, PALMING THEM, SWITCHING THEM, VANISHING THEM.

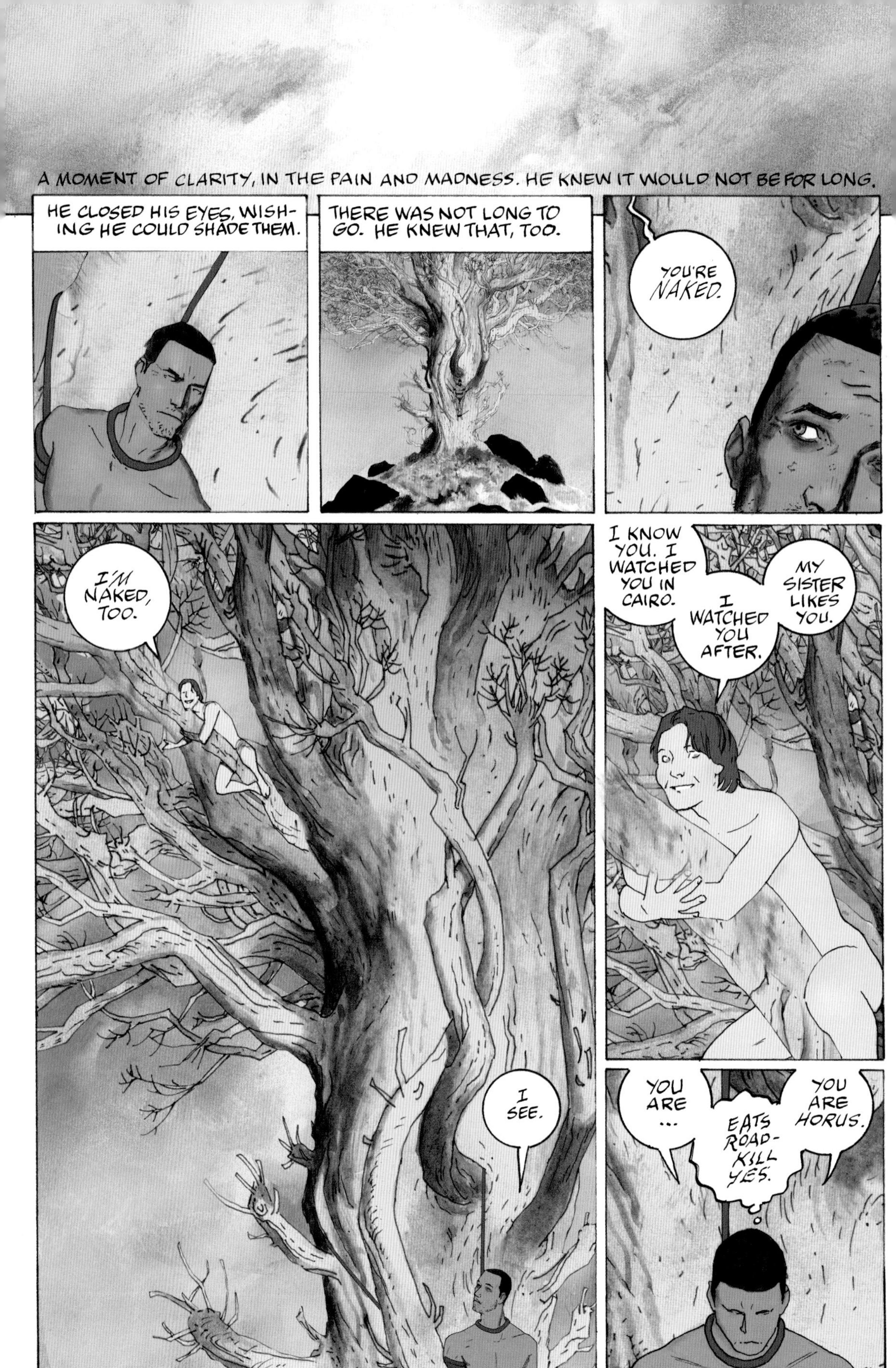
A MOMENT OF CLARITY, IN THE PAIN AND MADNESS. HE KNEW IT WOULD NOT BE FOR LONG.
HE CLOSED HIS EYES, WISHING HE COULD SHADE THEM.
THERE WAS NOT LONG TO GO. HE KNEW THAT, TOO.
YOU'RE NAKED.
I'M NAKED, TOO.
I SEE.
I KNOW YOU. I WATCHED YOU IN CAIRO.
I WATCHED YOU AFTER.
MY SISTER LIKES YOU.
YOU ARE ...
EATS ROAD-KILL YES.
YOU ARE HORUS.

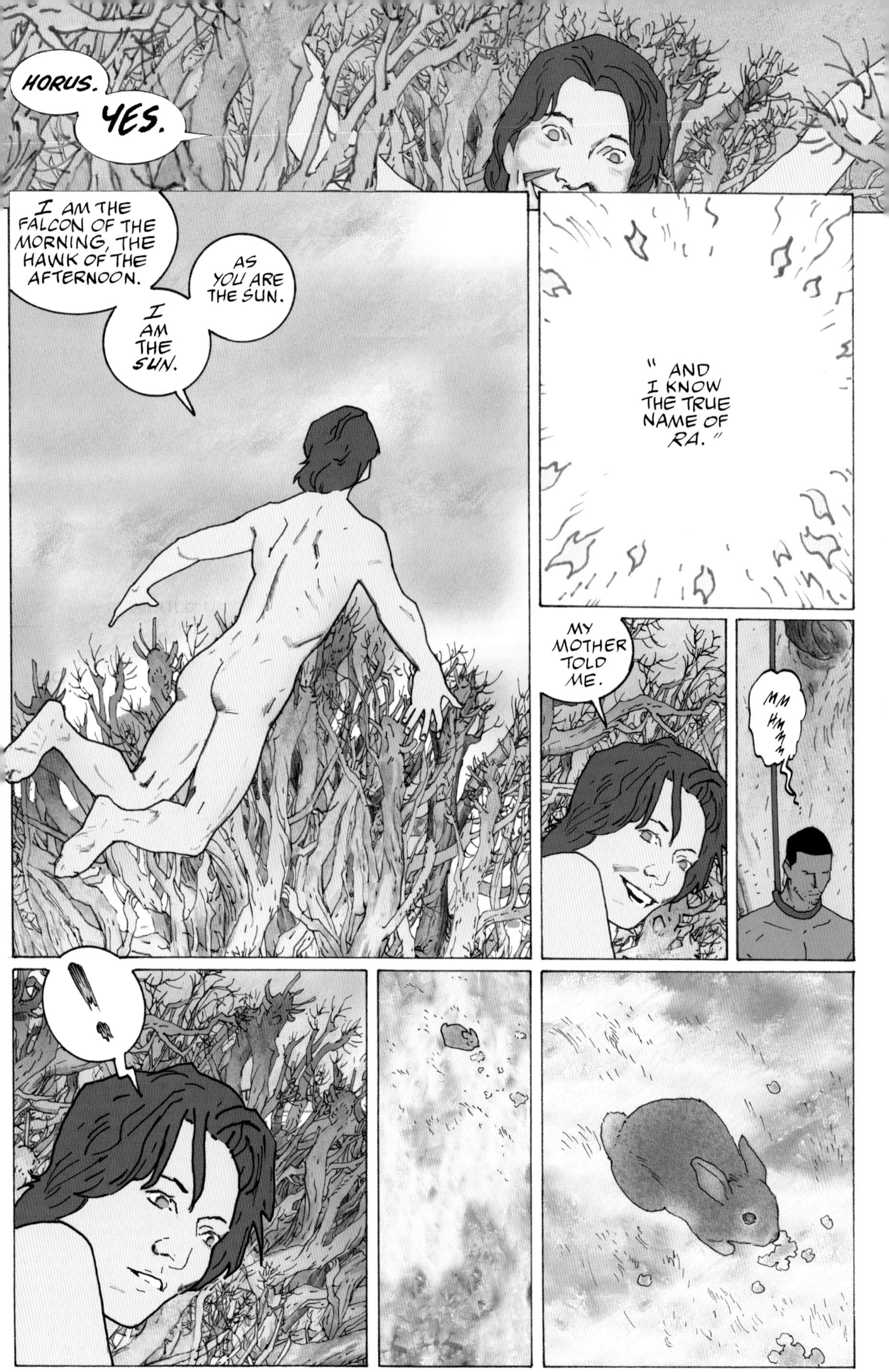
HORUS.
YES.
I AM THE FALCON OF THE MORNING, THE HAWK OF THE AFTERNOON.
I AM THE SUN.
AS YOU ARE THE SUN.
" AND I KNOW THE TRUE NAME OF RA."
MY MOTHER TOLD ME.
MM HMMM
!

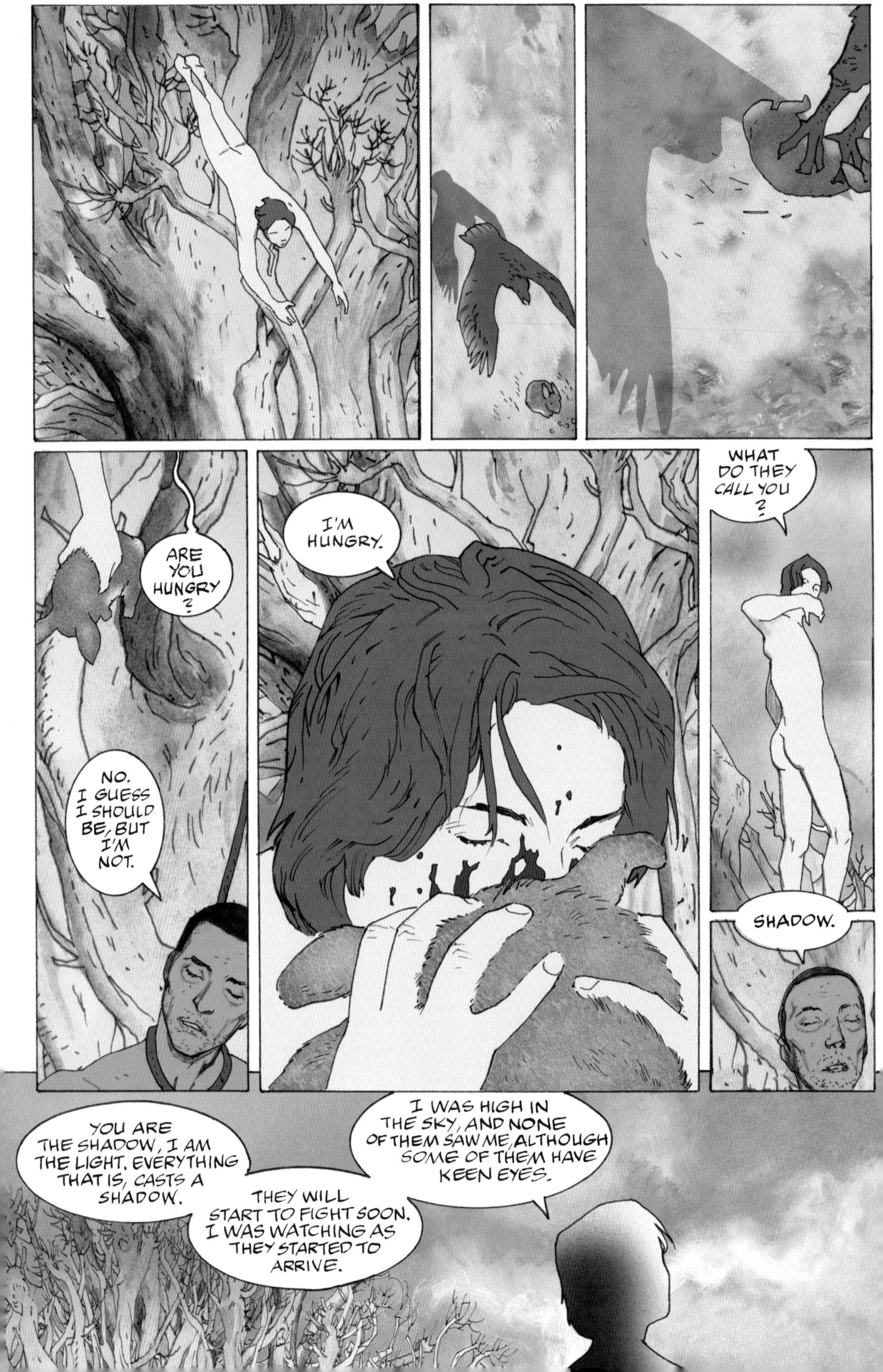
ARE YOU HUNGRY ?
I'M HUNGRY.
WHAT DO THEY CALL YOU ?
NO. I GUESS I SHOULD BE, BUT I'M NOT.
SHADOW.
YOU ARE THE SHADOW, I AM THE LIGHT. EVERYTHING THAT IS, CASTS A SHADOW.
I WAS HIGH IN THE SKY, AND NONE OF THEM SAW ME, ALTHOUGH SOME OF THEM HAVE KEEN EYES.
THEY WILL START TO FIGHT SOON. I WAS WATCHING AS THEY STARTED TO ARRIVE.

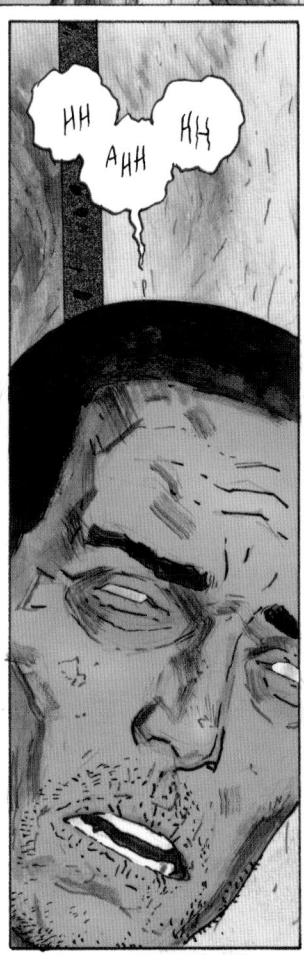

HH AHH HH

YOU'RE DYING. AREN'T YOU?

BUT SHADOW COULD NO LONGER SPEAK. EVERYTHING WAS VERY FAR AWAY.

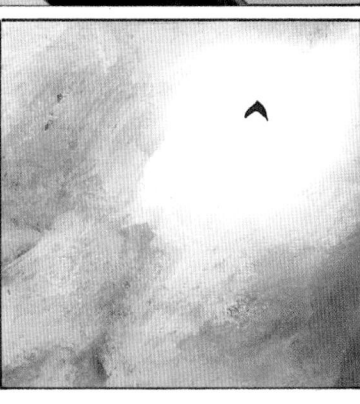

A COUGH SHOOK SHADOW'S FRAME, A RACKING PAINFUL COUGH THAT STABBED HIS CHEST AND HIS THROAT.

KAK KA HAK HUNGK KAK
HK HUNGK

HE GAGGED FOR BREATH.

AHUH AHUH

HEY, PUPPY.

HE TRIED TO SPEAK, BUT...

HK HK K

YOU KNOW, THAT DOESN'T SOUND GOOD.

THE MOONLIGHT BURNED BRIGHTLY THROUGH THE BRANCHES. THERE WAS A WOMAN STANDING IN THE MOONLIGHT ON THE GROUND BELOW, HER FACE A PALE OVAL.

HI, PUPPY.

HELLO, LAURA, HOW DID YOU FIND ME?

YOU ARE THE NEAREST THING I HAVE TO LIFE, THE ONLY THING THAT ISN'T BLEAK AND FLAT AND GREY. I COULD BE BLINDFOLDED AND DROPPED INTO THE DEEPEST OCEAN, COULD BE BURIED A HUNDRED MILES UNDERGROUND, AND I WOULD KNOW WHERE TO FIND YOU.

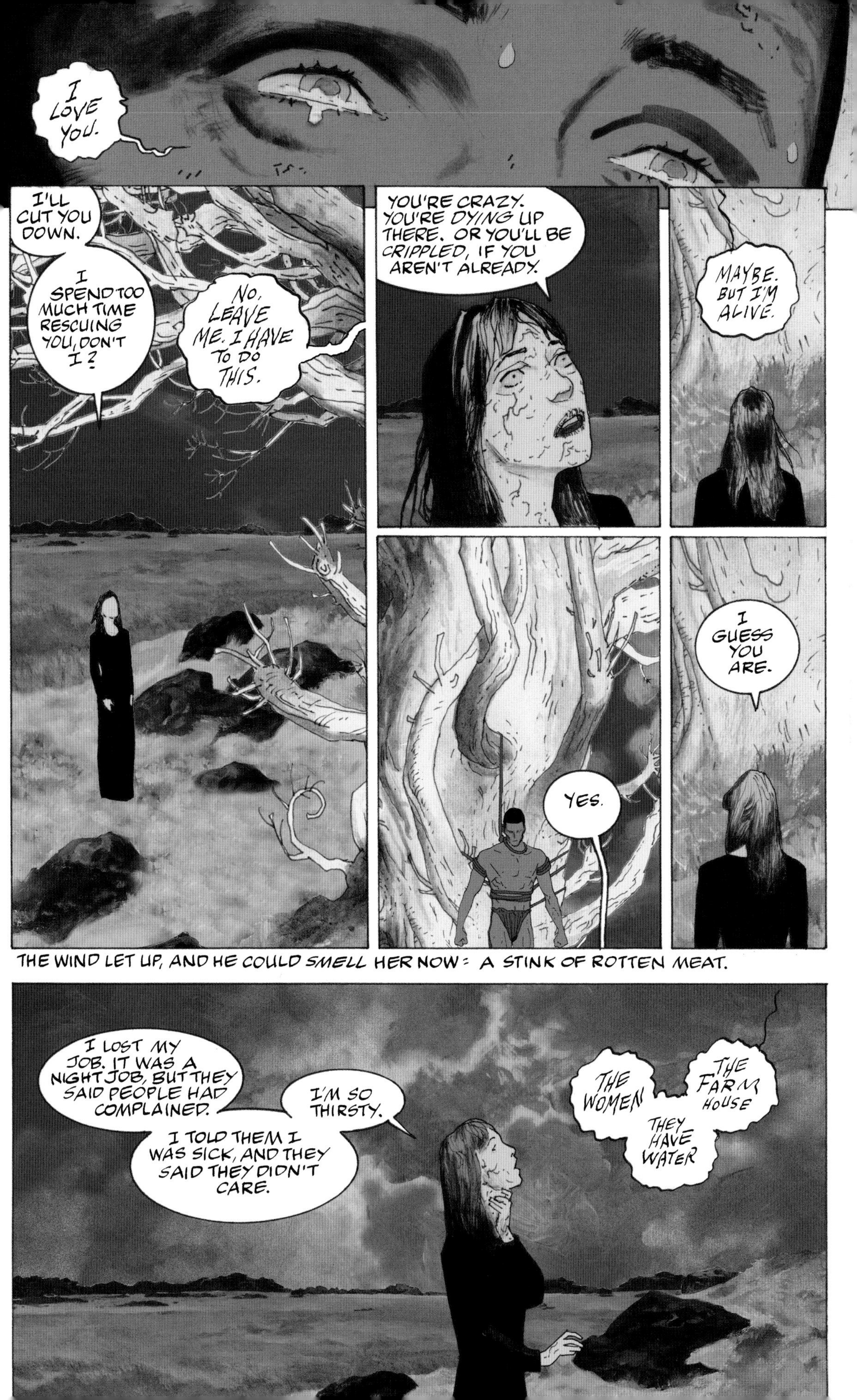

I LOVE YOU.
I'LL CUT YOU DOWN.
I SPEND TOO MUCH TIME RESCUING YOU, DON'T I?
NO. LEAVE ME. I HAVE TO DO THIS.
YOU'RE CRAZY. YOU'RE DYING UP THERE. OR YOU'LL BE CRIPPLED, IF YOU AREN'T ALREADY.
MAYBE. BUT I'M ALIVE.
YES.
I GUESS YOU ARE.
THE WIND LET UP, AND HE COULD SMELL HER NOW: A STINK OF ROTTEN MEAT.
I LOST MY JOB. IT WAS A NIGHT JOB, BUT THEY SAID PEOPLE HAD COMPLAINED.
I TOLD THEM I WAS SICK, AND THEY SAID THEY DIDN'T CARE.
I'M SO THIRSTY.
THE WOMEN
THE FARM HOUSE
THEY HAVE WATER

PUPPY ...

TELL THEM

TELL THEM I SAID TO GIVE YOU WATER

I SHOULD GO... I...

GAK

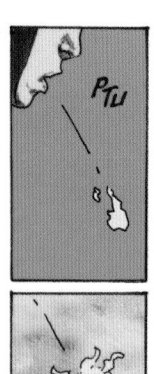

PTU

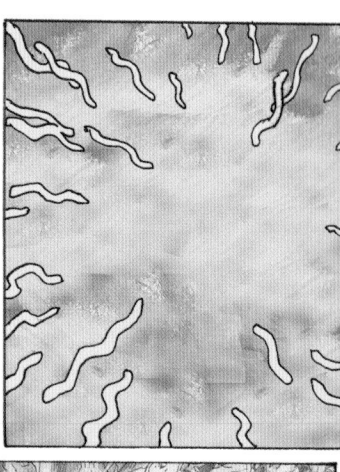

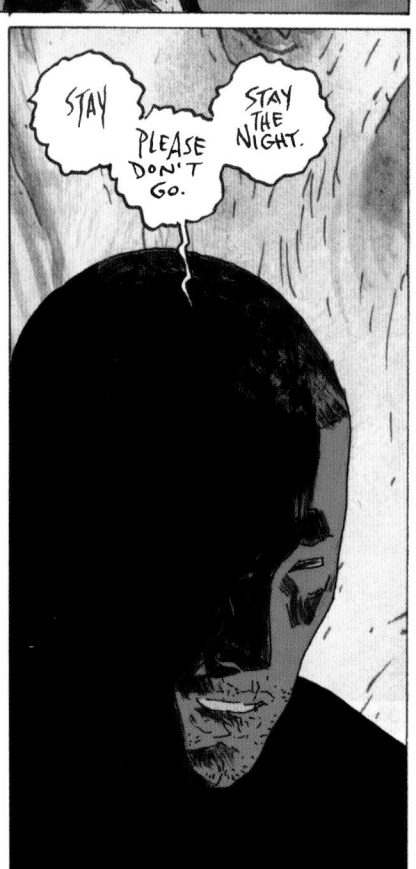

STAY PLEASE DON'T GO.

STAY THE NIGHT.

I'LL STOP AWHILE. NOTHING'S GONNA HURT YOU WHEN I'M HERE. YOU KNOW THAT?

SHADOW COUGHED ONCE MORE. HE CLOSED HIS EYES... ONLY FOR A MOMENT, HE THOUGHT.

BUT WHEN HE OPENED THEM AGAIN, THE MOON HAD SET AND HE WAS ALONE.

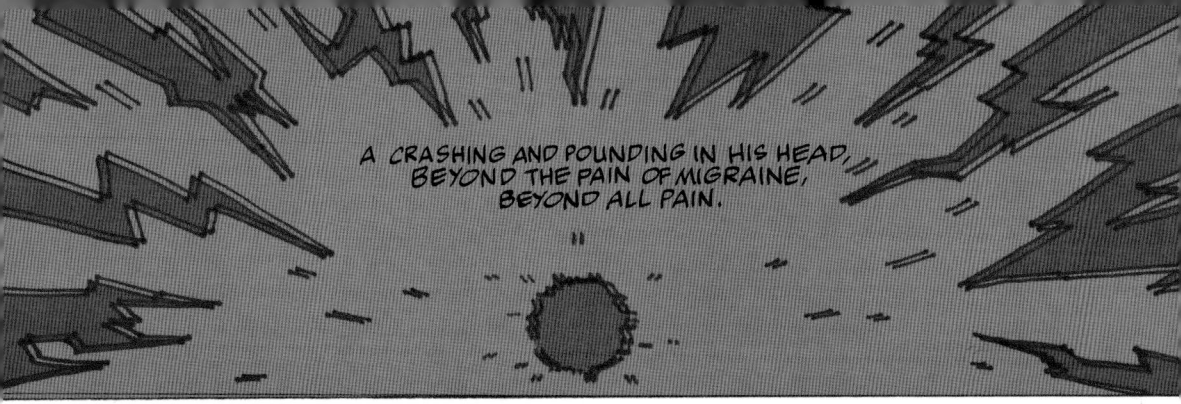

A CRASHING AND POUNDING IN HIS HEAD, BEYOND THE PAIN OF MIGRAINE, BEYOND ALL PAIN.

EVERYTHING DISSOLVED INTO TINY BUTTERFLIES WHICH CIRCLED HIM LIKE A MULTI-COLORED DUST STORM AND THEN EVAPORATED INTO THE NIGHT.

THE WHITE SHEET WRAPPED ABOUT THE BODY AT THE BASE OF THE TREE FLAPPED NOISILY IN THE WIND.

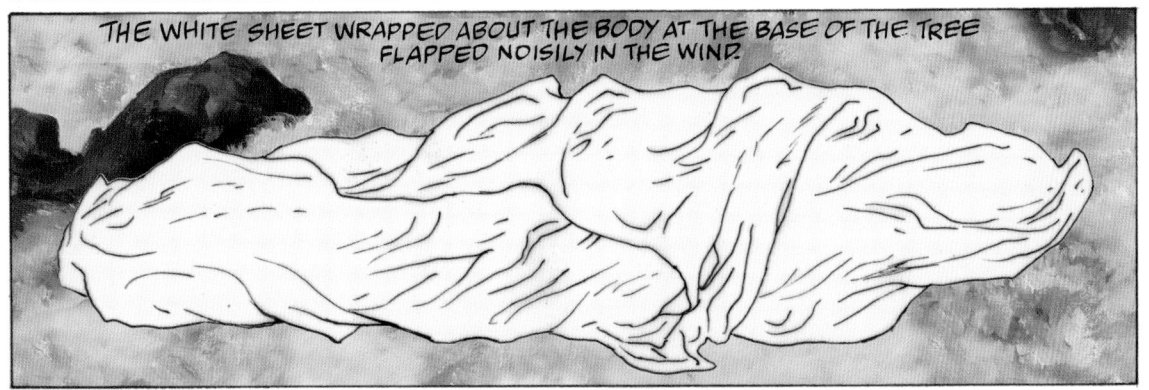

THE POUNDING EASED. EVERYTHING SLOWED.

THERE WAS NOTHING LEFT TO MAKE HIM KEEP BREATHING.

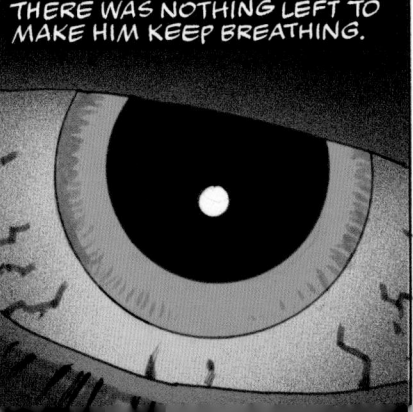

HIS HEART CEASED TO BEAT IN HIS CHEST.

THE
DARKNESS
THAT HE
ENTERED
THIS
TIME
WAS
DEEP
AND
LIT
BY A
SINGLE
STAR,
AND
IT
WAS
FINAL.

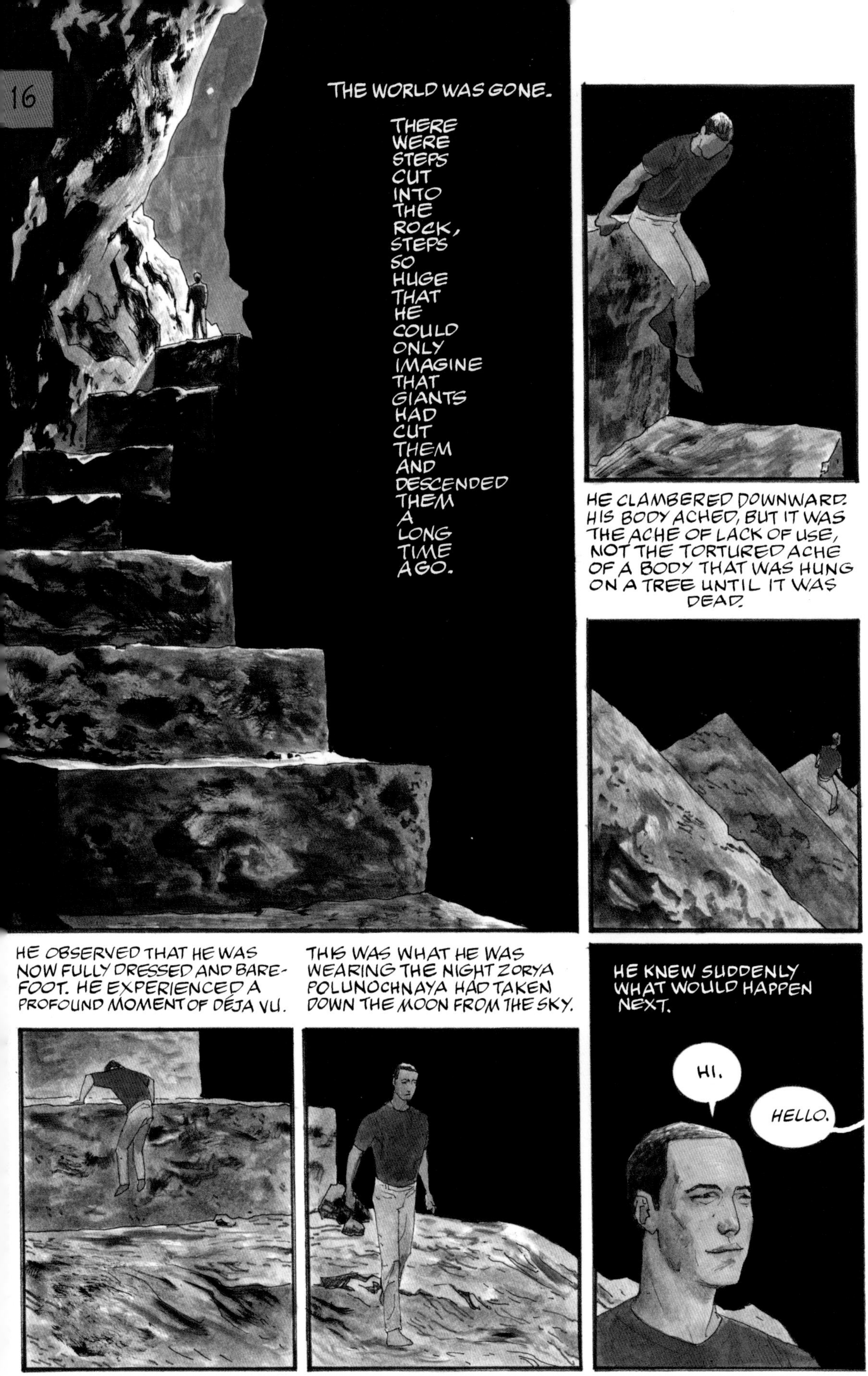
THE WORLD WAS GONE.
THERE WERE STEPS CUT INTO THE ROCK, STEPS SO HUGE THAT HE COULD ONLY IMAGINE THAT GIANTS HAD CUT THEM AND DESCENDED THEM A LONG TIME AGO.
HE CLAMBERED DOWNWARD. HIS BODY ACHED, BUT IT WAS THE ACHE OF LACK OF USE, NOT THE TORTURED ACHE OF A BODY THAT WAS HUNG ON A TREE UNTIL IT WAS DEAD.
HE OBSERVED THAT HE WAS NOW FULLY DRESSED AND BAREFOOT. HE EXPERIENCED A PROFOUND MOMENT OF DÉJA VU.
THIS WAS WHAT HE WAS WEARING THE NIGHT ZORYA POLUNOCHNAYA HAD TAKEN DOWN THE MOON FROM THE SKY.
HE KNEW SUDDENLY WHAT WOULD HAPPEN NEXT.
HI.
HELLO.

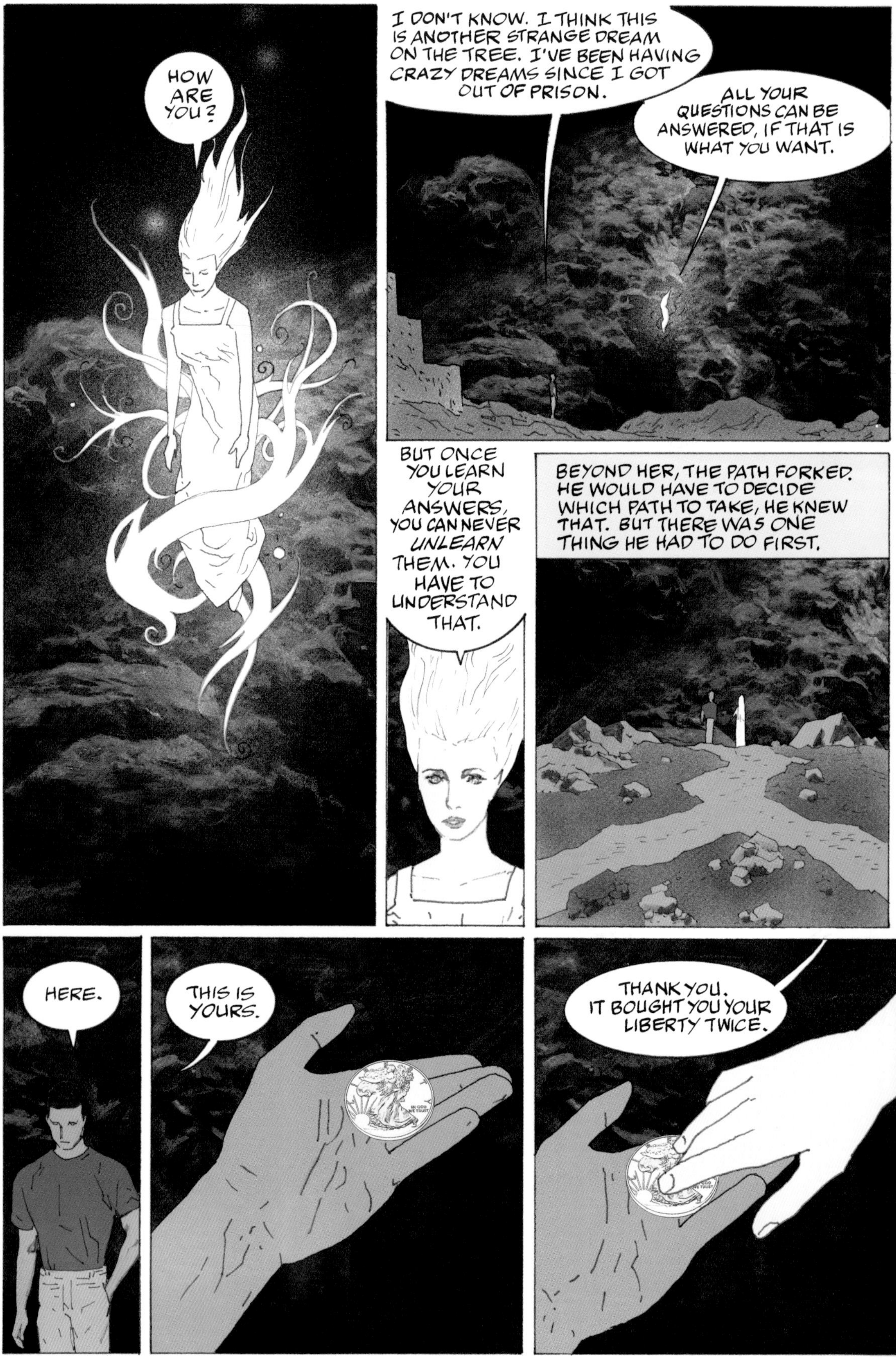
HOW ARE YOU?
I DON'T KNOW. I THINK THIS IS ANOTHER STRANGE DREAM ON THE TREE. I'VE BEEN HAVING CRAZY DREAMS SINCE I GOT OUT OF PRISON.
ALL YOUR QUESTIONS CAN BE ANSWERED, IF THAT IS WHAT YOU WANT.
BUT ONCE YOU LEARN YOUR ANSWERS, YOU CAN NEVER UNLEARN THEM. YOU HAVE TO UNDERSTAND THAT.
BEYOND HER, THE PATH FORKED. HE WOULD HAVE TO DECIDE WHICH PATH TO TAKE, HE KNEW THAT. BUT THERE WAS ONE THING HE HAD TO DO FIRST.
HERE.
THIS IS YOURS.
THANK YOU. IT BOUGHT YOU YOUR LIBERTY TWICE.

AND NOW IT WILL LIGHT YOUR WAY INTO DARK PLACES.

WHICH PATH SHOULD I TAKE?

WHICH WAY WOULD YOU WALK-- THE WAY OF HARD TRUTHS, OR THE WAY OF FINE LIES?

TRUTHS. I'VE COME TOO FAR FOR MORE LIES.

THERE WILL BE A PRICE.

I'LL PAY IT. WHAT IS THE PRICE?

YOUR NAME. YOUR REAL NAME. YOU WILL HAVE TO GIVE IT TO ME.

HOW?

LIKE THIS.

HE FELT HER FINGERS PENETRATE DEEP INTO HIS HEAD. SOME-THING TICKLED IN HIS HEAD AND ALL DOWN HIS SPINE.

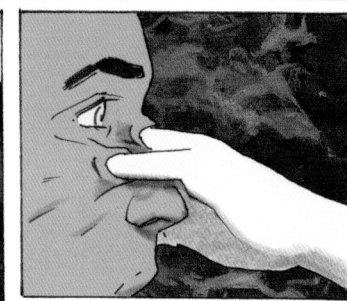

SHE PULLED HER HAND OUT OF HIS HEAD.

IT WAS.

THAT WAY.
FOR NOW.

IS THAT *MY* NAME?

NAMELESS, SHADOW WALKED DOWN THE RIGHT-HAND PATH IN THE MOONLIGHT. WHEN HE TURNED AROUND TO THANK HER, HE SAW NOTHING BUT DARKNESS.

IF THIS IS THE AFTERLIFE, IT'S A LOT LIKE THE HOUSE ON THE ROCK: PART DIORAMA, PART NIGHTMARE.

HE WAS LOOKING AT HIMSELF IN PRISON BLUES AS THE WARDEN TOLD HIM THAT LAURA HAD DIED IN A CAR CRASH. HE SAW THE NAKEDNESS AND FEAR ON HIS FACE.

HE HURRIED ON.

HE SAW HIMSELF INSIDE THE VCR STORE BEATING THE LIVING *CRAP* OUT OF TWO MEN. HE WAS ONLY THE *DRIVER* AT THE BANK ROBBERY, BUT THEY SHOULDN'T HAVE RIPPED HIM OFF.

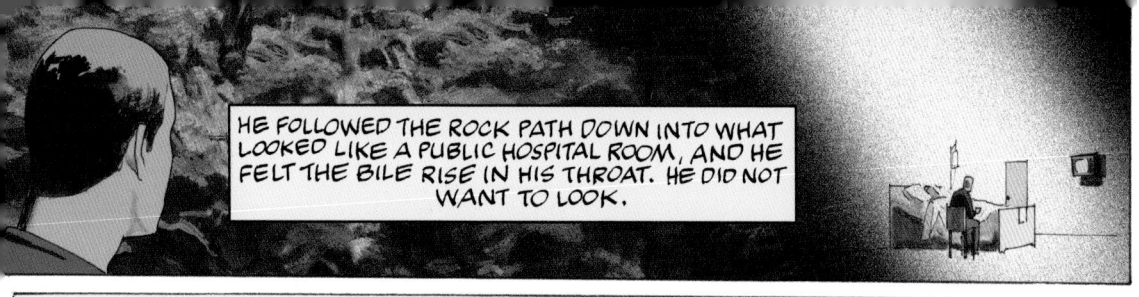

HE FOLLOWED THE ROCK PATH DOWN INTO WHAT LOOKED LIKE A PUBLIC HOSPITAL ROOM, AND HE FELT THE BILE RISE IN HIS THROAT. HE DID NOT WANT TO LOOK.

HIS MOTHER WAS DYING AGAIN, AS SHE'D DIED WHEN HE WAS SIXTEEN, AND HERE HE WAS, A LARGE, CLUMSY BOY, SITTING AT HER BEDSIDE, UNABLE TO LOOK AT HER. AND SO SHE DIED, WHILE HE SAT IN THE CHAIR NEXT TO HER, READING A FAT BOOK.

SHADOW WALKED AWAY FROM THE HOSPITAL ROOM DOWN THE WINDING CORRIDOR, DEEP INTO THE BOWELS OF THE EARTH.

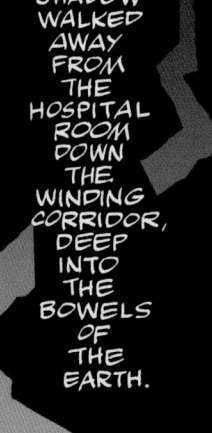

HE'S JUST A SHRIMP OF A KID NOW, AND HE'S ARGUING WITH HIS MOTHER IN SOME EMBASSY RENTAL IN NORTHERN EUROPE.

TELL ME ABOUT MY FATHER.

HE'S *DEAD.* DON'T ASK ABOUT HIM.

BUT WHO WAS HE?

FORGET HIM. DEAD AND GONE AND YOU AIN'T MISSED *NOTHING.*

I WANT TO SEE A PICTURE OF HIM.

I AIN'T *GOT* A PICTURE.

THEN HE IS STANDING IN THE FLOATING DISCO-GLITTER OF A MIRROR BALL, STARING AT A WOMAN WHO LOOKED JUST LIKE HIS MOTHER NEVER LOOKED IN ALL THE YEARS HE KNEW HER. SHE'S LITTLE MORE THAN A CHILD AFTER ALL....AND SHE IS DANCING.

THEY HAVE BEEN DRINKING MARGARITAS, AND SHE HAS SALT ON HER LIPS AND SALT CLINGING TO THE BACK OF HER HAND.

SHADOW FOUND THAT HE WAS COMPLETELY UNSUR-PRISED WHEN HE RECOG-NIZED THE MAN WHO DANCES WITH HER.

HE HAD NOT CHANGED THAT MUCH IN THIRTY-THREE YEARS.

CHAPTER FOUR

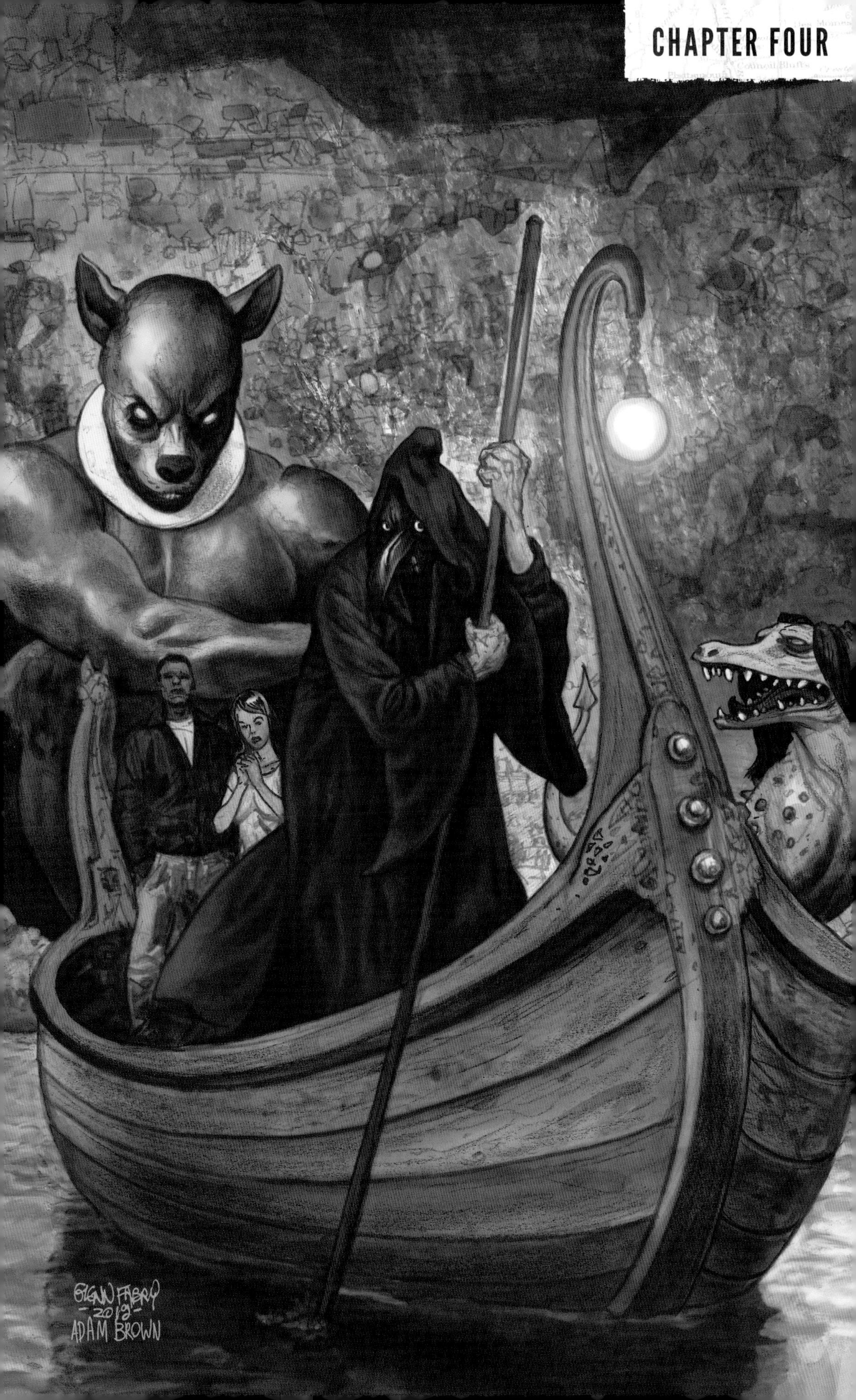
GLENN FABRY
-2019-
ADAM BROWN

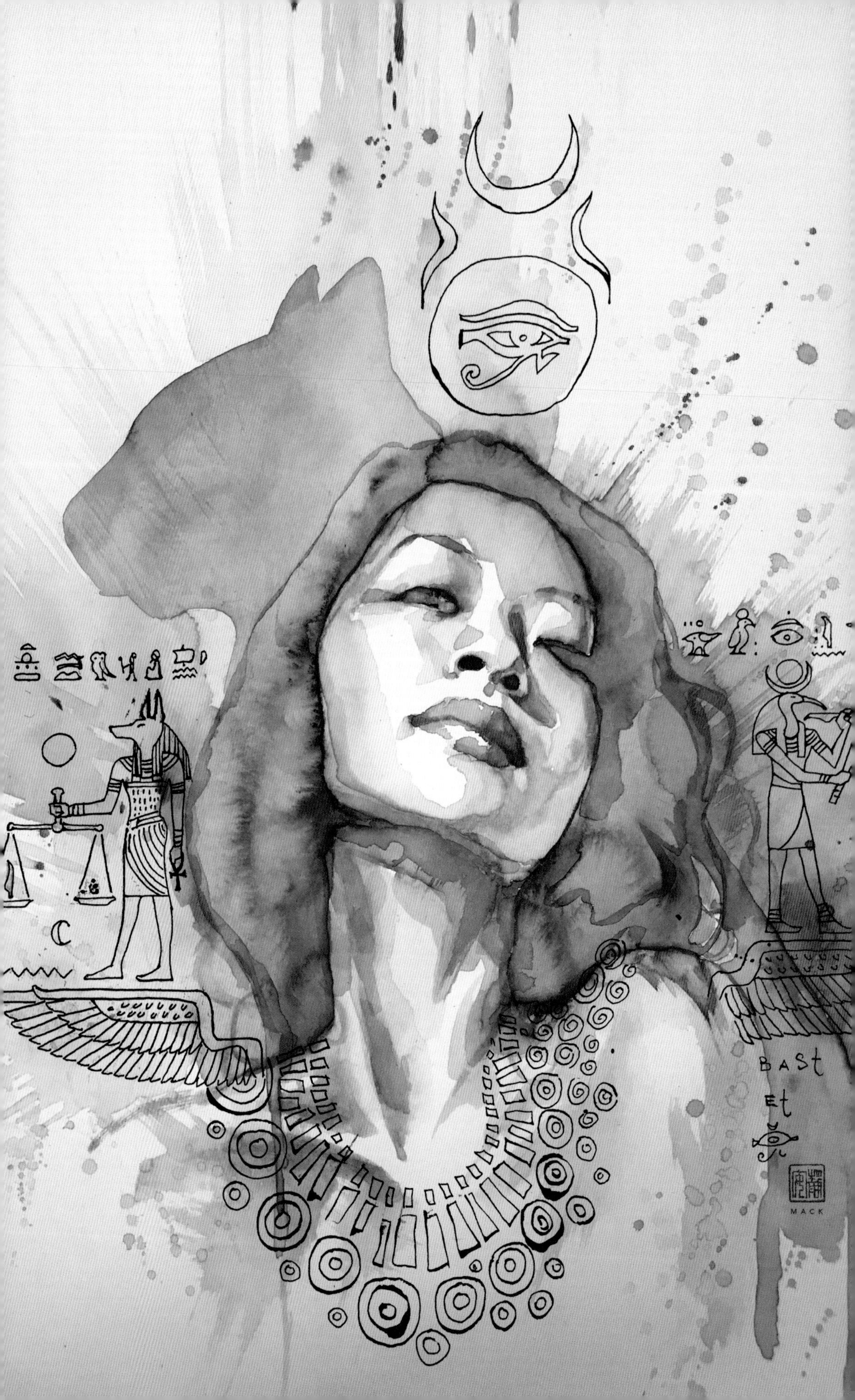
BASt
Et
MACK

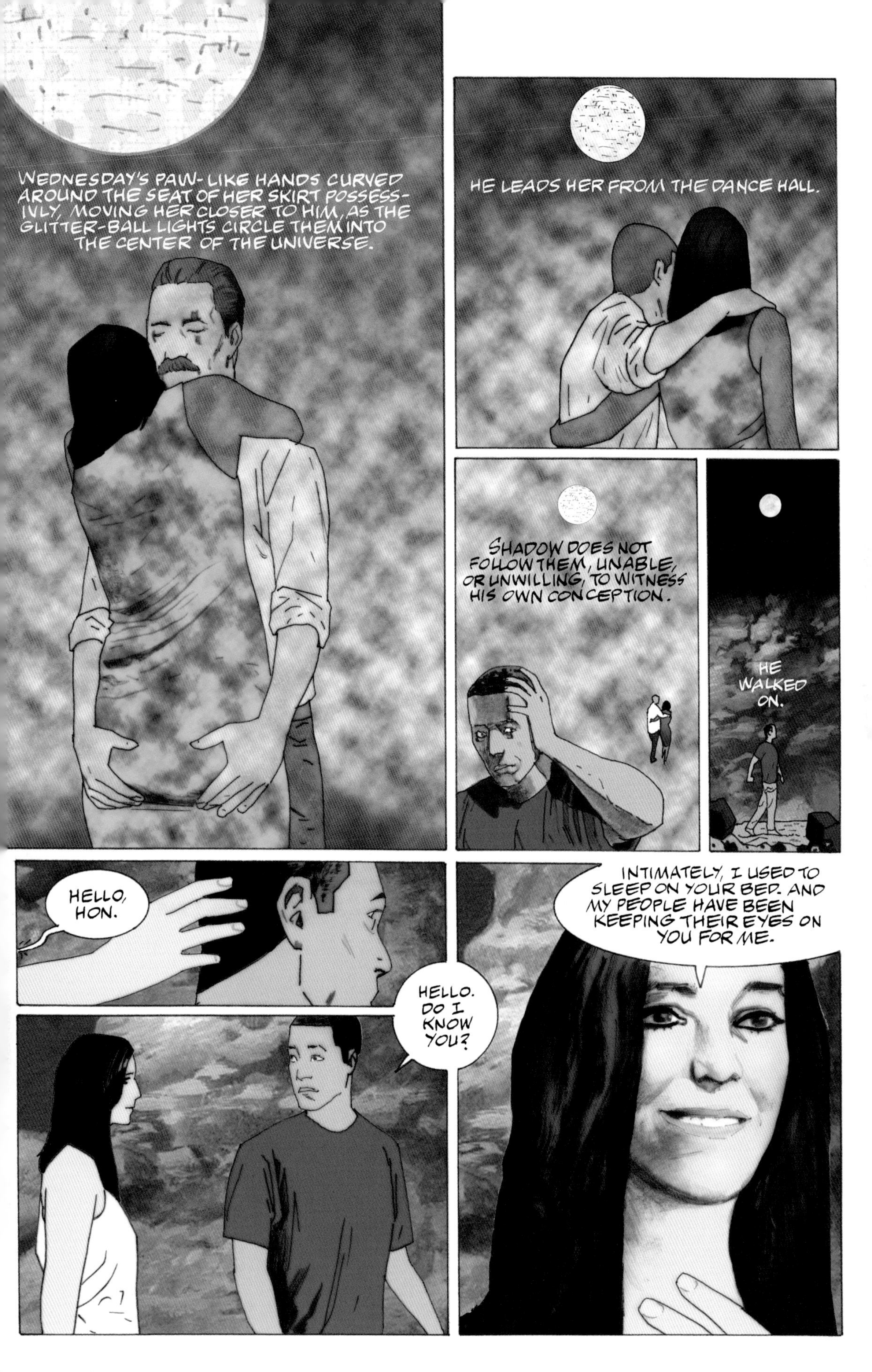
WEDNESDAY'S PAW-LIKE HANDS CURVED AROUND THE SEAT OF HER SKIRT POSSESS-IVLY, MOVING HER CLOSER TO HIM, AS THE GLITTER-BALL LIGHTS CIRCLE THEM INTO THE CENTER OF THE UNIVERSE.
HE LEADS HER FROM THE DANCE HALL.
SHADOW DOES NOT FOLLOW THEM, UNABLE, OR UNWILLING, TO WITNESS HIS OWN CONCEPTION.
HE WALKED ON.
HELLO, HON.
HELLO. DO I KNOW YOU?
INTIMATELY, I USED TO SLEEP ON YOUR BED. AND MY PEOPLE HAVE BEEN KEEPING THEIR EYES ON YOU FOR ME.

OKAY. ONE WAY WILL MAKE YOU WISE. ONE WAY WILL MAKE YOU WHOLE. AND ONE WAY WILL *KILL YOU*.

I'M ALREADY DEAD, I THINK. I DIED ON THE TREE.

THERE'S DEAD...

AND THERE'S *DEAD*...

AND THERE'S *DEAD*.

SO, WHICH WAY DO YOU WANT TO GO?

I DON'T KNOW.

SHE TIPPED HER HEAD, A PERFECTLY FELINE GESTURE AND SUDDENLY SHADOW KNEW HER. HE FELT HIMSELF BEGINNING TO BLUSH.

" IF YOU TRUST ME, I CAN CHOOSE FOR YOU. "

I TRUST YOU.

DO YOU WANT TO KNOW WHAT IT'S GOING TO COST YOU?

I'VE ALREADY LOST MY NAME, AND AS REVELATIONS GO, IT WAS KIND OF PERSONAL.

THEY ALL ARE. THAT'S WHY ALL REVELATIONS ARE SUSPECT.

I DON'T UNDERSTAND.

NO, YOU DON'T.

I'LL TAKE YOUR HEART.

WE'LL NEED IT LATER.

SHE PULLED IT OUT. IT WAS RUBY AND PULSING. IT WAS THE COLOR OF PIGEON'S BLOOD AND IT WAS MADE OF PURE LIGHT. RHYTHMICALLY, IT EXPANDED AND CONTRACTED.

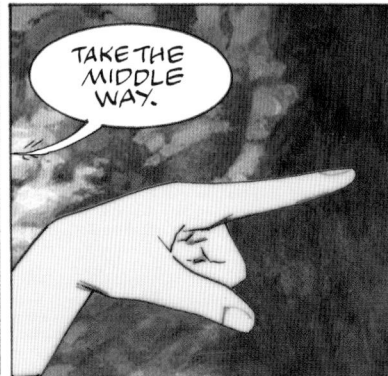

TAKE THE MIDDLE WAY.

WHAT ARE YOU?

WHAT *ARE* YOU PEOPLE?

THINK OF US AS SYMBOLS -- WE'RE THE DREAM HUMANITY CREATES TO MAKE SENSE OF THE SHADOWS ON THE CAVE WALL.

NOW GO ON, KEEP MOVING. YOUR BODY IS ALREADY GROWING COLD.

THE FOOLS ARE GATHERING ON THE MOUNTAIN.

THE CLOCK IS TICKING.

THE FIRST PATH OPENED INTO A VAST CHAMBER, THE PLACE HE HAD DREAMED OF IN THE MOTEL, SO LONG AGO: THE ENDLESS MEMORIAL HALL TO THE FORGOTTEN GODS.

NO.

HE LOOKED TO THE PATH ON THE FAR SIDE. THERE WAS A DISNEYLAND QUALITY TO THE CORRIDOR. COLORED LIGHTS BLINKED LIKE THE LIGHTS ON A TELEVISION STARSHIP.

NO.

NEITHER WAY SEEMED RIGHT. HE WAS DONE WITH PATHS. THE MIDDLE WAY. THE WAY THE CAT-WOMAN TOLD HIM TO WALK. NO DEALS TO MAKE, NO MORE BARGAINS.

NOTHING TO DO BUT ENTER.

HE WAS NOT AFRAID. NOT ANYMORE. FEAR HAD DIED ON THE TREE, AS SHADOW HAD DIED.

SOMETHING SPLASHED IN THE DISTANCE, AND THE SPLASH ECHOED INTO THE VASTNESS.

HELLO HELLO HELLO HELLO HELLO HELLO HELLO

GET IN.

I KNOW YOU.

YOU DO, INDEED. YOU WORKED FOR ME.

I'M AFRAID WE HAD TO INTER LILA GOODCHILD WITHOUT YOU.

MISTER IBIS?

GOOD TO SEE YOU, SHADOW. DO YOU KNOW WHAT A PSYCHOPOMP IS?

I THINK SO. IT'S... UM....

IT IS A FANCY TERM FOR AN ESCORT. I ESCORT THE LIVING TO THE WORLD OF THE DEAD.

I THOUGHT THIS WAS THE WORLD OF THE DEAD.

NO. NOT PER SE. IT'S MORE OF A PRELIMINARY.

YOU PEOPLE TALK 'BOUT THE LIVING AND THE DEAD AS IF THEY'RE TWO MUTUALLY EXCLUSIVE CATEGORIES. AS IF YOU CANNOT HAVE A RIVER THAT IS ALSO A ROAD, OR A SONG THAT IS ALSO A COLOR.

YOU CAN'T. CAN YOU?

WHAT YOU HAVE TO REMEMBER IS THAT LIFE AND DEATH ARE TWO SIDES OF THE SAME COIN. LIKE THE HEADS AND TAILS OF A QUARTER.

AND IF I HAD A DOUBLE-HEADED QUARTER?

YOU DON'T. THEY ONLY BELONG TO FOOLS AND GODS.

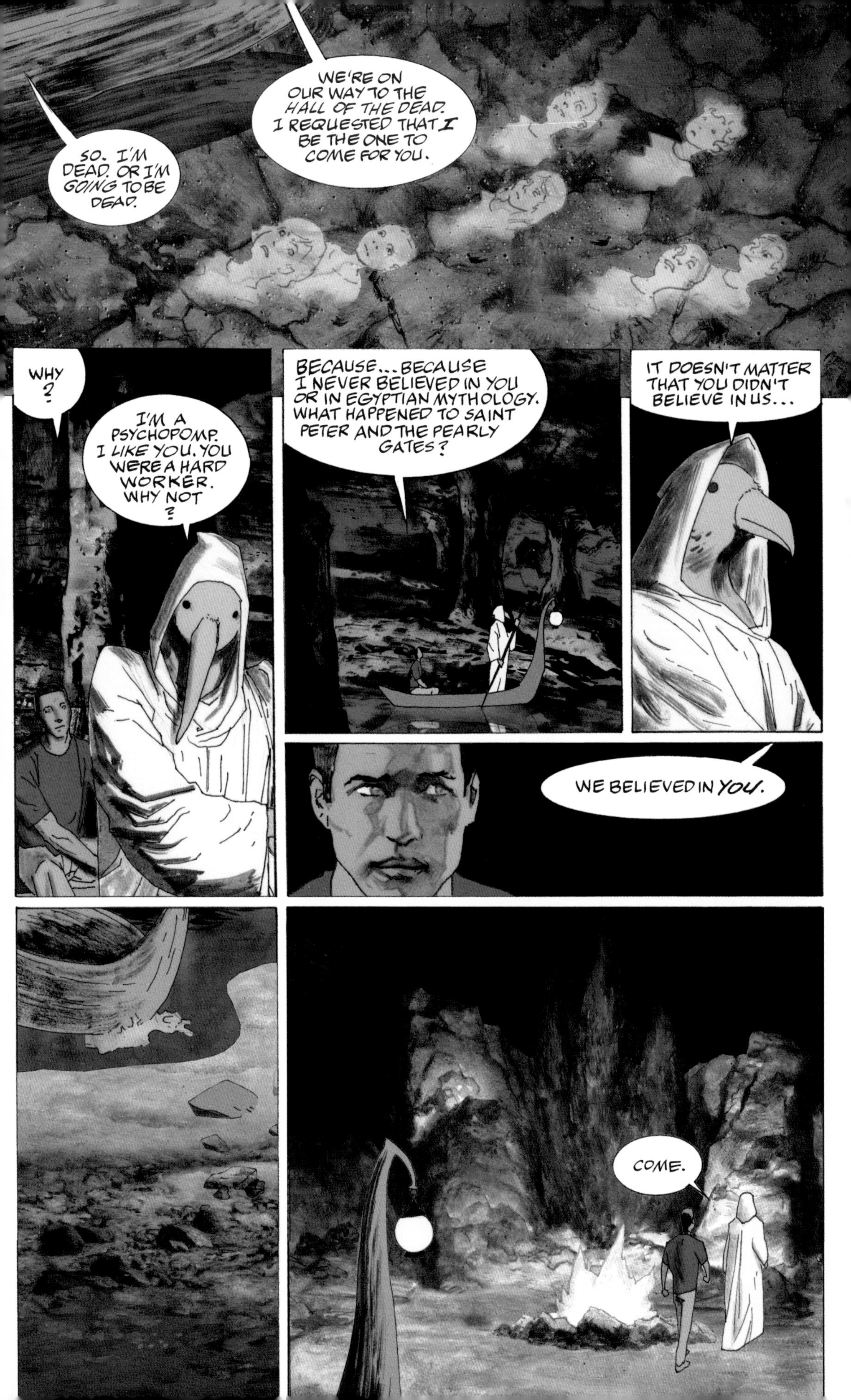
SO. I'M DEAD. OR I'M GOING TO BE DEAD.
WE'RE ON OUR WAY TO THE HALL OF THE DEAD. I REQUESTED THAT I BE THE ONE TO COME FOR YOU.
WHY?
I'M A PSYCHOPOMP. I LIKE YOU. YOU WERE A HARD WORKER. WHY NOT?
BECAUSE... BECAUSE I NEVER BELIEVED IN YOU OR IN EGYPTIAN MYTHOLOGY. WHAT HAPPENED TO SAINT PETER AND THE PEARLY GATES?
IT DOESN'T MATTER THAT YOU DIDN'T BELIEVE IN US...
WE BELIEVED IN YOU.
COME.

ARE YOU SCARED?

WELL, TRY TO CULTIVATE THE EMOTIONS OF TRUE AWE AND TERROR AS WE WALK. THEY ARE THE APPROPRIATE FEELINGS FOR THE SITUATION AT HAND.

NOT REALLY.

SHADOW WAS NOT SCARED OF THE SHIFTING DARKNESS NOR OF BEING DEAD...

...NOR EVEN OF THE LARGE DOG-HEADED CREATURE THAT STARED AT THEM AS THEY APPROACHED.

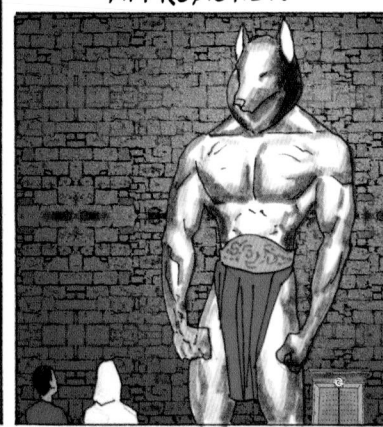

IT GROWLED, DEEP IN ITS THROAT, AND SHADOW FELT HIS NECK HAIRS PRICKLE.

SHADOW. NOW IS THE TIME OF JUDGMENT.

MISTER JACQUEL?

THE JACKEL HEAD EXAMINED HIM AS DISPASSIONATELY AS MR. JACQUEL HAD EXAMINED THE DEAD GIRL ON THE SLAB. HE WAS, IN SOME WAY, DISSECTED, SLICED, AND TASTED.

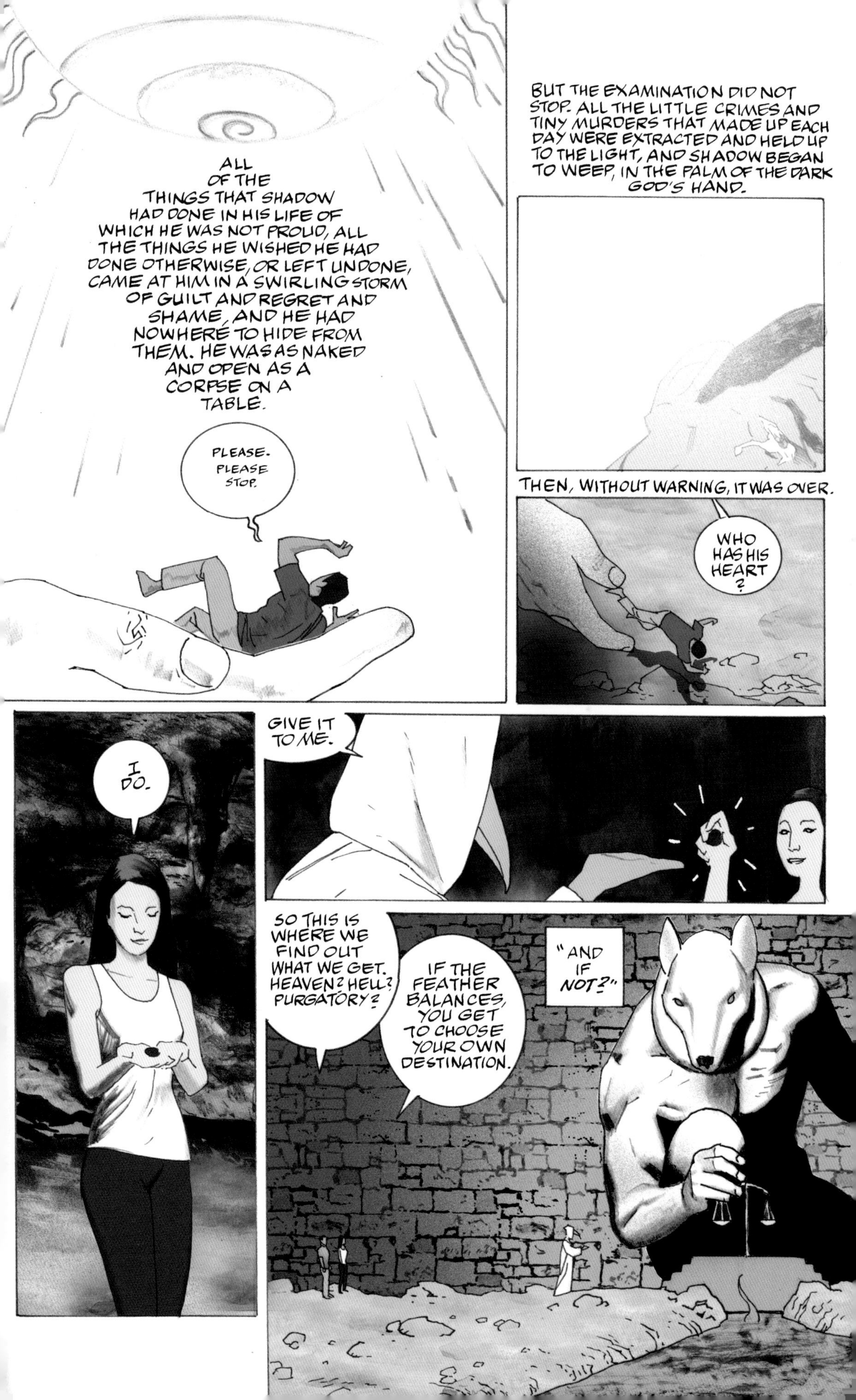

ALL OF THE THINGS THAT SHADOW HAD DONE IN HIS LIFE OF WHICH HE WAS NOT PROUD, ALL THE THINGS HE WISHED HE HAD DONE OTHERWISE, OR LEFT UNDONE, CAME AT HIM IN A SWIRLING STORM OF GUILT AND REGRET AND SHAME, AND HE HAD NOWHERE TO HIDE FROM THEM. HE WAS AS NAKED AND OPEN AS A CORPSE ON A TABLE.
PLEASE. PLEASE STOP.
BUT THE EXAMINATION DID NOT STOP. ALL THE LITTLE CRIMES AND TINY MURDERS THAT MADE UP EACH DAY WERE EXTRACTED AND HELD UP TO THE LIGHT, AND SHADOW BEGAN TO WEEP, IN THE PALM OF THE DARK GOD'S HAND.
THEN, WITHOUT WARNING, IT WAS OVER.
WHO HAS HIS HEART?
I DO.
GIVE IT TO ME.
SO THIS IS WHERE WE FIND OUT WHAT WE GET. HEAVEN? HELL? PURGATORY?
IF THE FEATHER BALANCES, YOU GET TO CHOOSE YOUR OWN DESTINATION.
"AND IF *NOT?*"

"THEN WE FEED YOUR HEART AND YOUR SOUL TO AMMET, THE EATER OF SOULS..."

"MAYBE, MAYBE I CAN GET SOME SORT OF... HAPPY ENDING."

"NOT ONLY ARE THERE NO HAPPY ENDINGS, THERE AREN'T EVEN ANY *ENDINGS*."

ON ONE OF THE PANS OF THE SCALE ANUBIS PLACED A FEATHER. ON THE OTHER, HE PLACED SHADOW'S HEART.

SOMETHING MOVED IN THE SHADOWS UNDER THE SCALES AS THEY TIPPED AND SWUNG WORRYINGLY.

BUT THEY BALANCED IN THE END, AND THE CREATURE IN THE SHADOWS SKULKED AWAY, UNSATISFIED.

SO THAT'S THAT. A PITY. I HAD HOPED YOU WOULD DO SOME GOOD IN THE CURRENT TROUBLES.

YOU WON'T BE THERE?

I DON'T LIKE OTHER PEOPLE PICKING MY BATTLES FOR ME.

THERE WAS SILENCE, THEN, IN THE VAST HALL OF DEATH.

SO NOW I GET TO CHOOSE WHERE I GO NEXT?

CHOOSE-- OR WE CAN CHOOSE FOR YOU.

NO. IT'S OKAY. IT'S MY CHOICE.

!WELL?

I WANT TO REST NOW. THAT'S WHAT I WANT.

I WANT NOTHING. NO HEAVEN, NO HELL, NO ANYTHING.

JUST LET IT END.

YOU'RE CERTAIN?

YES.

MR. JACQUEL OPENED THE LAST DOOR FOR SHADOW, AND BEHIND THAT DOOR THERE WAS NOTHING. NOT DARKNESS. NOT EVEN OBLIVION. ONLY NOTHING.

SHADOW ACCEPTED IT COMPLETELY AND WITHOUT RESERVATION. WHAT HE FELT WAS STRANGE-- AND FIERCE.

HE FELT JOY.

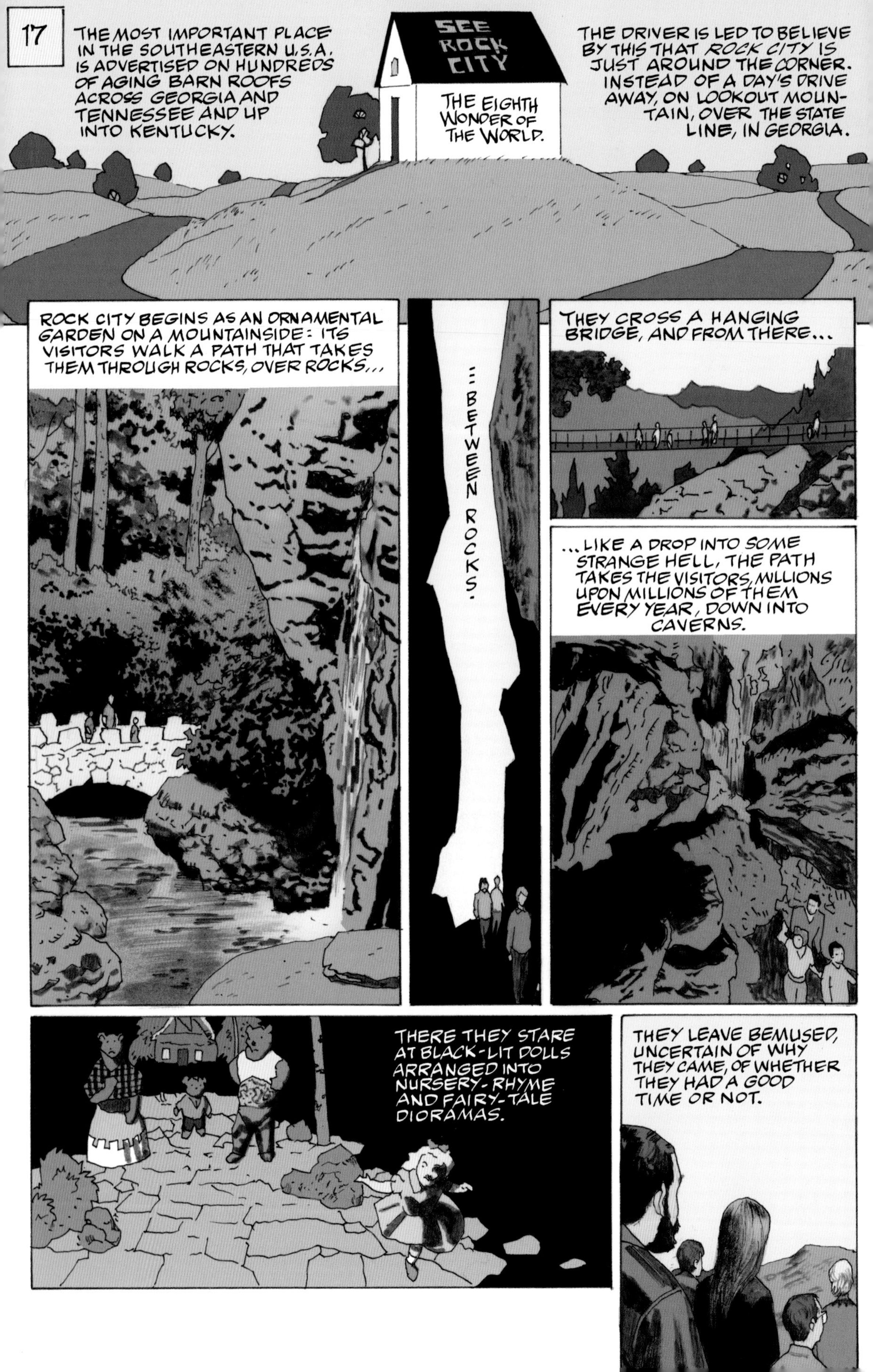
17
THE MOST IMPORTANT PLACE IN THE SOUTHEASTERN U.S.A. IS ADVERTISED ON HUNDREDS OF AGING BARN ROOFS ACROSS GEORGIA AND TENNESSEE AND UP INTO KENTUCKY.
SEE ROCK CITY
THE EIGHTH WONDER OF THE WORLD.
THE DRIVER IS LED TO BELIEVE BY THIS THAT *ROCK CITY* IS JUST AROUND THE CORNER. INSTEAD OF A DAY'S DRIVE AWAY, ON LOOKOUT MOUNTAIN, OVER THE STATE LINE, IN GEORGIA.
ROCK CITY BEGINS AS AN ORNAMENTAL GARDEN ON A MOUNTAINSIDE: ITS VISITORS WALK A PATH THAT TAKES THEM THROUGH ROCKS, OVER ROCKS...
...BETWEEN ROCKS.
THEY CROSS A HANGING BRIDGE, AND FROM THERE...
...LIKE A DROP INTO SOME STRANGE HELL, THE PATH TAKES THE VISITORS, MILLIONS UPON MILLIONS OF THEM EVERY YEAR, DOWN INTO CAVERNS.
THERE THEY STARE AT BLACK-LIT DOLLS ARRANGED INTO NURSERY-RHYME AND FAIRY-TALE DIORAMAS.
THEY LEAVE BEMUSED, UNCERTAIN OF WHY THEY CAME, OF WHETHER THEY HAD A GOOD TIME OR NOT.

THEY CAME TO LOOKOUT MOUNTAIN FROM ALL ACROSS THE UNITED STATES. THEY WERE NOT TOURISTS. THEY CAME BY CAR, BY PLANE, AND BY BUS, BY RAILROAD, AND ON FOOT.

SOME OF THEM FLEW--BUT ONLY IN THE DARK OF THE NIGHT. SEVERAL OF THEM TRAVELED THEIR OWN WAYS BENEATH THE EARTH.

MANY OF THEM HITCH-HIKED, CADGING RIDES FROM NERVOUS MOTORISTS OR FROM TRUCK DRIVERS.

THOSE WHO HAD CARS OR TRUCKS WOULD SEE THE ONES WHO HAD NOT AND, RECOGNIZING THEM, WOULD OFFER THEM RIDES.

THEY STARTED ARRIVING EARLY IN THE MORNING.

A SECOND WAVE OF THEM ARRIVED AT DUSK.

AND FOR SEVERAL DAYS THEY SIMPLY KEPT COMING.

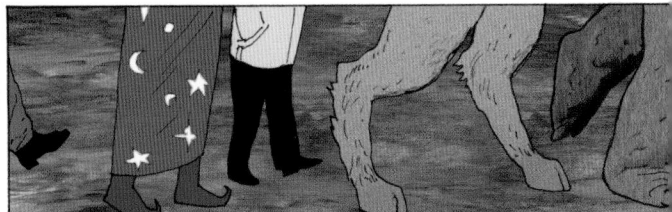

FOUR MEXICANS ARRIVED, ALL SMILES. THEY PASSED AMONG THEMSELVES A BEER BOTTLE, ITS CONTENTS A BITTER MIXTURE OF POWDERED CHOCOLATE, LIQUOR, AND BLOOD.

A SMALL, DARK-BEARDED MAN CAME FROM ACROSS THE FIELD. HIS COMPANION WAS THE BLANK GREY COLOR OF GOOD POLISH CLAY.

SEVERAL RAKSHASAS, DEMONS OF THE INDIAN SUBCONTINENT, MILLED AROUND UNTIL THEY FOUND MAMA-JI.

HER HANDS RUBBED A NECKLACE OF SKULLS. HER BROWN SKIN SLOWLY BECAME THE JET-BLACK OF OBSIDIAN. HER LONG WHITE TEETH WERE VERY SHARP.

SHE OPENED ALL HER EYES, AND BECKONED THE RAKSHASAS TO HER, AND GREETED THEM AS SHE WOULD HAVE GREETED HER OWN CHILDREN.

SEVERAL LOCAL MEN AND WOMEN CAME WALKING OVER THE MEADOWS, THEIR BODIES MOVING IN UNFAMILIAR WAYS; THEIR VOICES, WHEN THEY SPOKE, WERE THE VOICES OF THE LOA WHO RODE THEM.

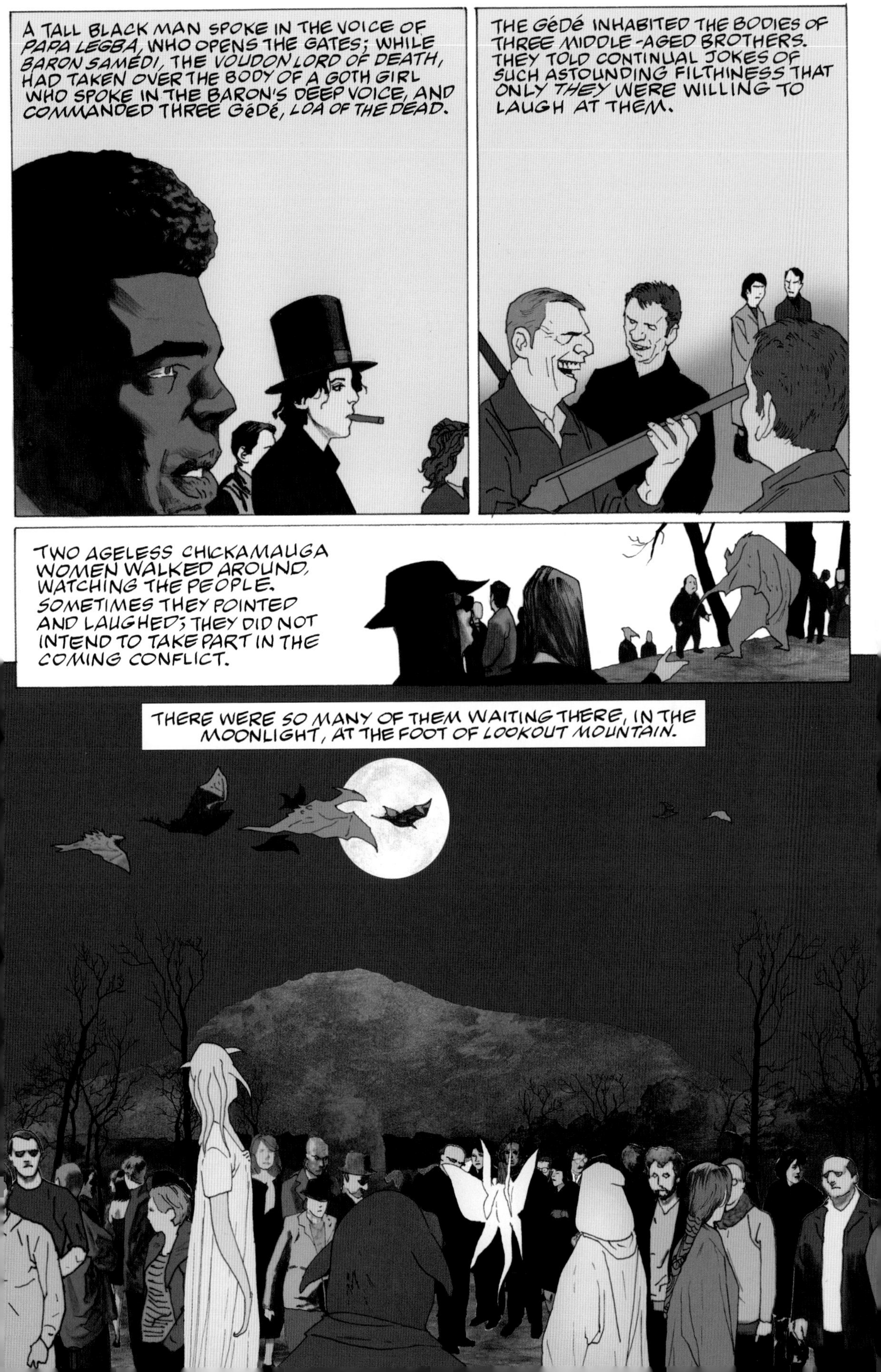
A TALL BLACK MAN SPOKE IN THE VOICE OF PAPA LEGBA, WHO OPENS THE GATES; WHILE BARON SAMEDI, THE VOUDON LORD OF DEATH, HAD TAKEN OVER THE BODY OF A GOTH GIRL WHO SPOKE IN THE BARON'S DEEP VOICE, AND COMMANDED THREE GéDé, LOA OF THE DEAD.
THE GéDé INHABITED THE BODIES OF THREE MIDDLE-AGED BROTHERS. THEY TOLD CONTINUAL JOKES OF SUCH ASTOUNDING FILTHINESS THAT ONLY THEY WERE WILLING TO LAUGH AT THEM.
TWO AGELESS CHICKAMAUGA WOMEN WALKED AROUND, WATCHING THE PEOPLE. SOMETIMES THEY POINTED AND LAUGHED; THEY DID NOT INTEND TO TAKE PART IN THE COMING CONFLICT.
THERE WERE SO MANY OF THEM WAITING THERE, IN THE MOONLIGHT, AT THE FOOT OF LOOKOUT MOUNTAIN.

LAURA WAS THIRSTY.

SOMETIMES LIVING PEOPLE BURNED STEADILY IN HER MIND LIKE CANDLES, AND SOMETIMES THEY FLAMED LIKE TORCHES. SHADOW HAD BURNED SO STRANGELY, WITH HIS OWN LIGHT, UP ON THAT TREE.

SHE HAD CHIDED HIM ONCE, ON THAT DAY IN THE CEMETERY, FOR NOT BEING ALIVE.

NOW, DYING ON THE TREE, SHADOW WAS UTTERLY ALIVE.

HE HAD FORGIVEN HER... PERHAPS. IT DID NOT MATTER. HE HAD CHANGED; THAT WAS ALL SHE KNEW.

SHADOW HAD TOLD HER TO GO TO THE FARM-HOUSE, THAT THEY WOULD GIVE HER WATER.

SOMETHING MOVED IN HER LEFT LUNG. SOMETHING THAT PUSHED AND SQUIRMED.

OH.

HELLO. IS THIS YOUR FARM?

SHADOW-- THAT'S THE GUY HANGING ON THE TREE. HE SAID YOU WOULD GIVE ME WATER.

SOMETHING **LARGE** SHIFTED IN HER BOWELS. IT SQUIRMED AND THEN WAS STILL.

LAURA COULD HEAR DOORS OPENING AND CLOSING, THROUGH THE FARMHOUSE.

FROM OUTSIDE, A SERIES OF LOUD CREAKS. EACH FOLLOWED BY A SPLASH OF WATER.

THEN ...

THANK YOU.

THE WATER FLOWED INTO HER, COLDER THAN SHE EVER IMAGINED WATER COULD BE. IT WAS LIKE DRINKING LIQUID ICE.

THE WOMEN WERE OBSERVING HER DISPASSIONATELY AND SHE FOUND HERSELF THINKING OF JURIES, OR SCIENTISTS OBSERVING A LABORATORY ANIMAL.

SUDDENLY, AND CONVULSIVELY...

HK HK

SHE BEGAN TO VOMIT BILE AND FORMALIN, CENTIPEDES, AND MAGGOTS. SHE FELT HERSELF STARTING TO VOID AND TO PISS: STUFF WAS BEING PUSHED VIOLENTLY, WETLY, FROM HER BODY. SHE WOULD HAVE SCREAMED IF SHE COULD.

BUT THEN THE FLOORBOARDS CAME UP TO MEET HER AND TIME RUSHED OVER AND INTO HER.

SHE WAS LOST IN A DEPARTMENT STORE AND HER FATHER WAS NOWHERE TO BE FOUND.

SHE WAS SITTING IN THE BAR AT CHI-CHI'S, ORDERING A STRAWBERRY DAIQUIRI AND CHECKING OUT HER BLIND DATE.

AND SHE WAS IN THE CAR AS IT ROLLED OVER, AND ROBBIE WAS SCREAMING AT HER UNTIL THE METAL POST STOPPED THE CAR BUT NOT ITS CONTENTS.

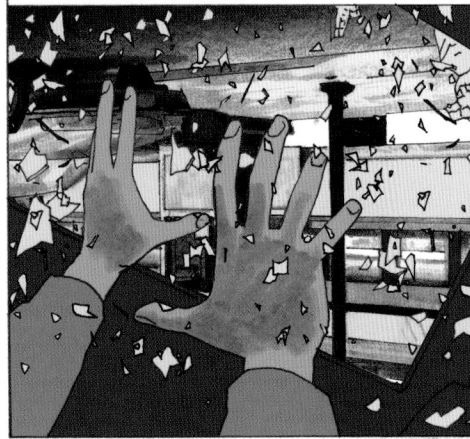

WHEN LAURA WOKE IN THE EMPTY FARM-HOUSE ROOM, SHE WAS SHIVERING, AND HER BREATH ACTUALLY STEAMED IN THE MORNING AIR.

THERE WAS A SCRAPE ON THE BACK OF HER HAND.

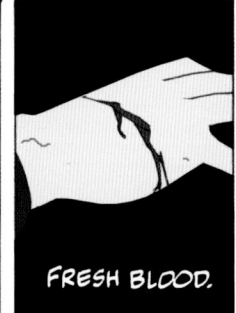

FRESH BLOOD.

SHE KNEW WHERE SHE HAD TO GO. SHE HAD DRUNK FROM THE WATER OF TIME, WHICH COMES THE SPRING OF FATE. SHE COULD SEE THE MOUNTAIN IN HER MIND.

SHE BEGAN TO WALK.

IT WAS A WET MARCH DAY, AND IT WAS UNSEASONABLY COLD. THERE WERE FEW REAL TOURISTS AT ROCK CITY. STILL, IF YOU HAD WALKED ITS PATHS THAT DAY, YOU MIGHT HAVE NOTICED PEOPLE WHO LOOKED LIKE MOVIE STARS AND PEOPLE WHO LOOKED LIKE ALIENS.

ALL THEY HAD IN COMMON WAS A SPECIFIC LOOK. IT SAID, *YOU KNOW ME; OR PERHAPS, YOU OUGHT TO KNOW ME.*

THE FAT KID MOVED AMONG THEM, BLACK COAT FLAPPING IN THE WIND.

KFF

IT WILL BE A MIGHTY BATTLE.

HELL YES

IT'S NOT GOING TO BE A BATTLE. ALL WE'RE FACING HERE IS A FUCKING PARADIGM SHIFT. IT'S A SHAKEDOWN. MODALITIES LIKE BATTLE ARE SO FUCKING LAO TZU.

WAITING.

WHATEVER. I'M LOOKING FOR MISTER WORLD. YOU SEEN HIM?

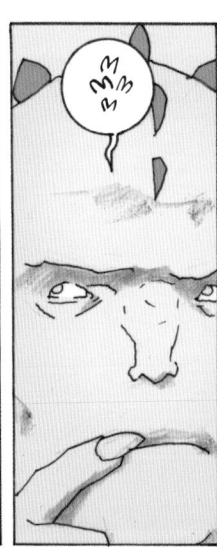

MM MM

OVER THERE.

IT WILL BE A BATTLE.

HELL YES

SO HOW DOES THAT MAKE YOU FEEL?

IT BLINKED, AND THEN IT BEGAN TO TELL HER.

CHAPTER FIVE

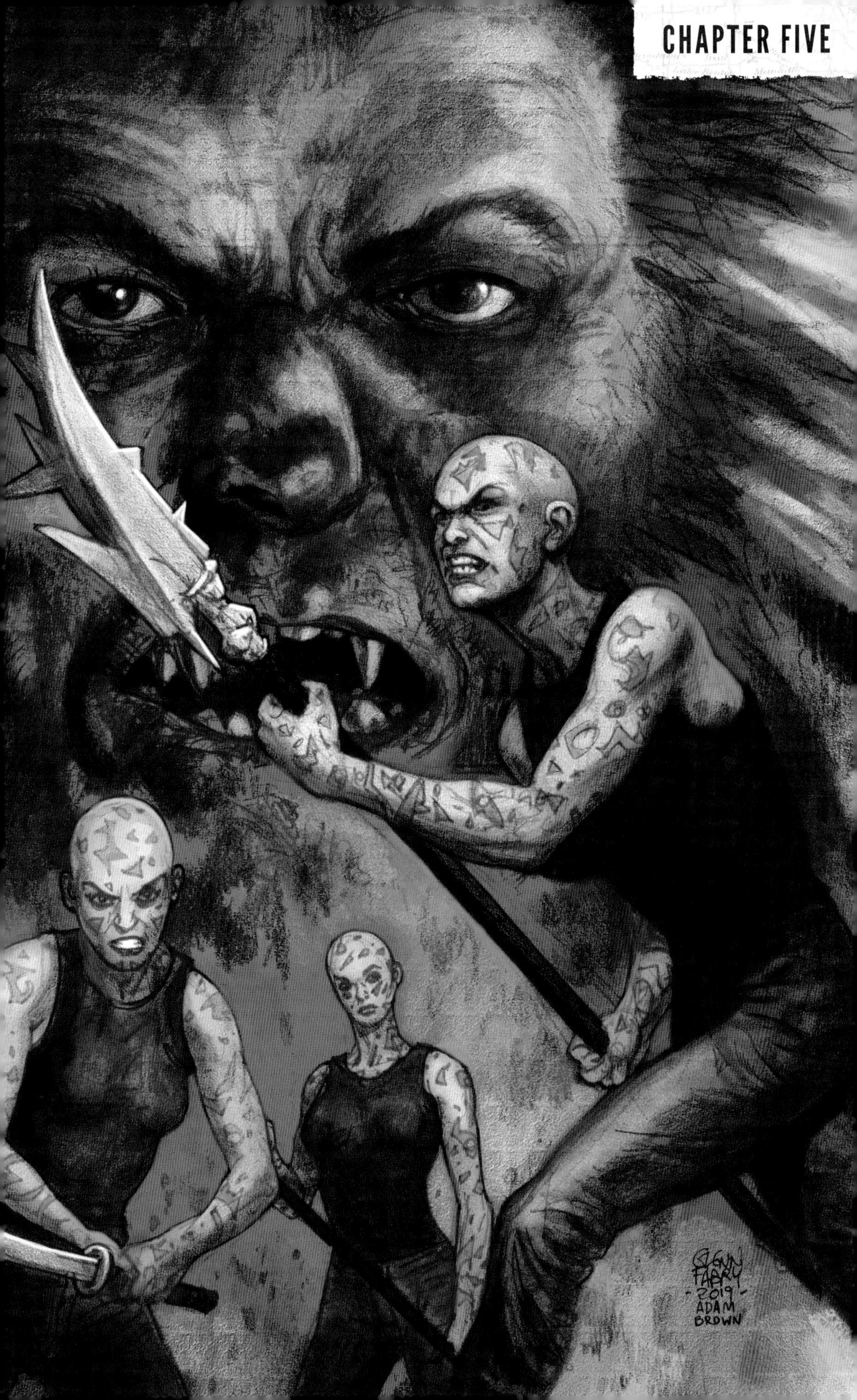
FABRY
-2019-
ADAM
BROWN

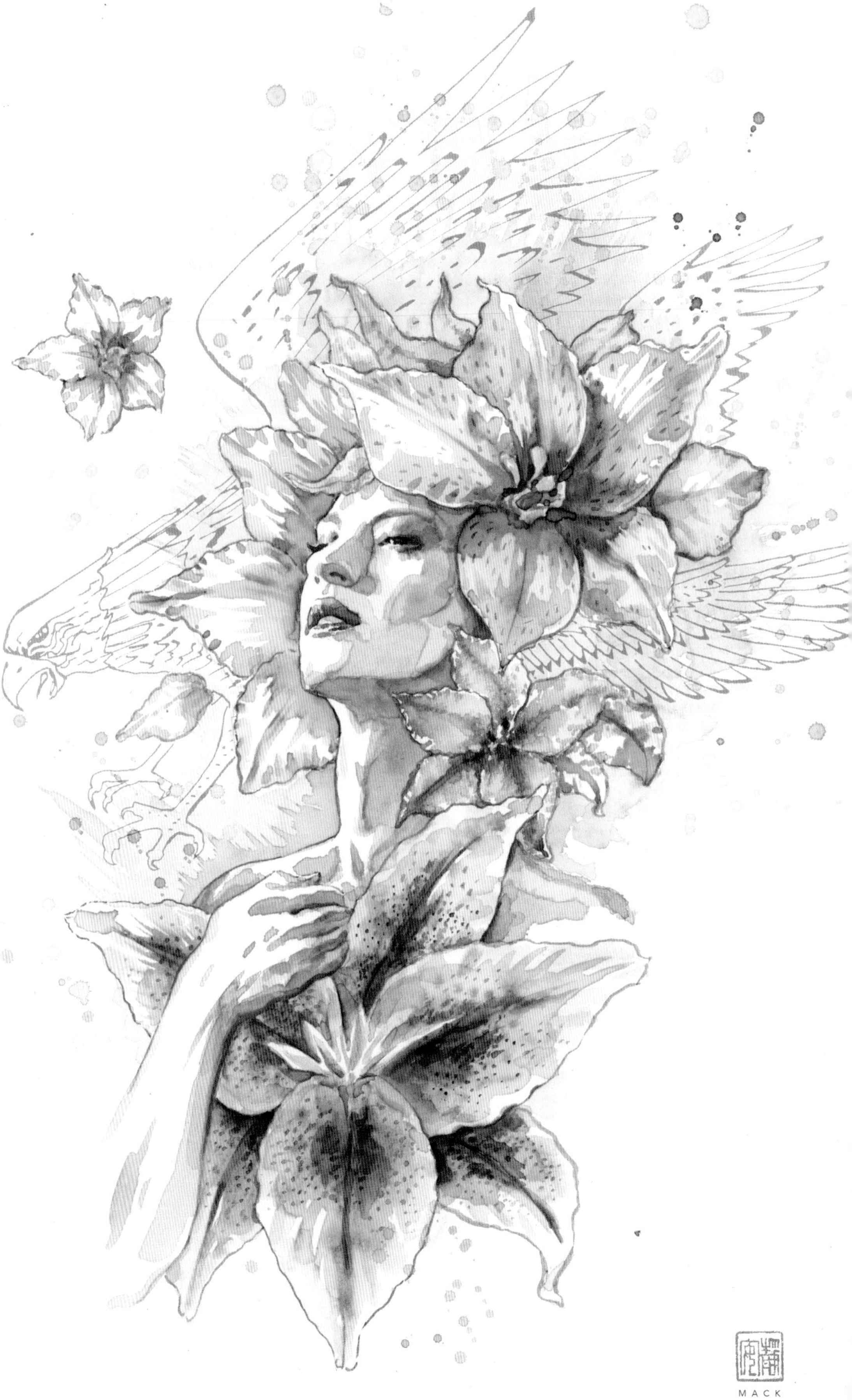
MACK

MR. TOWN'S HATRED OF SHADOW HAD BECOME A PART OF HIM. EVEN AS HE FELL ASLEEP HE WOULD SEE THAT FACE AND HIS JAWS WOULD CLENCH, HIS TEMPLES TENSE, AND HIS GULLET BURN.

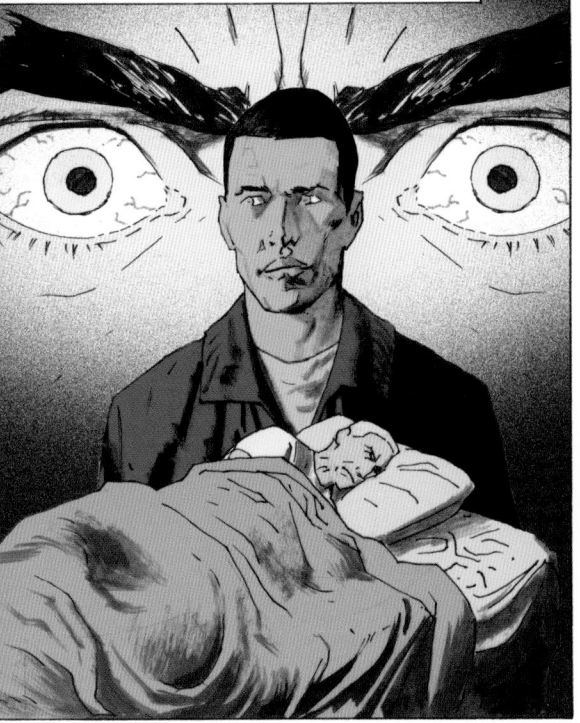

WHEN HE'D TRANSFERRED TO THE AGENCY IT HAD ALL SEEMED SO SIMPLE.

NOW IT WAS MERELY BIZARRE. HE HAD BEEN SITTING IN MR. WORLD'S OFFICE AT TWO THAT MORNING...

YOU GOT IT? CUT ME A STICK. IT DOESN'T HAVE TO BE LONGER THAN A COUPLE FEET.

FIND THE TREE. DO THE JOB. MEET ME DOWN IN CHATTANOOGA. DON'T WASTE ANY TIME.

WHAT ABOUT THE ASSHOLE?

SHADOW? DON'T TOUCH HIM. DON'T EVEN MESS WITH HIM. THERE'S NO ROOM FOR MARTYRS IN THE CURRENT GAME-PLAN.

HE SMILED HIS SCARRED SMILE. MR. WORLD WAS EASILY AMUSED. IT HAD AMUSED HIM TO PLAY CHAUFFEUR IN KANSAS, AFTER ALL.

LOOK.

NO MARTYRS, TOWN.

AND TOWN HAD NODDED AND PUSHED THE RAGE THAT WELLED UP INSIDE HIM DOWN DEEP AND AWAY.

TOWN HAD A GLOBAL POSITIONING DEVICE, BUT HE STILL GOT LOST. THE ROADS HE DROVE SEEMED TO BEAR LITTLE RELATIONSHIP TO THE TANGLE OF LINES ON THE MAP OF THE SCREEN.

HE WAS ON THE VERGE OF GIVING UP ON THE FARM WHEN HE DROVE UP A HILL AND SAW THE SIGN.

ASH

6:38

HELLO, ASSHOLE.

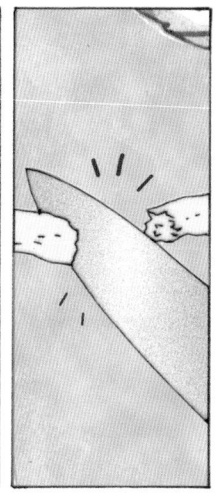

GOD, I HATE YOU.

TOWN JABBED THE STICK IN THE AIR TOWARD THE HANGING MAN, AN INSTINCTIVE GESTURE CONTAINING ALL HIS RAGE AND FRUSTRATION.

HE IMAGINED THAT HE WAS HOLDING A SPEAR AND TWISTING IT INTO SHADOW'S GUTS.

COME ON. TIME TO GET MOVING.

FIRST SIGN OF MADNESS... TALKING TO YOURSELF.

FROM THE CORNER OF HIS EYE, HE THOUGHT HE SAW SOMETHING MOVE IN THE FARMHOUSE.

?

FOR A MOMENT, IN A HALF-DREAM, HE IMAGINED HE SAW THREE WOMEN SITTING IN A DARK PARLOR.

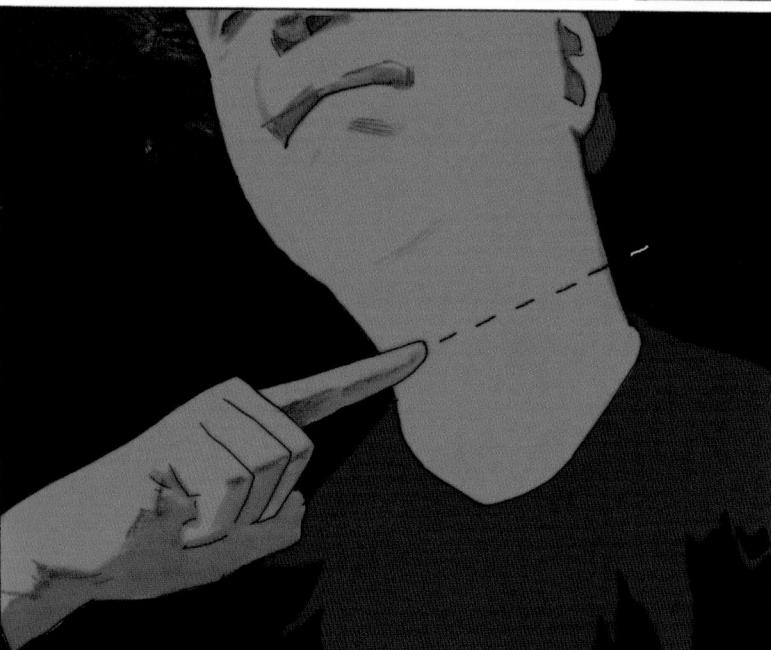

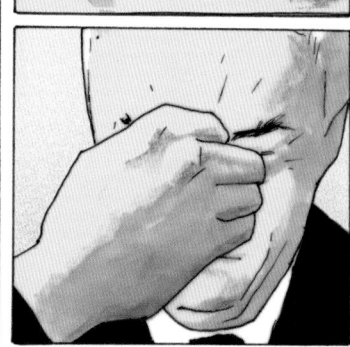

BUT THERE WAS NOBODY THERE AT ALL.

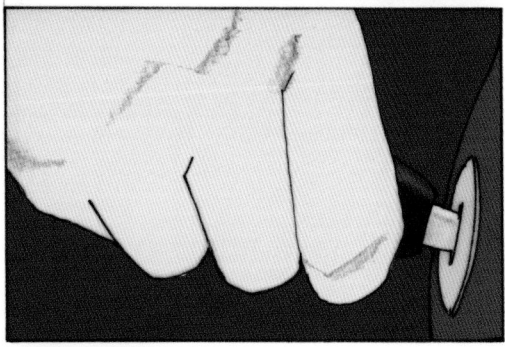

6:37

GREAT. I WAS EITHER UP ON THAT TREE FOR EIGHT HOURS OR FOR MINUS A MINUTE.

ON THE TREE, SHADOW'S BODY BEGAN TO BLEED.

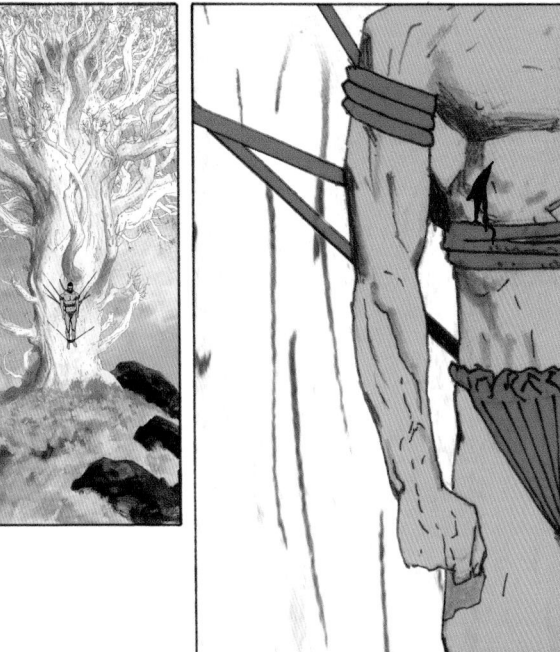

EASTER SAT SOME DISTANCE FROM THE CROWD AT THE FOOT OF LOOKOUT MOUNTAIN. THE FOLK WERE STILL COMING BY ONES AND TWOS. NOBODY FROM THE OUTSIDE WORLD EVEN SEEMED TO NOTICE THEY WERE THERE.

GOOD MORNING, LADY. THE BATTLE WILL START SOON NOW.

HOW DO YOU KNOW?

I AM *MACHA*, OF THE *MORRIGAN*. WHEN WAR COMES, I CAN SMELL IT IN THE AIR. I AM A WAR GODDESS, AND I SAY, *BLOOD SHALL BE SPILLED THIS DAY.* WE SHALL KILL THEM *EVERY ONE*, AND THE *CROWS* SHALL HAVE THEIR EYES AND THEIR CORPSES.

OH. WELL. THERE YOU GO.

IS THAT SOME HIDDEN WAR GODDESS THING? THE WHOLE 'WHO'S GOING TO WIN' THING?

NO. I CAN SMELL THE BATTLE, BUT THAT'S ALL. WE *HAVE* TO WIN. I SAW WHAT THEY DID TO THE ALL-FATHER. IT'S THEM OR US.

YES...

I SUPPOSE IT IS.

CAN I HELP YOU?

THE HAWK LOOKED UP AT HER WITH MAD EYES.

HELLO, CUTIE. NOW WHAT DO YOU REALLY LOOK LIKE?

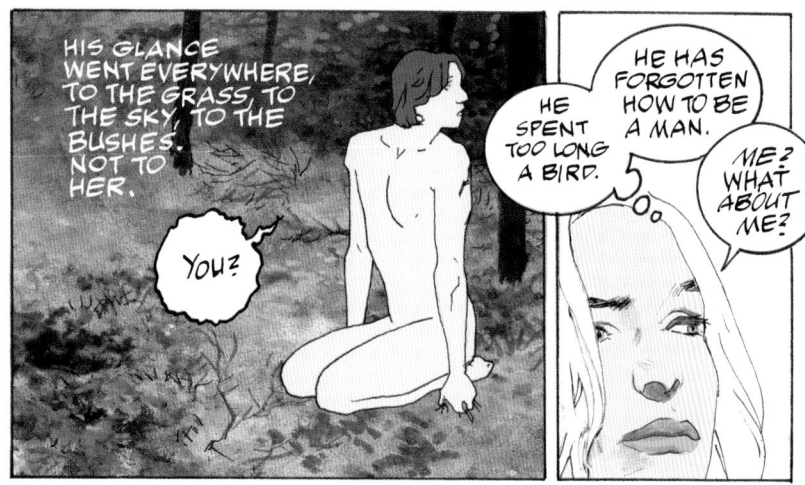

HIS GLANCE WENT EVERYWHERE, TO THE GRASS, TO THE SKY, TO THE BUSHES. NOT TO HER.

YOU?

HE SPENT TOO LONG A BIRD.

HE HAS FORGOTTEN HOW TO BE A MAN.

ME? WHAT ABOUT ME?

YOU ?

WILL YOU COME WITH ME? THE MAN ON THE TREE.

HE NEEDS YOU. A GHOST-HURT IN HIS SIDE.

THE BLOOD CAME. THEN IT STOPPED.

I THINK HE'S DEAD.

THERE'S A WAR ON. I CAN'T JUST GO RUNNING AWAY.

IF HE IS LOST, IT MATTERS NOT WHO WINS.

WHERE IS THIS? NEARBY?

AWAY.

WELL, I'M NEEDED HERE. AND I CAN'T JUST LEAVE. HOW DO YOU EXPECT ME TO GET THERE? I CAN'T FLY LIKE YOU.

NO. YOU CAN'T.

HE CAN.

TOWN HAD THOUGHT FINDING HIS WAY TO THE FARM AND THE GREAT SILVER ASH TREE HAD BEEN HARD; FINDING HIS WAY *AWAY* FROM THE FARM WAS MUCH HARDER.

IT DID NOT SEEM TO MATTER WHICH ROAD HE TOOK. WHICH DIRECTION HE DROVE DOWN THE NARROW ROADS-- EVENTUALLY HE WOULD FIND HIMSELF PASSING THE FARM ONCE MORE AND THE HAND-PAINTED SIGN...

THERE WERE HEAVY STORM CLOUDS MOVING IN AND HE HAD A LONG DRIVE AHEAD OF HIM: HE WOULD NEVER GET TO CHATTANOOGA ON TIME.

HIS CELL PHONE...

NO SERVICE

...THE FUEL GAUGE...

...A RUMBLE OF DISTANT THUNDER.

SO WHEN TOWN SAW THE WOMAN WALKING ALONG THE SIDE OF THE ROAD...

THANK GOD.

MA'AM? I'M KIND OF LOST. CAN YOU TELL ME HOW TO GET TO HIGHWAY 81 FROM HERE?

I DON'T THINK I CAN EXPLAIN IT. BUT I CAN SHOW YOU, IF YOU LIKE.

CLIMB IN.

THANKS. I NEEDED A RIDE.

LADY, IF YOU CAN GET ME TO A GAS STATION, AND BACK TO THE FREEWAY, I'LL TAKE YOU ALL THE WAY TO YOUR FRONT DOOR.

THANK YOU, BUT I'M GOING FURTHER THAN YOU ARE. IF YOU CAN GET ME TO THE FREEWAY, MAYBE A TRUCKER WILL PICK ME UP.

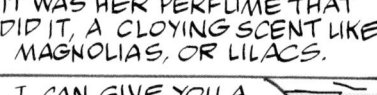

IT WAS HER PERFUME THAT DID IT, A CLOYING SCENT LIKE MAGNOLIAS, OR LILACS.

I CAN GIVE YOU A FINER RIDE THAN ANY TRUCKER.

I'M GOING TO GEORGIA. IT'S A LONG WAY.

I'M GOING TO CHATTANOOGA. I'LL TAKE YOU AS FAR AS I CAN.

MMM... WHAT'S YOUR NAME?

MACK. THE ONES THAT KNOW ME WELL CALL ME BIG MACK. WHAT'S YOUR NAME?

LAURA.

WELL, LAURA.. I'M SURE WE'RE GOING TO BE GREAT FRIENDS.

CAUTION
NO
ADMITTANCE
DURING
RENOVATION

EXCUSE ME-- MISTER WORLD?

YES?

IS EVERYTHING ON SCHEDULE?

I'VE SET UP EVERYTHING. I DON'T HAVE CONFIRMATION ON THE CHOPPERS.

THE HELICOPTERS WILL BE HERE WHEN WE NEED THEM.

GOOD.

GOOD.

MM...

IS THERE ANYTHING ELSE I CAN DO FOR YOU?

YES. OKAY. RIGHT. TWO THINGS:

OKAY. ONE: WHAT ARE WE FIGHTING FOR?

AND TWO. TWO IS HARDER.

LOOK ... WE HAVE THE GUNS. RIGHT. WE HAVE THE FIREPOWER.

THEY HAVE FUCKING SWORDS AND KNIVES AND FUCKING HAMMERS AND STONE AXES.

BUT. LOOK, EVER SINCE I DID THE JOB IN L.A., I'VE BEEN ... I'VE BEEN ...

YOU'VE BEEN TROUBLED.

YES. GOOD WORD. TROUBLED. YES. LIKE A HOME FOR TROUBLED TEENS.

YES.

FUNNY.

SO. THE OLD GODS.

THEY'LL DIE OUT ANY-WAY. YES? WHO CARES?

THIS WAY IT'S GOING TO BE A BLOODBATH.

IF WE JUST WAIT THEM OUT, WE GET THE WHOLE THING.

AH!

LOOK, I'M NOT THE ONLY ONE WHO FEELS THIS WAY.

THE CREW AT RADIO MODERN IS ALL FOR SETTLING THIS PEACEFULLY, AND THE INTANGIBLES ARE IN FAVOR OF LETTING MARKET FORCES TAKE CARE OF IT.

I'M BEING... YOU KNOW... THE VOICE OF REASON HERE.

YOU ARE INDEED. UNFORTUNATELY, THERE IS INFORMATION YOU DO NOT HAVE.

MISTER WORLD? WHAT HAPPENED TO YOUR LIPS?

THE TRUTH IS THAT SOMEBODY SEWED THEM TOGETHER--A LONG TIME AGO.

WHOA. SERIOUS OMERTA SHIT.

YOU WANT TO KNOW WHAT WE'RE WAITING FOR? WHY WE DIDN'T STRIKE LAST NIGHT?

YES?

WE DIDN'T STRIKE YET BECAUSE I'M WAITING FOR A STICK.

A STICK?

THAT'S RIGHT. A STICK, AND DO YOU KNOW WHAT I'M GOING TO DO WITH THE STICK?

OKAY. I'LL BITE. WHAT?

I COULD TELL YOU, BUT THEN I'D HAVE TO KILL YOU.

OKAY. HEE HEE OKAY.

HEE

GOT IT. MESSAGE RECEIVED ON PLANET TECHNICAL LOUD AND CLEAR. IXNAY ON THE ESTIONSQUAY.

WELL,,, SEEING THAT WE'RE FRIENDS, HERE IS THE ANSWER.

"I'M GOING TO TAKE THE STICK, AND I'M GOING TO THROW IT OVER THE ARMIES AS THEY COME TOGETHER. AS I THROW IT, IT WILL BECOME A SPEAR, AND THEN, AS THE SPEAR ARCS OVER THE BATTLE, I'M GOING TO SHOUT --

I DEDICATE THIS BATTLE TO ODIN!;

HUH? WHY?

POWER. AND FOOD. A COMBINATION OF THE TWO. YOU SEE, THE OUTCOME OF THE BATTLE IS UNIMPORTANT. WHAT MATTERS IS THE CHAOS, AND THE SLAUGHTER.

I DON'T GET IT.

LET ME SHOW YOU. IT'LL BE JUST LIKE THIS.

WATCH.

I DEDICATE THIS DEATH TO ODIN.

THE SMELL ON THE AIR WAS THAT OF BURNING INSULATION WIRE, AS IF SOMEWHERE A PLUG WAS OVERLOADING.

LOOK AT HIM. HE LOOKS AS IF HE JUST SAW A SEQUENCE OF ZEROES AND ONES TURNING INTO A CLUSTER OF BRIGHTLY COLORED BIRDS AND THEN JUST FLY AWAY.

THERE WAS NO REPLY FROM THE EMPTY ROCK CORRIDOR.

I'LL DISPOSE OF YOU ON THE BATTLEFIELD TONIGHT. ALMOST TOO EASY. NOBODY WILL NOTICE.

NOBODY WILL CARE.

FOR A LITTLE WHILE THERE WAS SILENCE IN THAT PLACE. AND THEN A GRUFF VOICE CLEARED ITS THROAT IN THE SHADOWS AND SAID...

GOOD START.

18

NONE OF THIS CAN ACTUALLY BE HAPPENING. IF IT MAKES YOU MORE COMFORTABLE, YOU COULD SIMPLY THINK OF IT AS A METAPHOR. RELIGIONS ARE, BY DEFINITION, METAPHORS. AFTER ALL, GOD IS A DREAM, A HOPE, A WOMAN, AN IRONIST, A FATHER, A CITY, A HOUSE OF MANY ROOMS, A WATCHMAKER WHO LEFT HIS CHRONOMETER IN THE DESERT. SOMEONE WHO LOVES YOU--EVEN, PERHAPS AGAINST ALL EVIDENCE, A CELESTIAL BEING WHOSE ONLY INTEREST IS TO MAKE SURE YOUR FOOTBALL TEAM, BUSINESS, ARMY, OR MARRIAGE THRIVES, PROSPERS, AND TRIUMPHS OVER ALL OPPOSITION.

RELIGIONS ARE PLACES TO STAND AND LOOK, AND ACT, VANTAGE POINTS FROM WHICH TO VIEW THE WORLD.

SO, NONE OF THIS IS HAPPENING. SUCH THINGS COULD NOT OCCUR IN THIS DAY AND AGE. NEVER A WORD OF IT IS LITERALLY TRUE, ALTHOUGH IT ALL HAPPENED AND THE NEXT THING THAT HAPPENED, HAPPENED LIKE THIS:

THEY WERE ARGUING.

SOMETHING THAT LOOKED A LITTLE LIKE A WOLF GRUNTED AND SPAT ON THE FOREST FLOOR.

WHEN BETTER TO ATTACK THEM, DEDUSHKA? SHALL WE WAIT TILL THE WEATHER CLEARS WHEN THEY LEAST EXPECT IT?

I SAY WE GO NOW. I SAY WE MOVE,

A MAN, IN AN ELEGANT SUIT, WHO UNTIL NOW SAID NOTHING, STEPPED INTO THE FIRELIGHT, AND MADE HIS POINT SUCCINCTLY AND CLEARLY TO NODS AND MURMURS OF AGREEMENT.

A VOICE CAME FROM ONE OF THE THREE WARRIOR-WOMEN.

GOOD TIME OR BAD TIME, THIS IS THE TIME, THEY WILL CONTINUE TO KILL US WHETHER WE FIGHT OR NOT. BETTER TO DIE TOGETHER, ON THE ATTACK, LIKE GODS, THAN TO DIE SINGLY, LIKE RATS.

A VERY TALL CHINESE MAN STOOD AND SPOKE.

THE FIRST HEAD IS MINE.

HE BEGAN TO WALK SLOWLY AND INTENTLY UP THE MOUNTAIN.

EVEN NOTHING CANNOT LAST FOREVER.

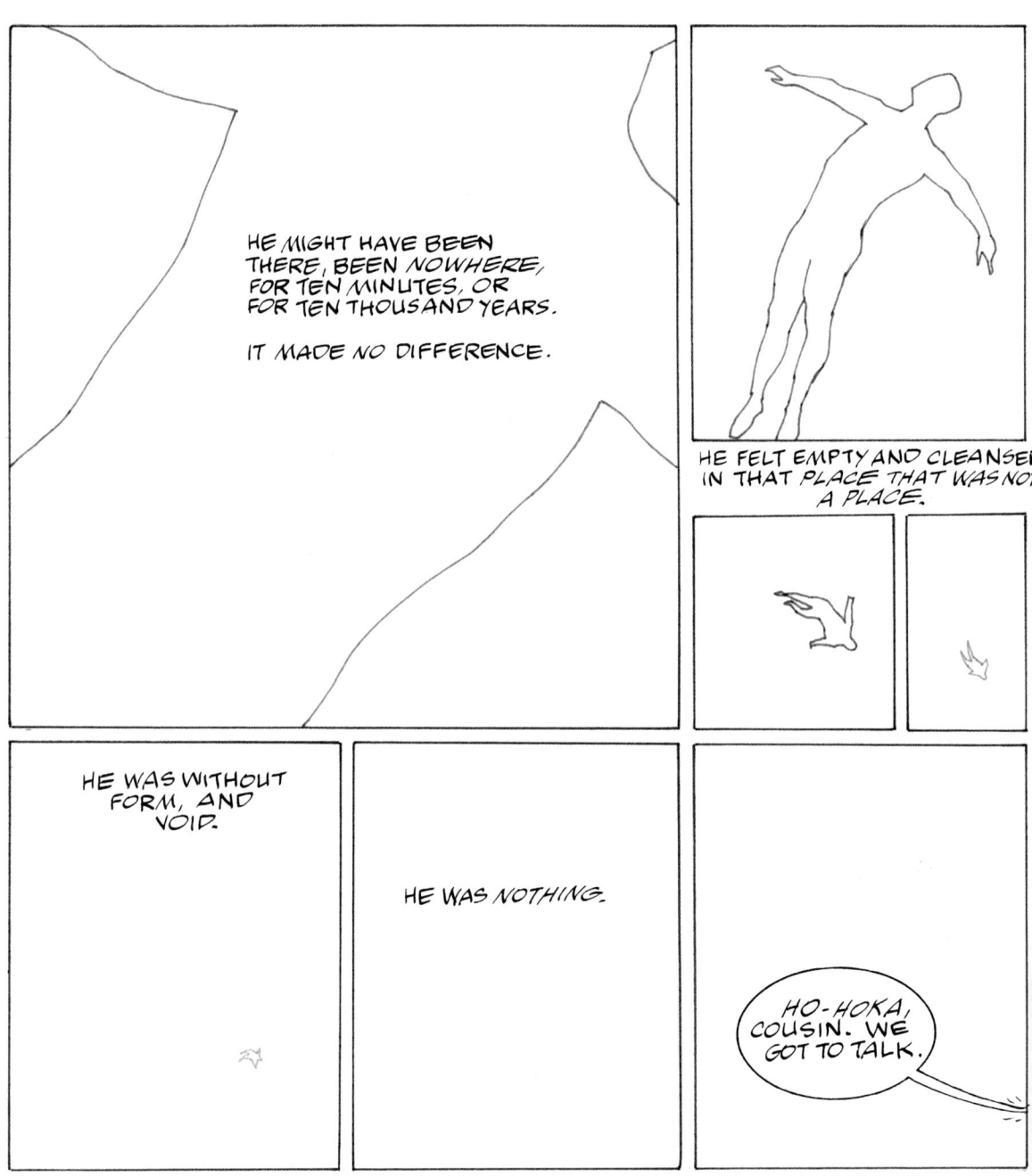

HE MIGHT HAVE BEEN THERE, BEEN *NOWHERE*, FOR TEN MINUTES, OR FOR TEN THOUSAND YEARS.

IT MADE *NO* DIFFERENCE.

HE FELT EMPTY AND CLEANSED IN THAT *PLACE THAT WAS NOT A PLACE.*

HE WAS WITHOUT FORM, AND VOID.

HE WAS *NOTHING.*

HO-HOKA, COUSIN. WE GOT TO TALK.

" WHISKEY JACK ? "

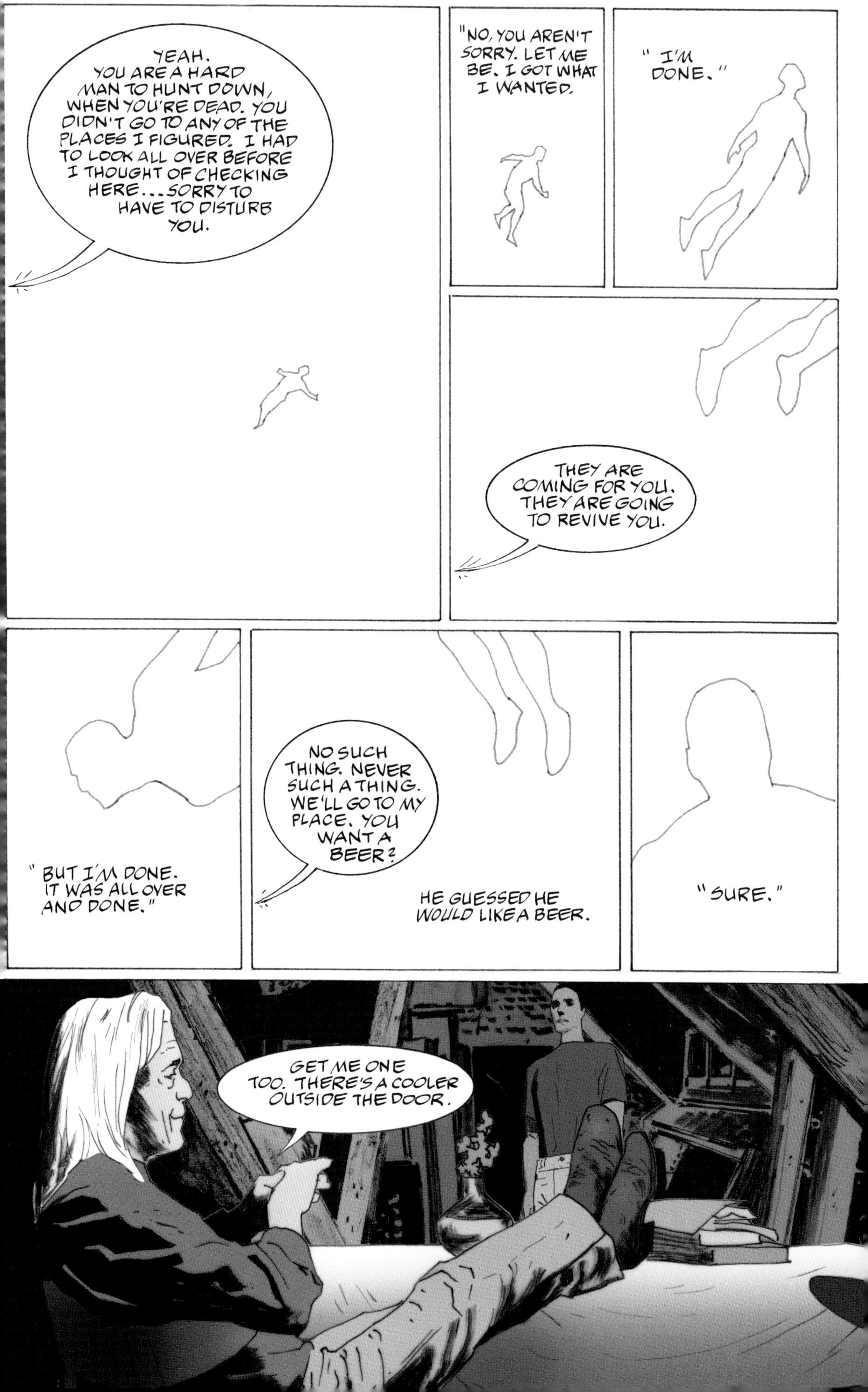
YEAH. YOU ARE A HARD MAN TO HUNT DOWN, WHEN YOU'RE DEAD. YOU DIDN'T GO TO ANY OF THE PLACES I FIGURED. I HAD TO LOOK ALL OVER BEFORE I THOUGHT OF CHECKING HERE... SORRY TO HAVE TO DISTURB YOU.
"NO, YOU AREN'T SORRY. LET ME BE. I GOT WHAT I WANTED.
" I'M DONE."
THEY ARE COMING FOR YOU. THEY ARE GOING TO REVIVE YOU.
" BUT I'M DONE. IT WAS ALL OVER AND DONE."
NO SUCH THING. NEVER SUCH A THING. WE'LL GO TO MY PLACE. YOU WANT A BEER?
HE GUESSED HE WOULD LIKE A BEER.
"SURE."
GET ME ONE TOO. THERE'S A COOLER OUTSIDE THE DOOR.

WHERE ARE WE?

OUT-SIDE MY PLACE.

YOU DIDN'T HAVE A WATERFALL OUTSIDE YOUR PLACE LAST TIME I WAS HERE.

YOU REMEMBER MY NEPHEW? *HARRY BLUEJAY?* THE POET? HE TRADED HIS BUICK FOR YOUR *WINNEBAGO.* REMEMBER?

SURE. I DIDN'T KNOW HE WAS A POET.

BEST DAMN POET IN AMERICA.

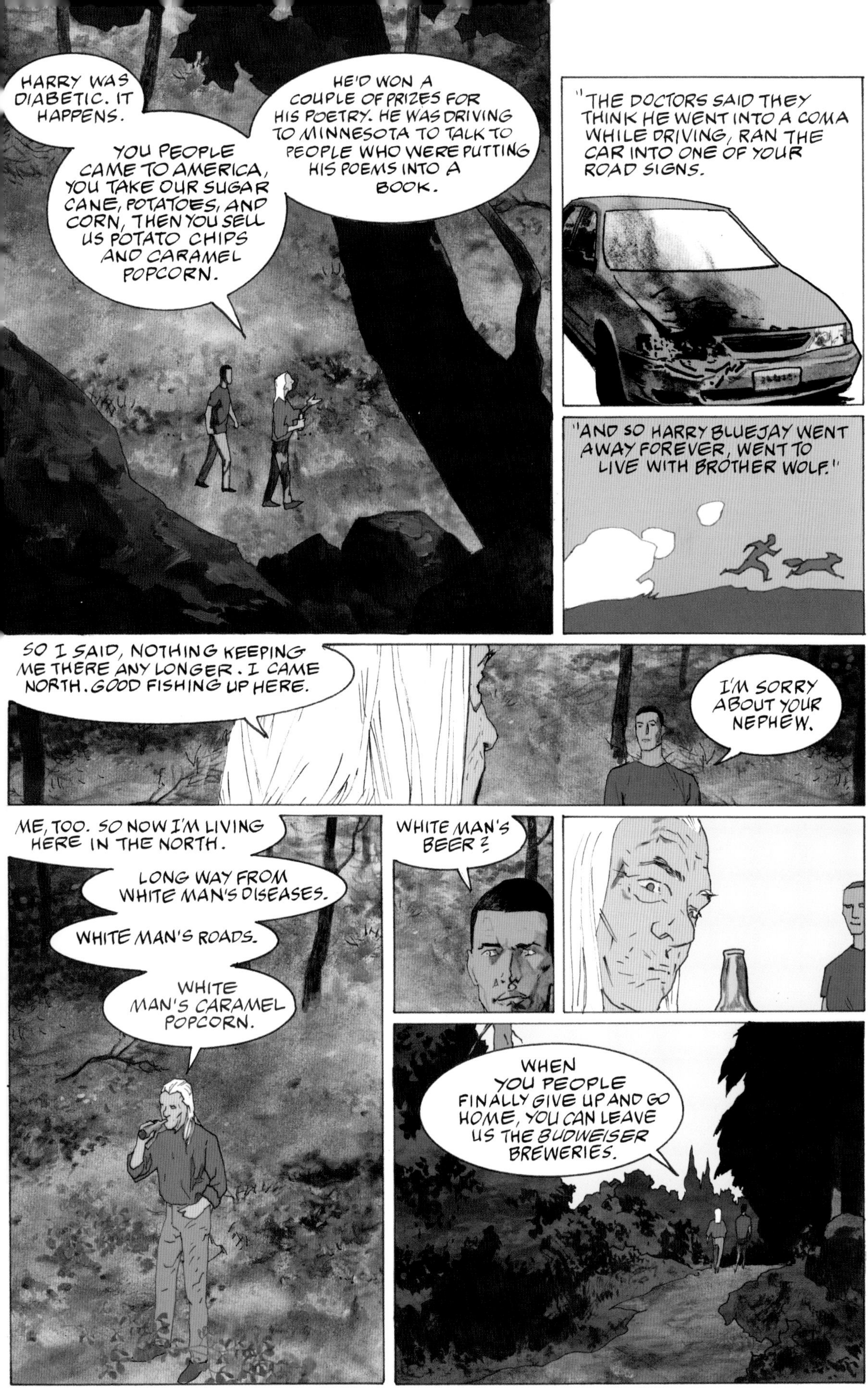
HARRY WAS DIABETIC. IT HAPPENS.
YOU PEOPLE CAME TO AMERICA, YOU TAKE OUR SUGAR CANE, POTATOES, AND CORN, THEN YOU SELL US POTATO CHIPS AND CARAMEL POPCORN.
HE'D WON A COUPLE OF PRIZES FOR HIS POETRY. HE WAS DRIVING TO MINNESOTA TO TALK TO PEOPLE WHO WERE PUTTING HIS POEMS INTO A BOOK.
"THE DOCTORS SAID THEY THINK HE WENT INTO A COMA WHILE DRIVING, RAN THE CAR INTO ONE OF YOUR ROAD SIGNS.
"AND SO HARRY BLUEJAY WENT AWAY FOREVER, WENT TO LIVE WITH BROTHER WOLF."
SO I SAID, NOTHING KEEPING ME THERE ANY LONGER. I CAME NORTH. GOOD FISHING UP HERE.
I'M SORRY ABOUT YOUR NEPHEW.
ME, TOO. SO NOW I'M LIVING HERE IN THE NORTH.
LONG WAY FROM WHITE MAN'S DISEASES.
WHITE MAN'S ROADS.
WHITE MAN'S CARAMEL POPCORN.
WHITE MAN'S BEER?
WHEN YOU PEOPLE FINALLY GIVE UP AND GO HOME, YOU CAN LEAVE US THE BUDWEISER BREWERIES.

WHERE ARE WE? AM I ON THE TREE? AM I DEAD? I THOUGHT EVERYTHING WAS FINISHED. WHAT'S REAL?

YES.

YES? WHAT KIND OF AN ANSWER IS YES?

A GOOD ANSWER. TRUE, TOO.

ARE YOU A GOD AS WELL?

I'M A CULTURE HERO. WE DO THE SAME SHIT GODS DO. WE JUST SCREW UP MORE, AND NOBODY WORSHIPS US.

LOOK, THIS IS NOT A GOOD COUNTRY FOR GODS. MY PEOPLE FIGURED THAT OUT EARLY ON. THERE ARE CREATOR SPIRITS WHO MADE THE EARTH AND SO WE SAY THANK YOU.

IT GAVE US SALMON AND CORN AND BUFFALO, AND WILD RICE.

BUT WE NEVER BUILT CHURCHES. THE LAND WAS THE CHURCH.

YOU FOLLOW THAT RIVER FOR A WAY, YOU'LL GET TO THE LAKES WHERE THE WILD RICE GROWS.

YOU GO FAR ENOUGH SOUTH, THERE ARE ORANGE TREES, LEMON TREES, AND THOSE SQUASHY GREEN THINGS...

AVOCADOS.

"WHAT I'M TRYING TO SAY IS THAT AMERICA IS LIKE THAT. IT'S NOT GOOD GROWING COUNTRY FOR GODS."

THEY'RE LIKE AVOCADOS TRYING TO GROW IN WILD RICE COUNTRY.

THEY MAY NOT GROW WELL, BUT THEY'RE GOING TO WAR.

THAT WAS THE ONLY TIME HE SAW WHISKEY JACK LAUGH. IT WAS ALMOST A BARK, AND HAD LITTLE HUMOR IN IT.

IT'S NOT GOING TO BE A **WAR**.

THEN WHAT IS IT?

LOOK AT THE WATER-FALL ---

THE WATERFALL SPRAY CAUGHT THE SUN. SHADOW THOUGHT IT WAS THE MOST BEAUTIFUL THING HE HAD EVER SEEN.

"...IT'S GOING TO BE A BLOODBATH."

SHADOW SAW IT THEN IN ALL ITS STARK SIMPLICITY, SHOOK HIS HEAD, AND BEGAN TO LAUGH.

YOU OKAY?

I'M FINE. I JUST SAW THE HIDDEN INDIANS.

IT'S NOT A WAR AT ALL, IS IT?

IT'S A TWO-MAN CON.

YOU'RE NOT SO DUMB.

I WISH I COULD STAY HERE WITH YOU. THIS SEEMS LIKE A GOOD PLACE.

THERE ARE A *LOT* OF GOOD PLACES. THAT'S KIND OF THE POINT.

LISTEN. GODS DIE WHEN THEY ARE FORGOTTEN. PEOPLE, TOO. BUT THE LAND'S STILL HERE.

THE LAND ISN'T GOING ANYWHERE, AND NEITHER AM I.

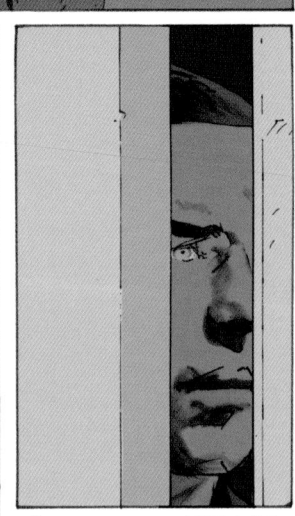

SHADOW CLOSED THE DOOR. SOMETHING WAS PULLING AT HIM.

HE WAS ALONE IN THE DARKNESS ONCE MORE.

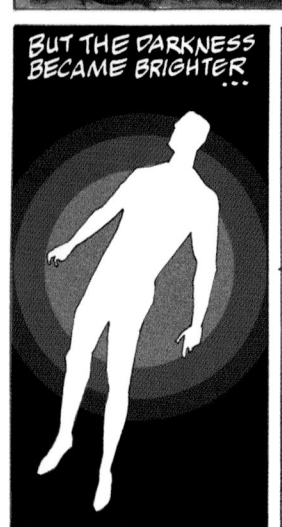

BUT THE DARKNESS BECAME BRIGHTER...

UNTIL IT WAS BURNING LIKE THE SUN.

AND THEN THE PAIN BEGAN.

CHAPTER SIX

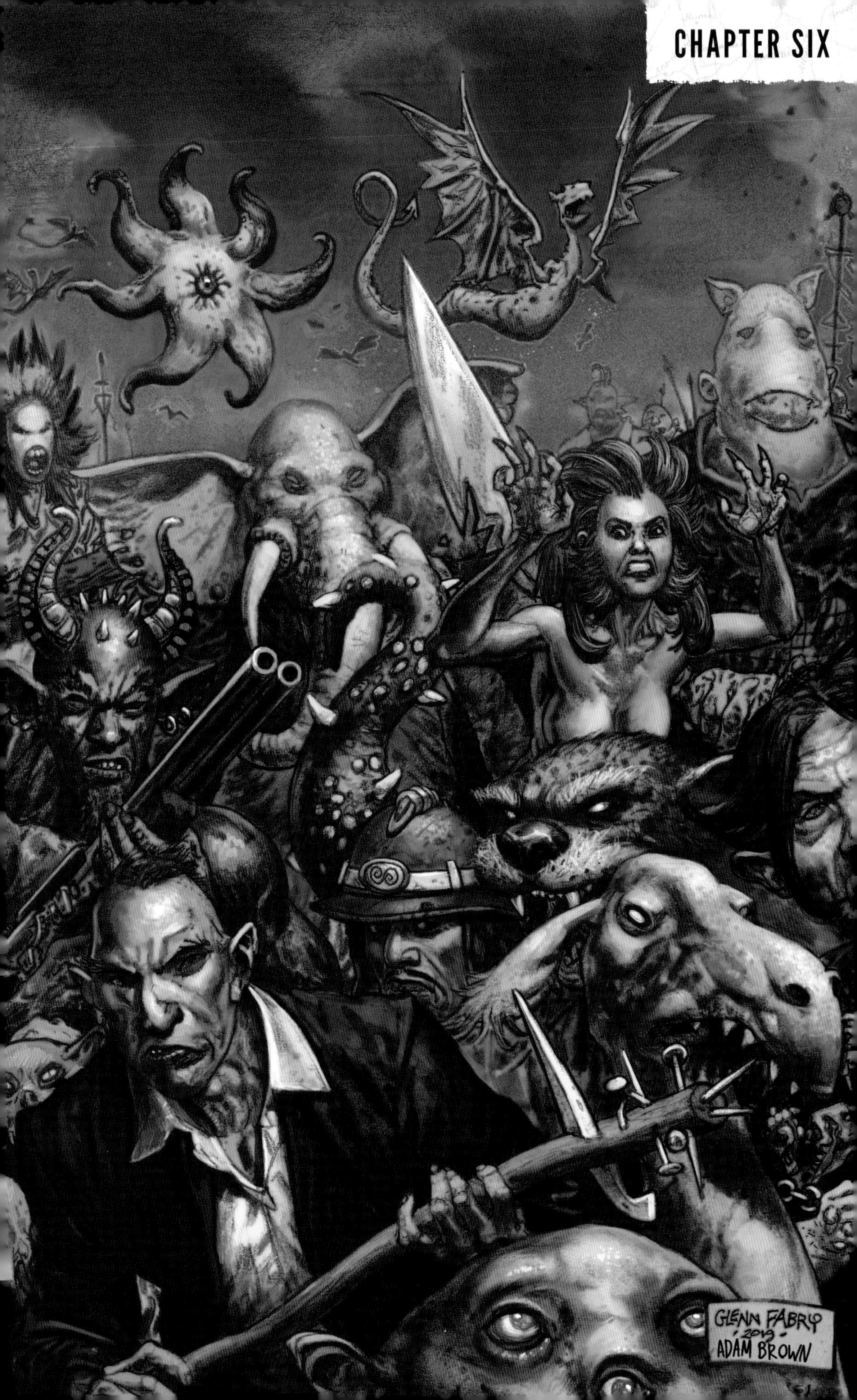
GLENN FABRY
2019
ADAM BROWN

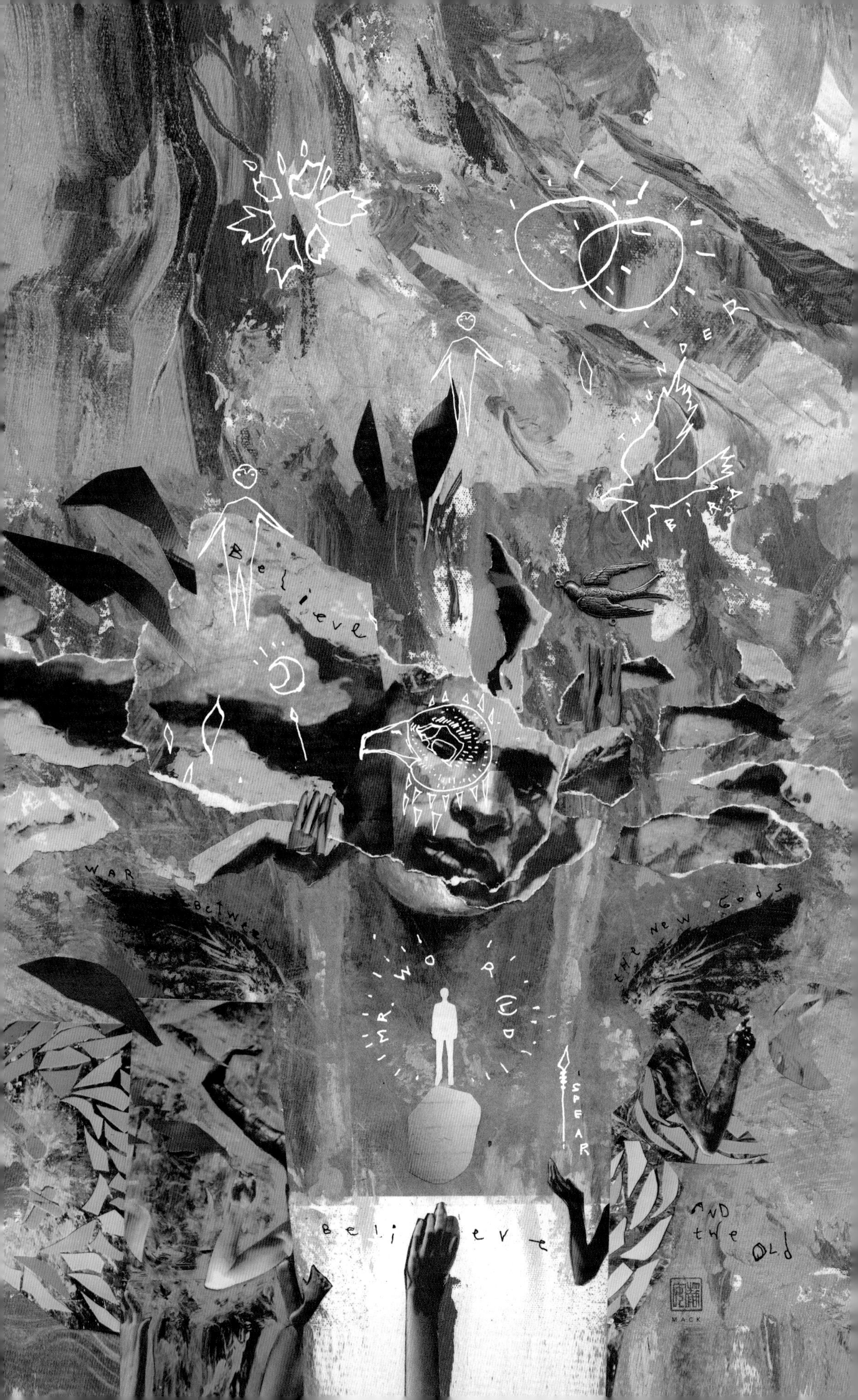
THUNDER BIRD
Believe
WAR Between the New Gods
MR. WORLD
SPEAR
Believe
AND the OLD
MACK

THERE WAS A WOMAN WHO WALKED THROUGH A MEADOW, AND SPRING FLOWERS BLOSSOMED WHERE SHE HAD PASSED. IN THIS PLACE AND IN THIS TIME SHE CALLED HERSELF *EASTER*.

THEY JUST AREN'T AS INTERESTING NAKED.

I CAN LOOK AT THE SUN WITHOUT EVEN BLINKING.

VERY CLEVER OF YOU. NOW LET'S GET HIM DOWN FROM THERE.

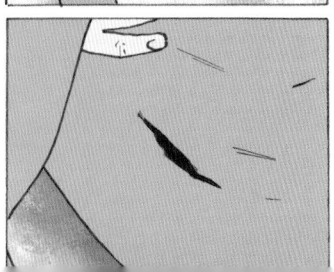

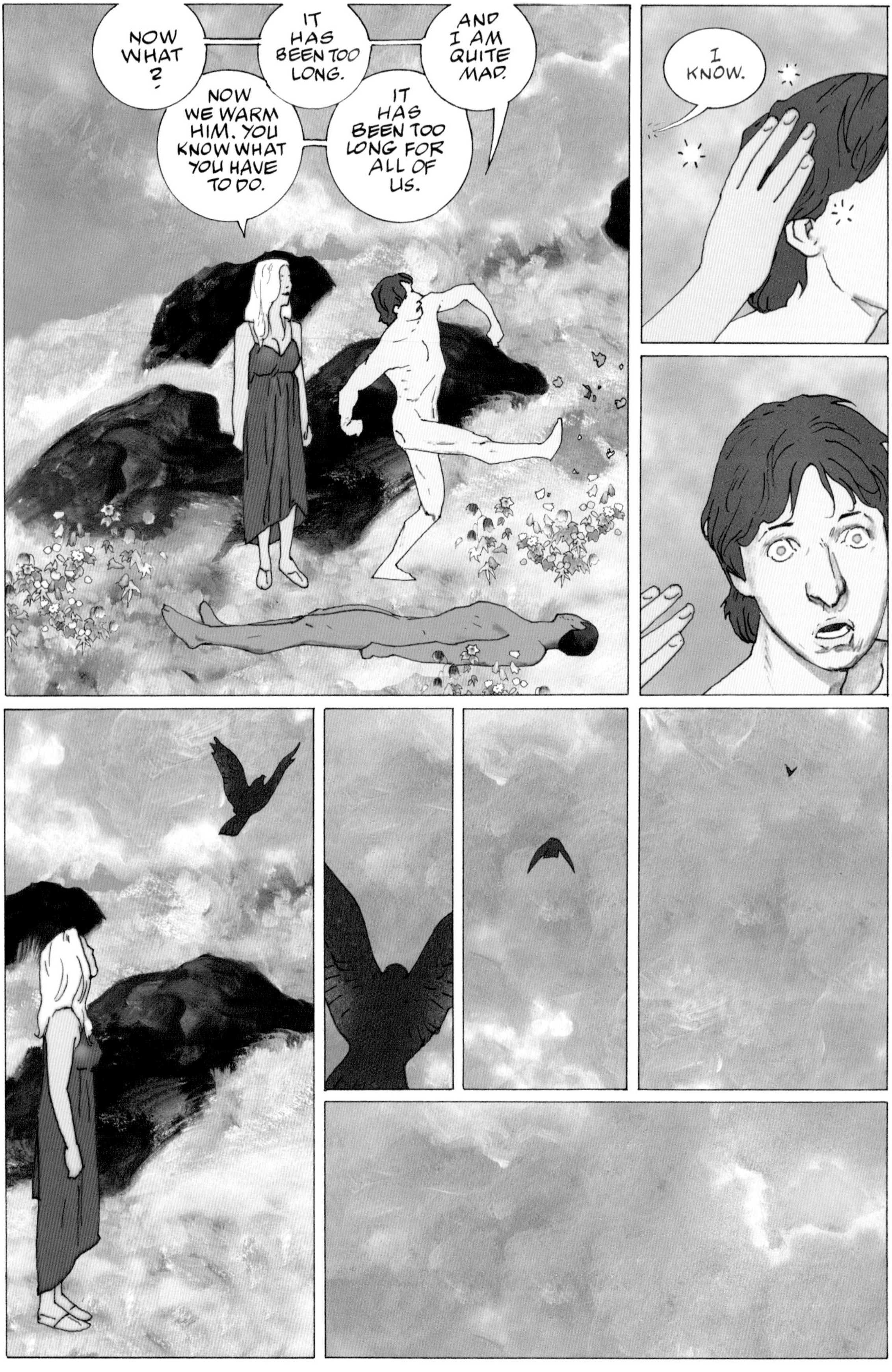
NOW WHAT ?
NOW WE WARM HIM. YOU KNOW WHAT YOU HAVE TO DO.
IT HAS BEEN TOO LONG.
IT HAS BEEN TOO LONG FOR ALL OF US.
AND I AM QUITE MAD.
I KNOW.

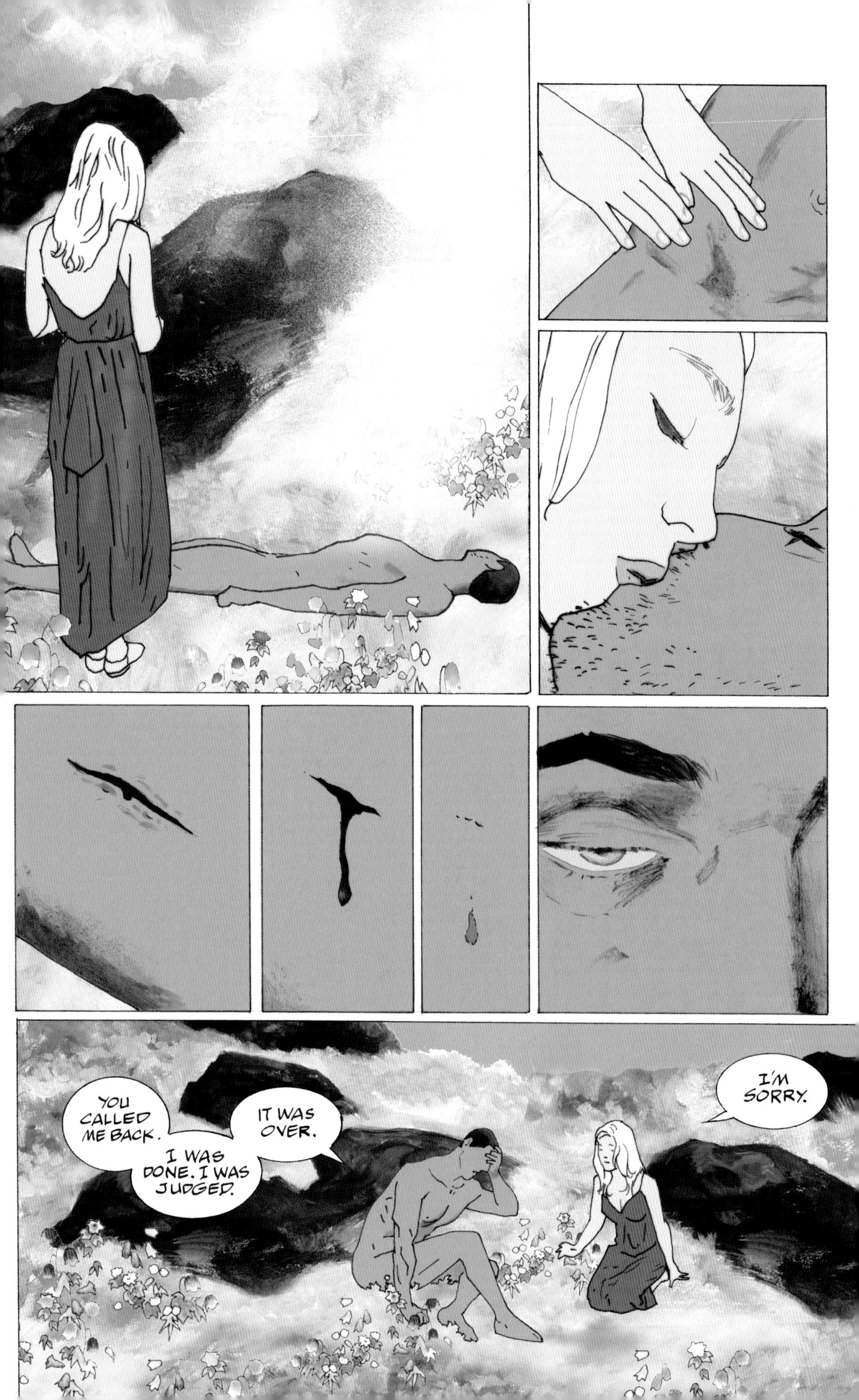
YOU CALLED ME BACK.
I WAS DONE. I WAS JUDGED.
IT WAS OVER.
I'M SORRY.

COME ON. TIME TO GET UP. IT'S ALL HAPPENING. YOU DON'T WANT TO MISS IT.

YOU CALLED ME BACK.

YES. I'M SORRY. DO YOU REMEMBER WHAT YOU LEARNED?

YES. IT WILL FADE THOUGH. LIKE A DREAM. I KNOW THAT. I LOST MY NAME AND I LOST MY HEART.

"AND YOU BROUGHT ME BACK."

I'M SORRY. THEY ARE GOING TO FIGHT SOON. THE OLD GODS AND THE NEW ONES.

YOU WANT ME TO FIGHT FOR YOU? YOU WASTED YOUR TIME.

I BROUGHT YOU BACK BECAUSE THAT IS WHAT I HAD TO DO. IT'S WHAT I'M BEST AT. WHAT YOU DO NOW IS WHATEVER YOU HAVE TO DO. YOUR CALL.

I DID MY PART.

SUDDENLY, SHE BECAME AWARE OF HIS NAKEDNESS.

IN THE RAIN AND THE CLOUD, SHADOWS MOVED UP THE SIDE OF THE MOUNTAIN, UP TO THE ROCK PATHWAYS.

THE PEOPLE CONTINUED UP THE HILL, ON TWO LEGS, ON FOUR LEGS, ON NO LEGS AT ALL.

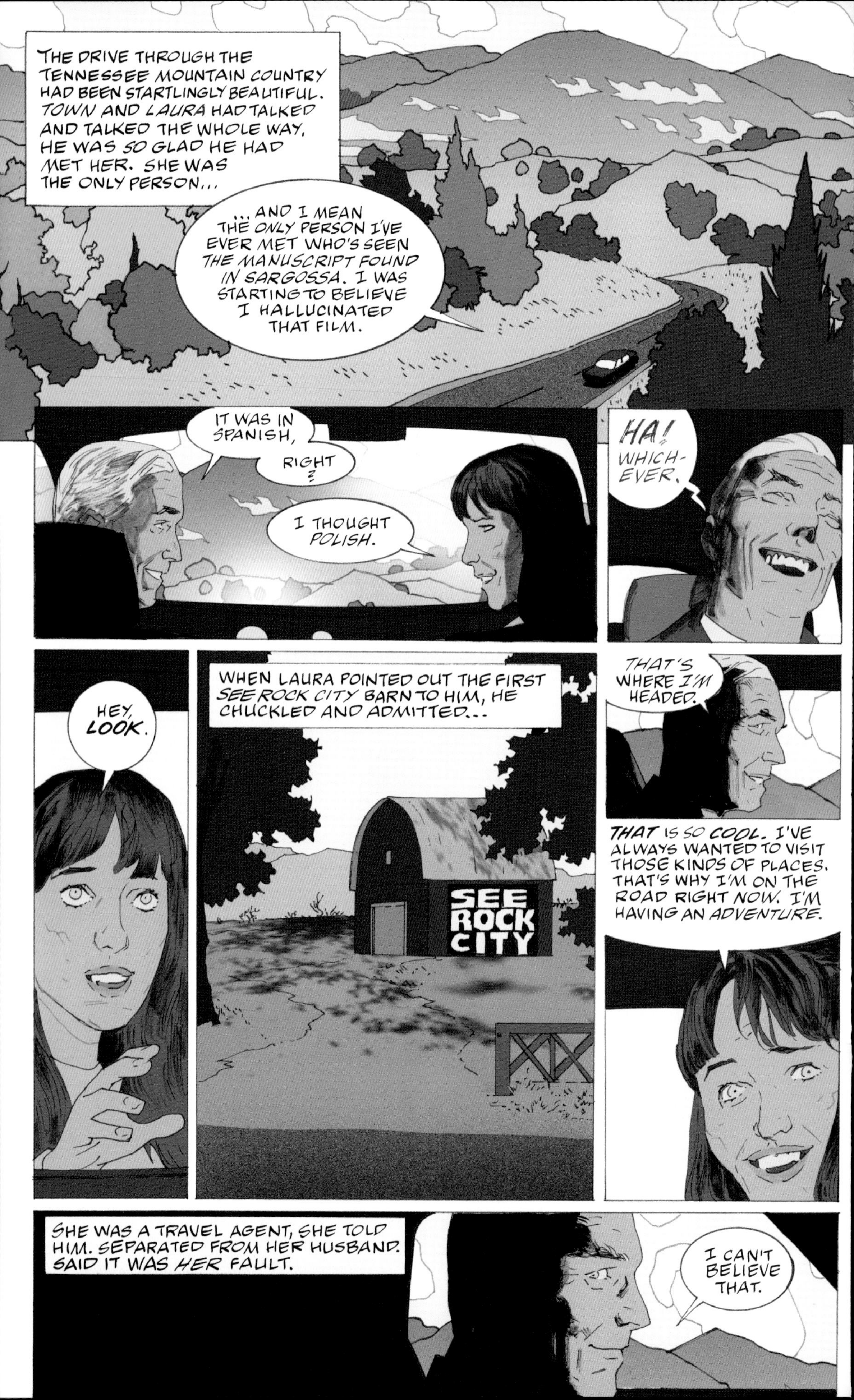
THE DRIVE THROUGH THE TENNESSEE MOUNTAIN COUNTRY HAD BEEN STARTLINGLY BEAUTIFUL. TOWN AND LAURA HAD TALKED AND TALKED THE WHOLE WAY. HE WAS SO GLAD HE HAD MET HER. SHE WAS THE ONLY PERSON...
...AND I MEAN THE ONLY PERSON I'VE EVER MET WHO'S SEEN THE MANUSCRIPT FOUND IN SARGOSSA. I WAS STARTING TO BELIEVE I HALLUCINATED THAT FILM.
IT WAS IN SPANISH,
RIGHT?
I THOUGHT POLISH.
HA! WHICH-EVER.
HEY, LOOK.
WHEN LAURA POINTED OUT THE FIRST SEE ROCK CITY BARN TO HIM, HE CHUCKLED AND ADMITTED...
SEE ROCK CITY
THAT'S WHERE I'M HEADED.
THAT IS SO COOL. I'VE ALWAYS WANTED TO VISIT THOSE KINDS OF PLACES. THAT'S WHY I'M ON THE ROAD RIGHT NOW. I'M HAVING AN ADVENTURE.
SHE WAS A TRAVEL AGENT, SHE TOLD HIM. SEPARATED FROM HER HUSBAND. SAID IT WAS HER FAULT.
I CAN'T BELIEVE THAT.

IT'S TRUE, MACK. I'M JUST NOT THE WOMAN HE MARRIED ANYMORE.

WELL, PEOPLE CHANGE.

AND BEFORE HE COULD THINK, HE WAS TELLING HER EVERYTHING HE *COULD* TELL HER ABOUT HIS LIFE, ABOUT *WOODY* AND *STONE* AND HOW THE TWO OF THEM WERE KILLED AND HOW...

YOU'D THINK YOU'D GET HARDENED TO THAT KIND OF THING IN *GOVERNMENT* WORK, BUT YOU *NEVER* DO.

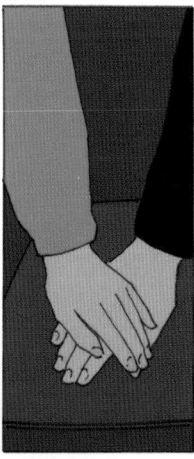

LUNCHTIME, THEY ATE BAD JAPANESE FOOD WHILE A THUNDERSTORM LOWERED ON KNOXVILLE, AND TOWN DIDN'T CARE THAT THE MISO WAS COLD OR THE SUSHI WAS WARM.

WELL, I HATED THE IDEA OF GETTING *STALE.* I WAS JUST *ROTTING AWAY* WHERE I WAS, SO I SET OFF WITHOUT MY CAR OR MY CREDIT CARDS. AND I'VE HAD THE *BEST* TIME.

AREN'T YOU SCARED? I MEAN, YOU COULD BE STRANDED. YOU COULD BE MUGGED.

I MET YOU, DIDN'T I?

THIS WAS LOVE.

WHEN THE MEAL WAS OVER THEY RAN THROUGH THE STORM HOLDING JAPANESE-LANGUAGE NEWSPAPERS TO COVER THEIR HEADS, AND THEY LAUGHED AS THEY RAN, LIKE SCHOOLCHILDREN IN THE RAIN.

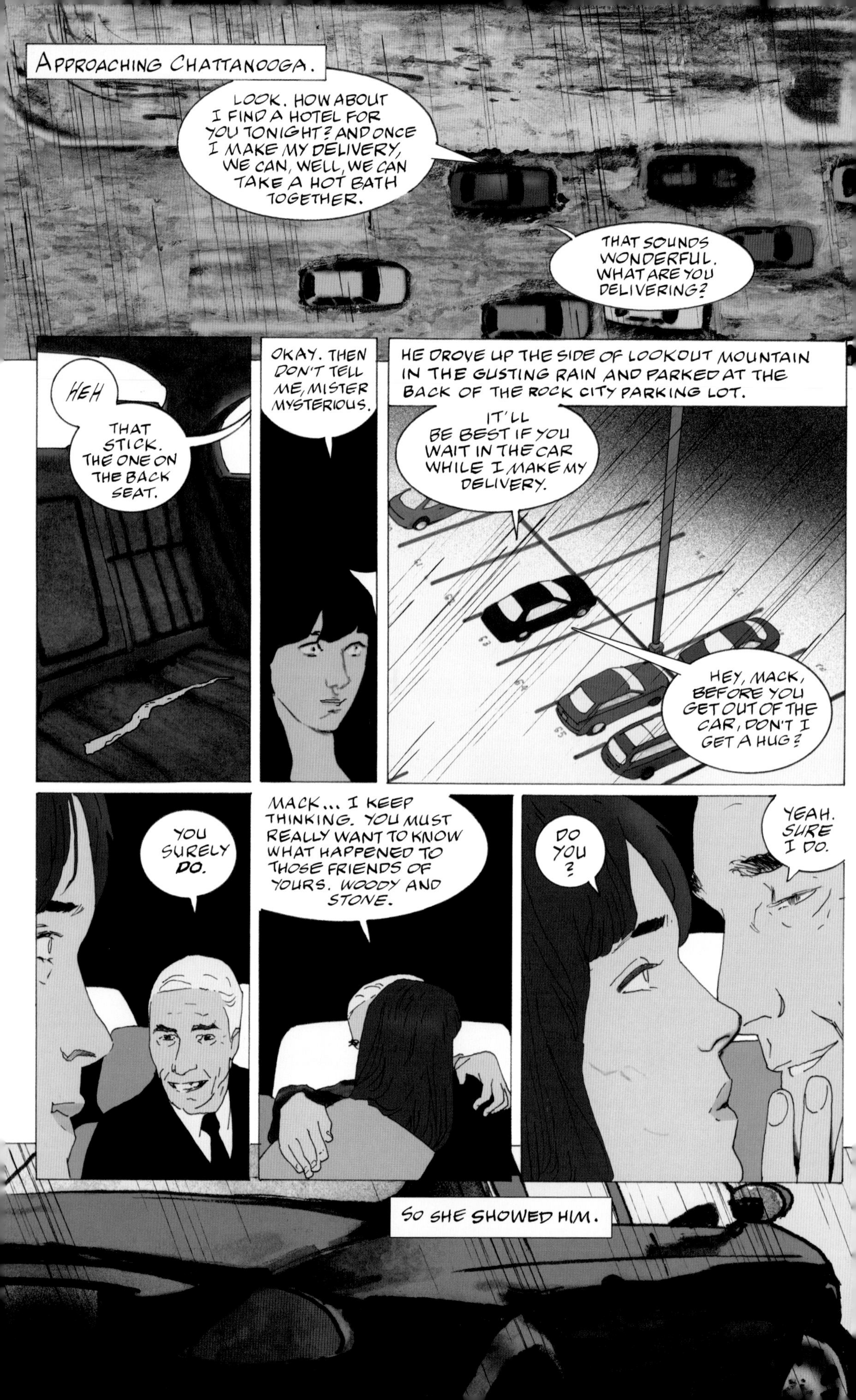
Approaching Chattanooga.
LOOK. HOW ABOUT I FIND A HOTEL FOR YOU TONIGHT? AND ONCE I MAKE MY DELIVERY, WE CAN, WELL, WE CAN TAKE A HOT BATH TOGETHER.
THAT SOUNDS WONDERFUL. WHAT ARE YOU DELIVERING?
HEH
THAT STICK. THE ONE ON THE BACK SEAT.
OKAY. THEN DON'T TELL ME, MISTER MYSTERIOUS.
HE DROVE UP THE SIDE OF LOOKOUT MOUNTAIN IN THE GUSTING RAIN AND PARKED AT THE BACK OF THE ROCK CITY PARKING LOT.
IT'LL BE BEST IF YOU WAIT IN THE CAR WHILE I MAKE MY DELIVERY.
HEY, MACK, BEFORE YOU GET OUT OF THE CAR, DON'T I GET A HUG?
YOU SURELY DO.
MACK... I KEEP THINKING. YOU MUST REALLY WANT TO KNOW WHAT HAPPENED TO THOSE FRIENDS OF YOURS. WOODY AND STONE.
DO YOU?
YEAH. SURE I DO.
SO SHE SHOWED HIM.

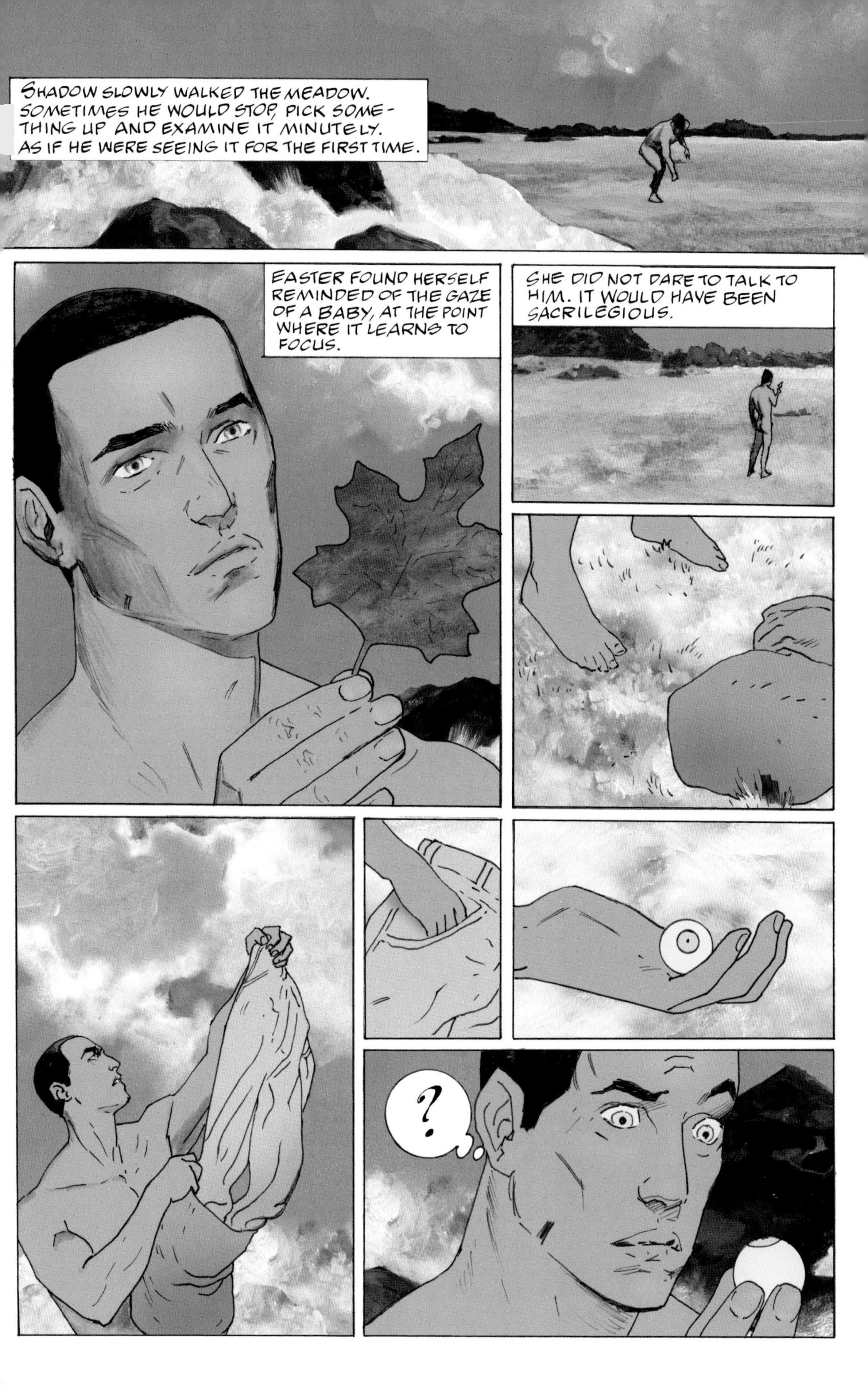
SHADOW SLOWLY WALKED THE MEADOW. SOMETIMES HE WOULD STOP, PICK SOMETHING UP AND EXAMINE IT MINUTELY. AS IF HE WERE SEEING IT FOR THE FIRST TIME.
EASTER FOUND HERSELF REMINDED OF THE GAZE OF A BABY, AT THE POINT WHERE IT LEARNS TO FOCUS.
SHE DID NOT DARE TO TALK TO HIM. IT WOULD HAVE BEEN SACRILEGIOUS.
?

Once he was dressed he looked more normal. Easter wondered how far he had traveled, and what it had cost him to return.

He was not the first whose return she had initiated.

NO COINS.

NO COINS?

IT WAS GOOD TO HAVE THE COINS. IT GAVE ME SOMETHING TO DO WITH MY HANDS.

Soon enough, she knew, the dreams and memories he brought back from the tree would fade.

COME.

AAWK

YOU RODE HIM HERE?

AWK

YES. YOU CAN RIDE HIM BACK IF HE LETS YOU.

HOW DO YOU RIDE HIM?

IT'S EASY. IF YOU DON'T FALL. LIKE RIDING THE LIGHTNING.

WILL I SEE YOU BACK THERE?

I'M DONE, HONEY. YOU GO DO WHATEVER YOU NEED TO DO. BRINGING YOU BACK LIKE THAT TOOK A LOT OUT OF ME. I NEED TO REST, TO SAVE UP MY ENERGIES UNTIL MY FESTIVAL BEGINS. GOOD LUCK.

WHISKEY JACK. I SAW HIM AFTER I PASSED ON, HE CAME AND FOUND ME. WE DRANK BEER TOGETHER.

WILL I EVER SEE YOU AGAIN?

YES. I'M SURE YOU DID.

I DOUBT IT.

THERE WAS AN OZONE TASTE IN HIS MOUTH, METALLIC AND BLUE. SOMETHING CRACKLED AND THE GROUND FELL AWAY BENEATH THEM. IT WAS *EXACTLY* LIKE RIDING THE LIGHTNING.

LAURA TOOK THE STICK FROM THE BACK SEAT OF
THE CAR, LEFT MR. TOWN IN THE FRONT SEAT, AND
WALKED THROUGH THE RAIN TO *ROCK CITY.*

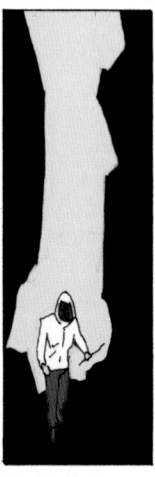

CAUTION
NO
ADMITTANCE
DURING
RENOVATION

WELCOME,
SPEAR-CARRIER.
I SHALL ASSUME
MISTER TOWN
IS DEAD.

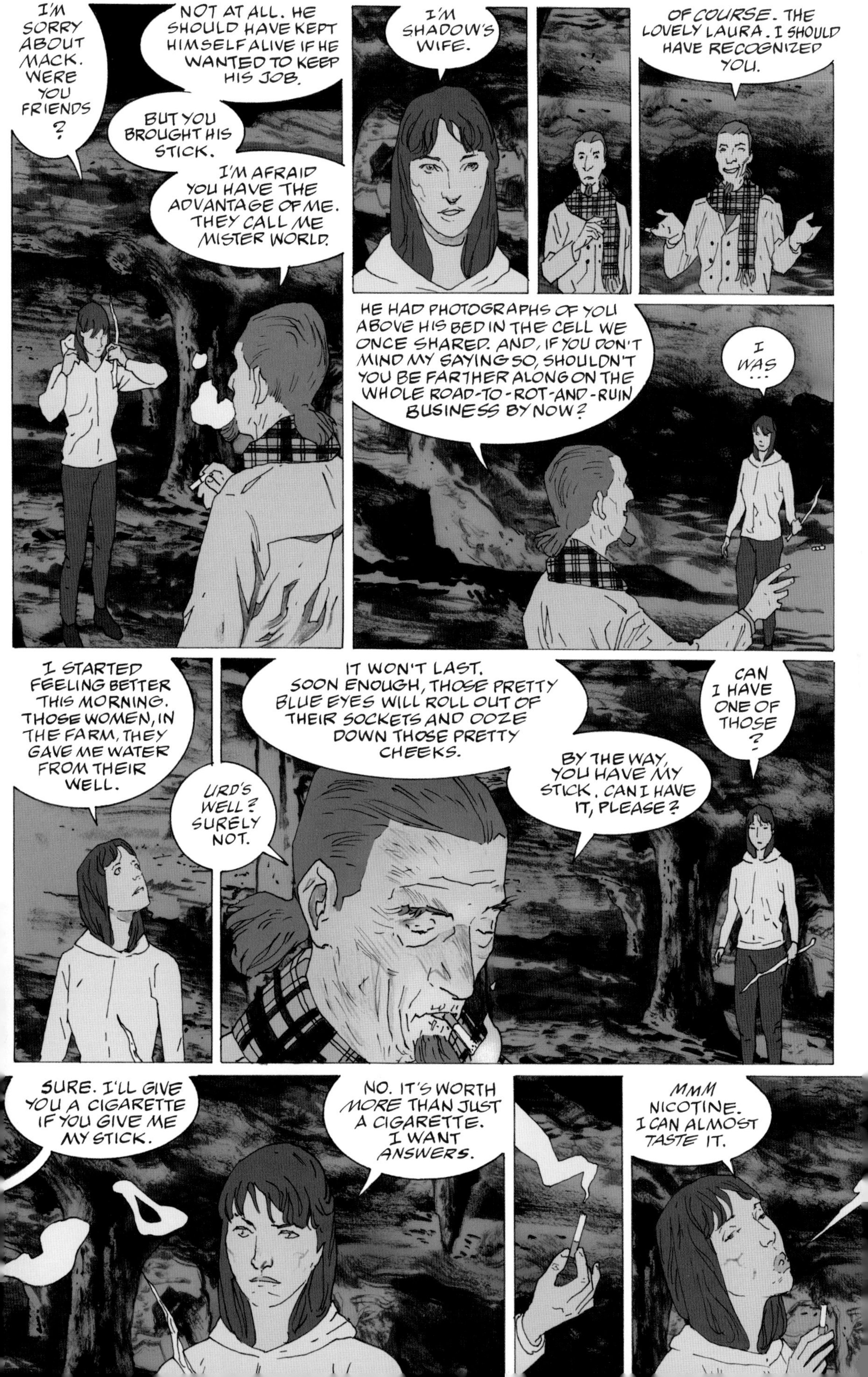
I'M SORRY ABOUT MACK. WERE YOU FRIENDS?
NOT AT ALL. HE SHOULD HAVE KEPT HIMSELF ALIVE IF HE WANTED TO KEEP HIS JOB.
BUT YOU BROUGHT HIS STICK.
I'M AFRAID YOU HAVE THE ADVANTAGE OF ME. THEY CALL ME MISTER WORLD.
I'M SHADOW'S WIFE.
OF COURSE. THE LOVELY LAURA. I SHOULD HAVE RECOGNIZED YOU.
HE HAD PHOTOGRAPHS OF YOU ABOVE HIS BED IN THE CELL WE ONCE SHARED. AND, IF YOU DON'T MIND MY SAYING SO, SHOULDN'T YOU BE FARTHER ALONG ON THE WHOLE ROAD-TO-ROT-AND-RUIN BUSINESS BY NOW?
I WAS...
I STARTED FEELING BETTER THIS MORNING. THOSE WOMEN, IN THE FARM, THEY GAVE ME WATER FROM THEIR WELL.
URD'S WELL? SURELY NOT.
IT WON'T LAST. SOON ENOUGH, THOSE PRETTY BLUE EYES WILL ROLL OUT OF THEIR SOCKETS AND OOZE DOWN THOSE PRETTY CHEEKS.
BY THE WAY, YOU HAVE MY STICK. CAN I HAVE IT, PLEASE?
CAN I HAVE ONE OF THOSE?
SURE. I'LL GIVE YOU A CIGARETTE IF YOU GIVE ME MY STICK.
NO. IT'S WORTH MORE THAN JUST A CIGARETTE. I WANT ANSWERS.
MMM NICOTINE. I CAN ALMOST TASTE IT.

YES. WHY DID YOU GO TO THE WOMEN IN THE FARMHOUSE?

SHADOW TOLD ME TO ASK THEM FOR WATER.

I WONDER IF HE KNEW WHAT IT WOULD DO? PROBABLY NOT. STILL, THAT'S THE GOOD THING ABOUT HAVING HIM DEAD ON THE TREE. HE'S OFF THE BOARD.

YOU SET HIM UP ALL THE WAY, YOU PEOPLE.

WHY DID YOU WANT HIM?

PATTERNS AND DISTRACTION.

" THAT'S WHAT THOSE MORONS FIGHTING OUT THERE HAVE NEVER BEEN ABLE TO GRASP. IT'S NEVER A MATTER OF THE OLD AND THE NEW. IT'S ONLY ABOUT PATTERNS. "

NOW... MY STICK, PLEASE.

WHY DO YOU WANT IT?

IT SYMBOLIZES A SPEAR, AND IN THIS SORRY WORLD, THE SYMBOL IS THE THING.

WHICH SIDE ARE YOU ON?

I'M ON THE WINNING SIDE. ALWAYS. IT'S WHAT I DO BEST.

I CAN SEE THAT. OKAY, I'LL GIVE YOU THE STICK.

GOOD GIRL.

SHE HAD TO WAIT UNTIL HE GOT CLOSE ENOUGH. SHE HAD THAT MUCH FIGURED OUT.

THEY SWEPT THROUGH THE STORM LIKE JAGGED BOLTS OF LIGHTNING, FLASHING FROM CLOUD TO CLOUD.

IN MY DREAM, I WAS HUNTING YOU. I HAD TO BRING BACK A FEATHER.

"YES. THEY CAME FOR THE FEATHERS, TO PROVE THAT THEY WERE MEN; AND THEY CAME TO CUT THE STONES FROM OUR HEADS, TO GIFT THEIR DEAD WITH OUR LIVES."

AN IMAGE FILLED HIS MIND THEN: OF A THUNDERBIRD LYING FRESHLY DEAD. A WOMAN WAS BREAKING OPEN ITS SKULL WITH A KNOB OF FLINT AND PICKING THROUGH THE WET SHARDS UNTIL SHE FOUND A SMOOTH CLEAR STONE, OPALESCENT FIRES FLICKERING IN ITS DEPTHS.

"EAGLE STONES."

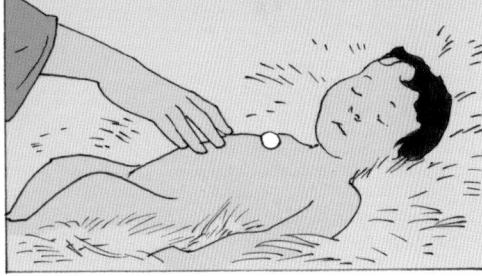

SHE WAS GOING TO TAKE IT TO HER INFANT SON, DEAD THESE LAST THREE NIGHTS, AND SHE WOULD LAY IT ON HIS COLD BREAST.

BY MORNING, THE BOY WOULD BE ALIVE AND LAUGHING, AND THE JEWEL WOULD BE CLOUDED AND, LIKE THE BIRD IT HAD BEEN STOLEN FROM...

...QUITE DEAD.

I UNDERSTAND.

THE BIRD THREW BACK ITS HEAD AND CROWED, AND ITS CRY WAS THE THUNDER.

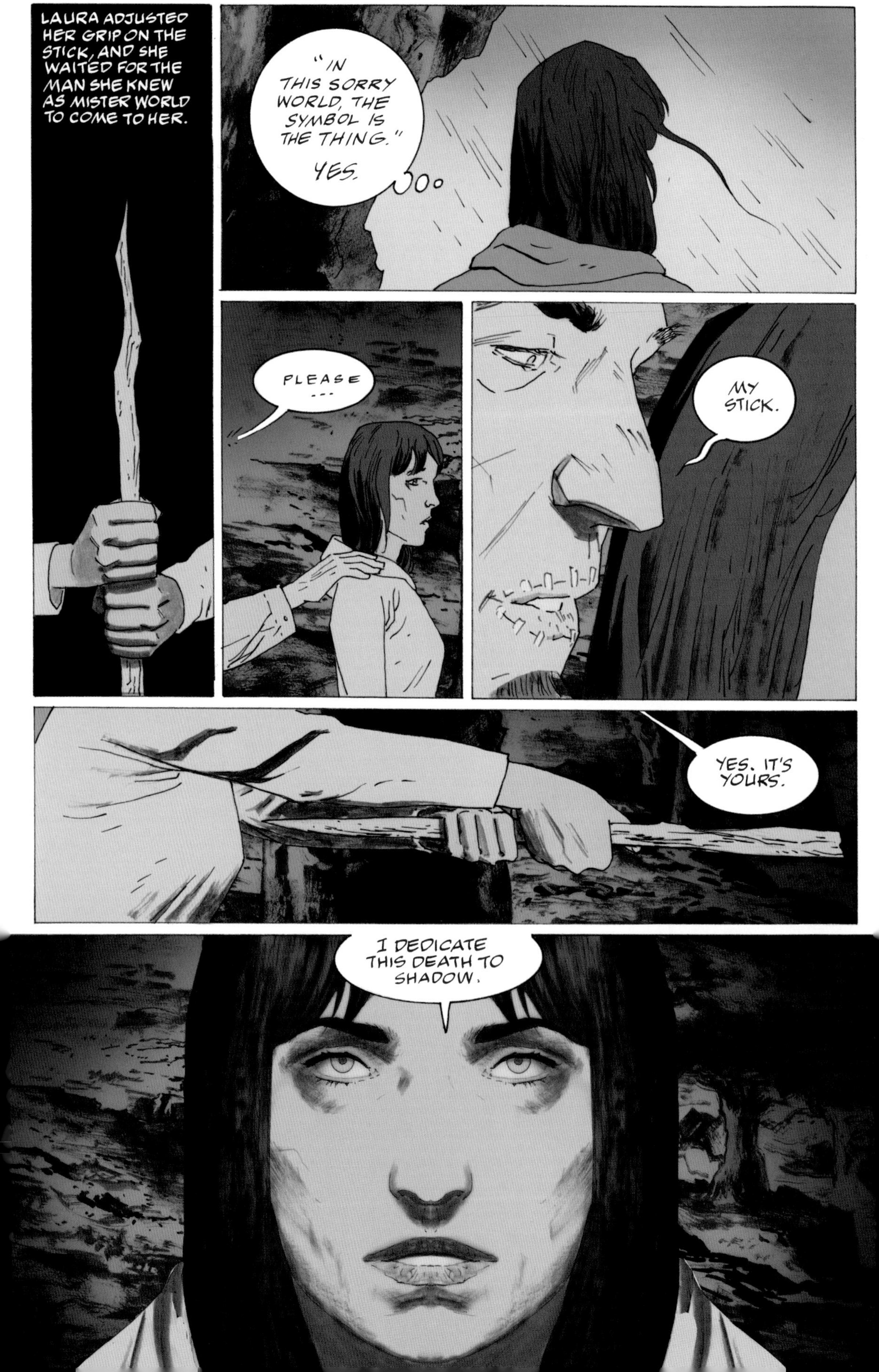
LAURA ADJUSTED HER GRIP ON THE STICK, AND SHE WAITED FOR THE MAN SHE KNEW AS MISTER WORLD TO COME TO HER.
"IN THIS SORRY WORLD, THE SYMBOL IS THE THING."
YES.
PLEASE ...
MY STICK.
YES. IT'S YOURS.
I DEDICATE THIS DEATH TO SHADOW.

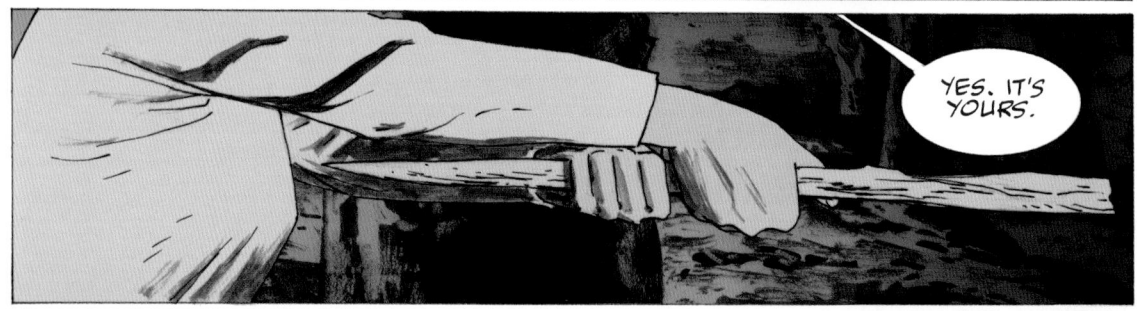

SHE STABBED THE STICK INTO HER CHEST, JUST BELOW THE BREASTBONE, FELT IT WRITHE AND CHANGE AS THE STICK BE- CAME A SPEAR.

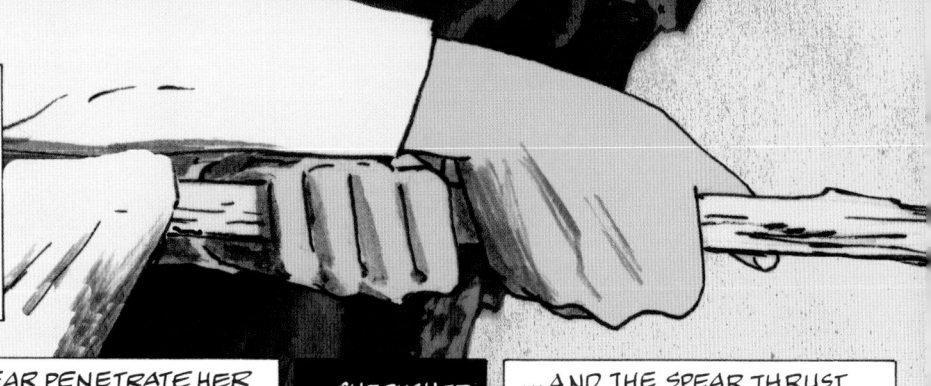

SHE FELT THE SPEAR PENETRATE HER CHEST, FELT IT PUSH THROUGH HER BACK. A MOMENT'S RESISTANCE...

... SHE PUSHED HARDER...

...AND THE SPEAR THRUST INTO MR. WORLD. HIS HOWLS WERE IN A LANGUAGE SHE DID NOT RECOGNIZE.

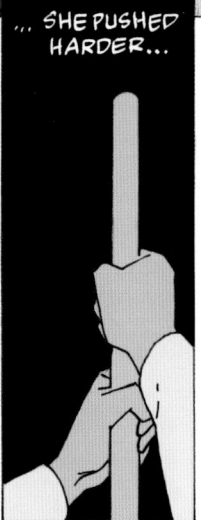

SHE COULD FEEL HIS HOT BLOOD SPURTING ONTO HER BACK. NOW THEY WERE JOINED BY THE POLE, IMPALED TOGETHER LIKE TWO FISH ON A SINGLE SPEAR.

BITCH. YOU FUCKING BITCH.

HE NOW HAD A KNIFE, SHE SAW, AND HE STABBED HER CHEST AND BREASTS RANDOMLY AND WILDLY, UNABLE TO SEE WHAT HE WAS DOING.

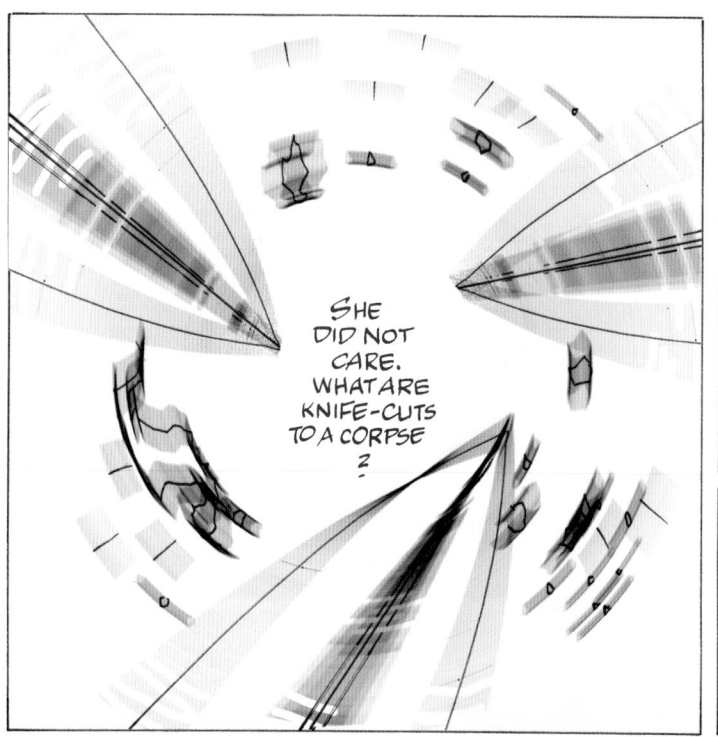

SHE DID NOT CARE. WHAT ARE KNIFE-CUTS TO A CORPSE?

SHE COULD FEEL HIS HOT TEARS ON HER NECK, HIS BLOOD SPURTING DOWN THE BACK OF HER LEGS, AND SHE SAID, WITH A CERTAIN DARK AMUSEMENT...

THIS MUST LOOK SO UNDIGNIFIED.

THE ROCK CITY PARKING LOT.

SOMETHING DEEPLY FAMILIAR...

?

MR. TOWN.

STILL WARM.

A SCENT ON THE AIR IN THE CAR; IT WAS FAINT, BUT SHADOW WOULD HAVE RECOGNIZED IT ANYWHERE.

HE FELT A SHARP PAIN IN HIS SIDE. SOMEWHERE A MAN'S VOICE CALLED OUT...

...TO ODIN!

THERE WAS NOBODY IN THE GIFT SHOP, NOBODY IN THE GARDENS. HE CALLED OUT AND IMAGINED HE HEARD SOMETHING ANSWERING.

CAUTION
NO
ADMITTANCE
DURING
RENOVATION

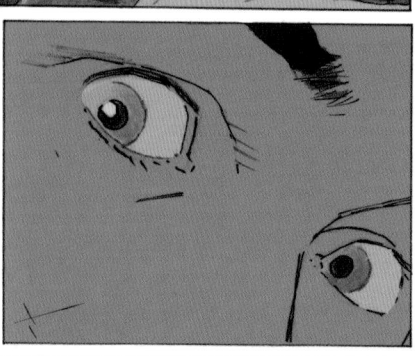

YOU HAVE NEVER DISAPPOINTED ME.

THAT'S WEIRD. I DISAPPOINTED MYSELF ALL THE WAY, EVERY TIME.

NOT AT ALL. YOU DID EVERYTHING YOU WERE MEANT TO DO. YOU TOOK EVERYBODY'S ATTENTION SO THEY NEVER LOOKED AT THE HAND WITH THE COIN IN IT.

AND THERE'S POWER IN THE SACRIFICE OF A SON-- POWER ENOUGH TO GET THE WHOLE BALL ROLLING

TO TELL THE TRUTH-- I'M PROUD OF YOU.

IT WAS CROOKED. ALL OF IT. IT WAS JUST A SET-UP FOR A MASSACRE.

EXACTLY. IT WAS CROOKED. BUT IT WAS THE ONLY GAME IN TOWN.

I WANT LAURA. I WANT LOKI. WHERE ARE THEY?

THERE WAS ONLY SILENCE.

YOU ARE TOO LATE.

I HAVE THROWN THE SPEAR.

AH HHHH

I HAVE DEDICATED THE BATTLE.

HHHHH

IT HAS BEGUN.

NO SHIT.

NO SHIT.

IT DOES NOT MATTER WHAT YOU DO ANYMORE. IT IS TOO LATE.

OKAY.

YOU SAY THERE'S SOME SPEAR YOU HAD TO THROW TO KICK OFF THE BATTLE, LIKE THE WHOLE *UPPSALA* THING. AM I RIGHT?

H H H H

I FIGURED IT OUT. I'M NOT SURE WHEN. MAYBE WHEN I WAS HANGING ON THE TREE. IT WAS FROM SOMETHING WEDNESDAY SAID TO ME AT CHRISTMAS.

"IT'S JUST A TWO-MAN CON. LIKE THE BISHOP AND THE DIAMOND NECKLACE AND THE COP. TWO MEN, WHO APPEAR TO BE ON OPPOSITE SIDES, PLAYING THE SAME GAME."

YOU'RE RIDICULOUS.

YOU CAN COME OUT WHEREVER YOU ARE. SHOW YOURSELF. I'M TIRED OF BEING PLAYED FOR A *SUCKER.*

THERE WAS A CHANGE IN THE SHADOWS AT THE BACK OF THE CAVE. SOMETHING BECAME MORE SOLID...

... SOMETHING SHIFTED.

YOU KNOW TOO DAMNED MUCH, M'BOY.

CHAPTER SEVEN

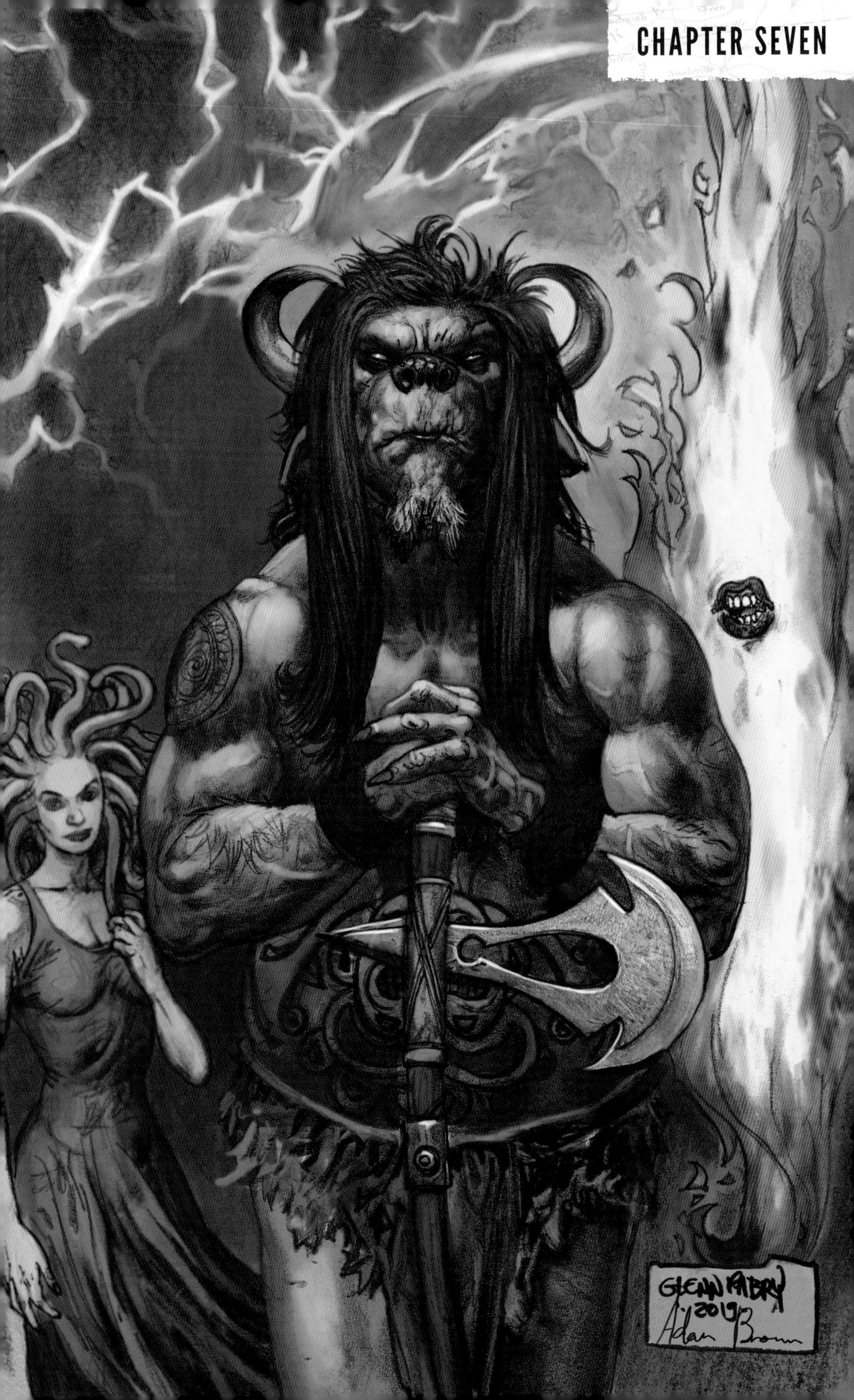
GLENN FABRY 2019
Adam Brown

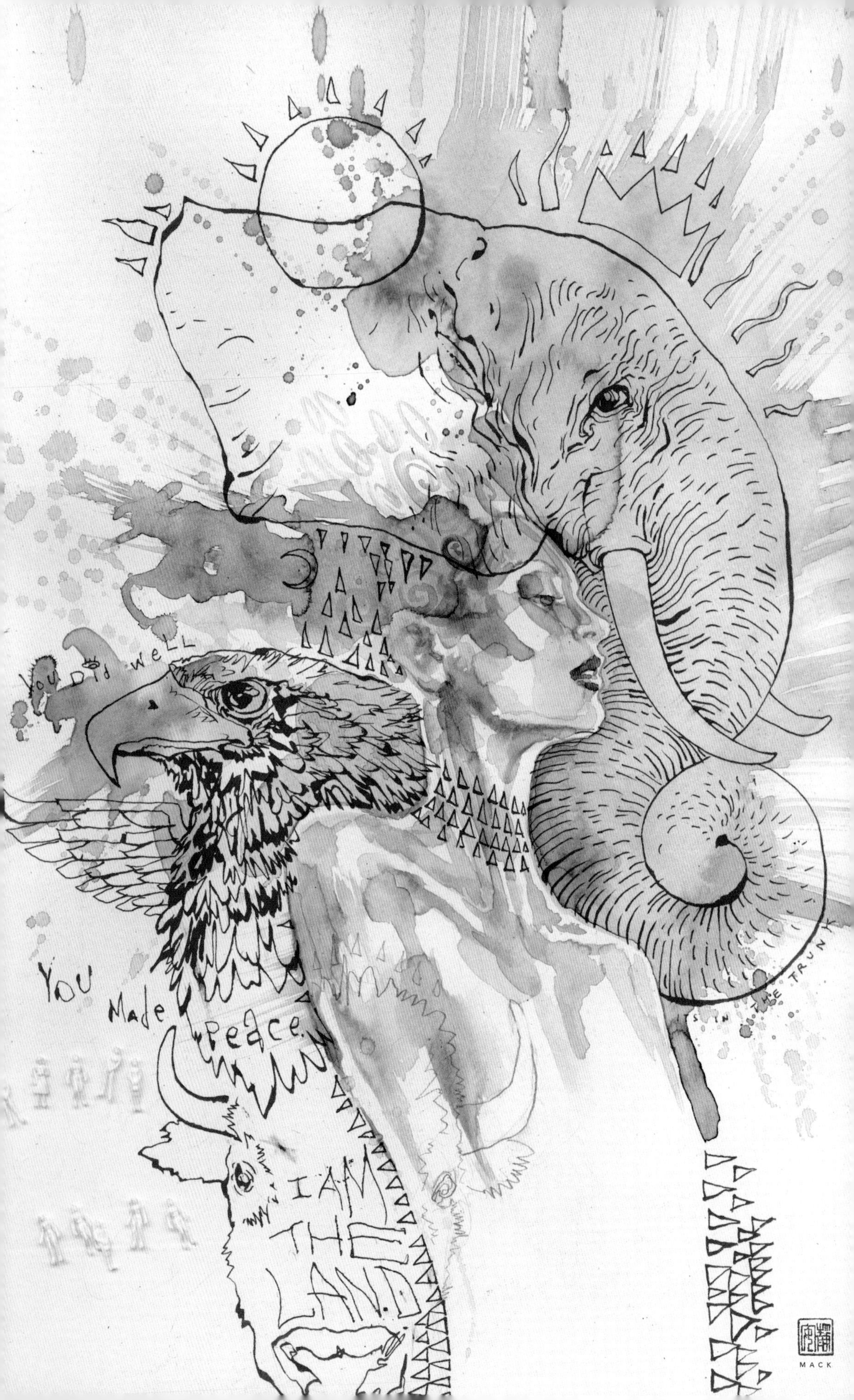

YOU DID WELL
YOU Made peace.
I AM THE LAND.
S IN THE TRUNK
MACK

HIS VOICE WAS FAINT-- NOT ACTUALLY QUIET-- BUT THERE WAS A QUALITY TO IT THAT MADE SHADOW THINK OF AN OLD RADIO NOT QUITE TUNED TO A DISTANT STATION.

NO. YOU WERE THE JUDAS GOAT.

SO THEY DIDN'T KILL YOU.

THEY KILLED ME.

NONE OF THIS WOULD HAVE WORKED IF THEY DIDN'T. IT WAS MY DEATH THAT DREW THEM ALL TOGETHER.

I WAS THE SACRIFICIAL LAMB.

NOT AT ALL. THAT IMPLIES THAT I WAS BETRAYING THE OLD GODS FOR THE NEW.

NOT AT ALL.

I CAN SEE THAT. YOU WEREN'T BETRAYING EITHER SIDE. YOU TWO WERE BETRAYING BOTH SIDES. YOU NEEDED A BLOOD SACRIFICE. A SACRIFICE OF GODS.

THE HOWL ACROSS THE CAVE DOOR BECAME A SCREECH. AS IF OF SOMETHING HUGE AND IN PAIN.

AND WHY THE HELL NOT. I'VE BEEN TRAPPED IN THIS DAMNED LAND FOR ALMOST TWELVE HUNDRED YEARS. MY BLOOD IS THIN. I'M HUNGRY.

AND YOU TWO FEED ON DEATH.

"YES. BUT YOUR MOTHER LEFT THE COUNTRY AFTER YOU'D BEEN CONCEIVED. IT TOOK US SO LONG TO FIND YOU.

"AND WHEN WE DID, YOU WERE IN PRISON.

"WE NEEDED TO FIND WHAT BUTTONS TO PRESS TO MAKE YOU MOVE.

"AND YOU HAD A WIFE TO GO HOME TO.

"IT WAS UNFORTUNATE. NOT INSURMOUNTABLE. IF IT COULD HAVE BEEN ANY OTHER WAY."

THIS TIME SHADOW KNEW WHAT HE MEANT.

AND IF SHE'D HAD THE GRACE...

TO STAY DEAD...

HHH

HHH

WOOD AND STONE WERE GOOD MEN. YOU WERE GOING...

...YOU WERE GOING TO BE ALLOWED TO ESCAPE WHEN THE TRAIN CROSSED THE DAKOTAS.

WHERE IS SHE?

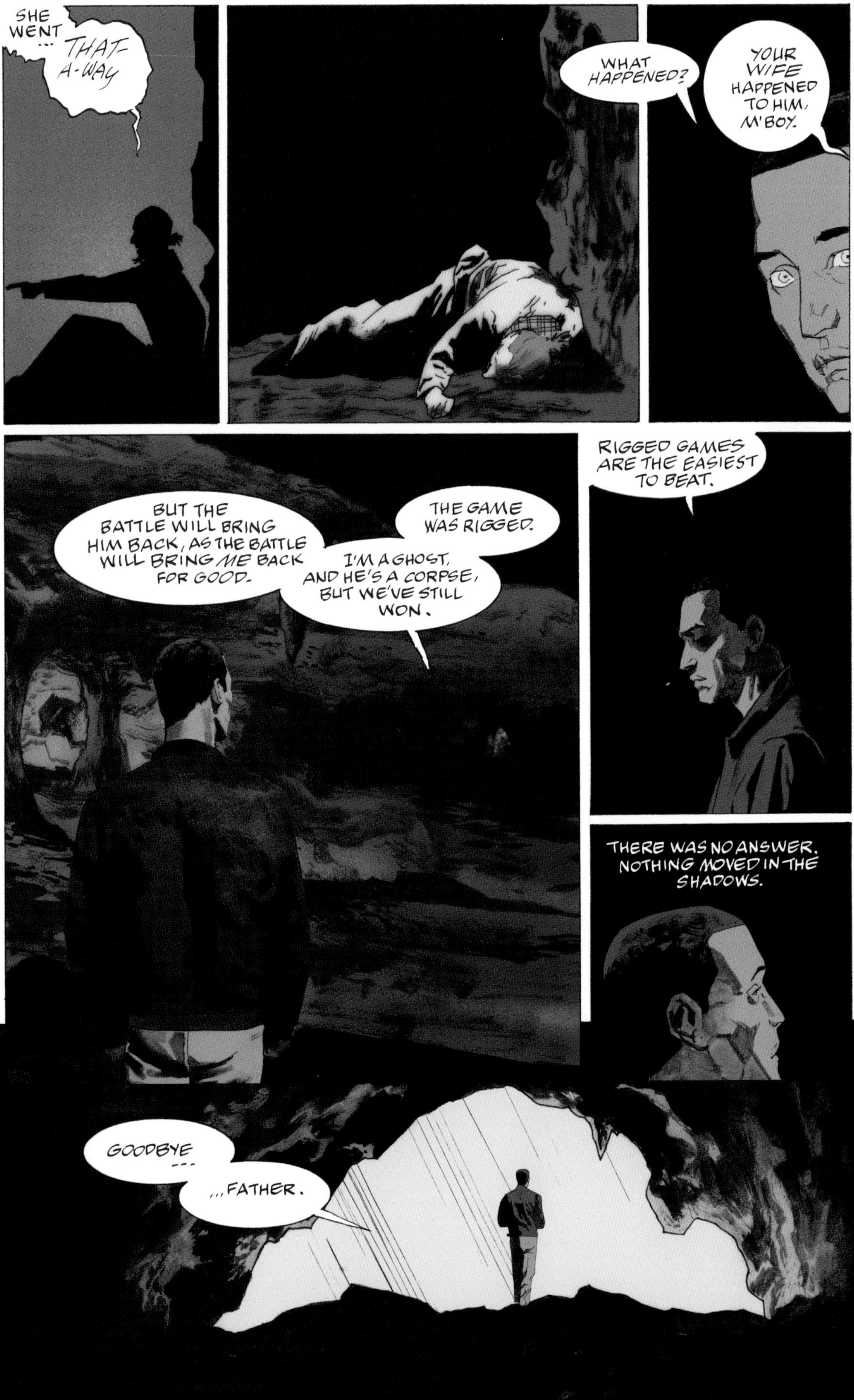
SHE WENT ... THAT-A-WAY
WHAT HAPPENED?
YOUR WIFE HAPPENED TO HIM, M'BOY.
THE GAME WAS RIGGED.
I'M A GHOST, AND HE'S A CORPSE, BUT WE'VE STILL WON.
BUT THE BATTLE WILL BRING HIM BACK, AS THE BATTLE WILL BRING ME BACK FOR GOOD.
RIGGED GAMES ARE THE EASIEST TO BEAT.
THERE WAS NO ANSWER. NOTHING MOVED IN THE SHADOWS.
GOODBYE ---
...FATHER.

DESERTED. BUT THIS WAS ROCK CITY, A PLACE OF AWE AND WORSHIP FOR A THOUSAND YEARS.

THE MILLIONS OF TOURISTS WHO PASSED THROUGH HAD THE SAME EFFECT AS WATER TURNING A MILLION PRAYER WHEELS.

AND SHADOW KNEW WHERE THE BATTLE MUST BE TAKING PLACE.

HE REMEMBERED HOW HE HAD *FELT* ON THE *CAROUSEL.*

HE REMEMBERED TURNING THE WINNEBAGO, SHIFTING IT AT RIGHT ANGLES TO *EVERYTHING.*

AND THEN, EASILY AND PERFECTLY, IT HAPPENED. WITH ONE STEP HE HAD MOVED FROM THE TOURIST PATH...

...TO SOMEWHERE REAL.

HE WAS BACKSTAGE.

THE SKY WAS LIT BY LIGHTNING HELD IN ONE FROZEN MOMENT. THIS WAS THE MOMENT OF THE STORM.

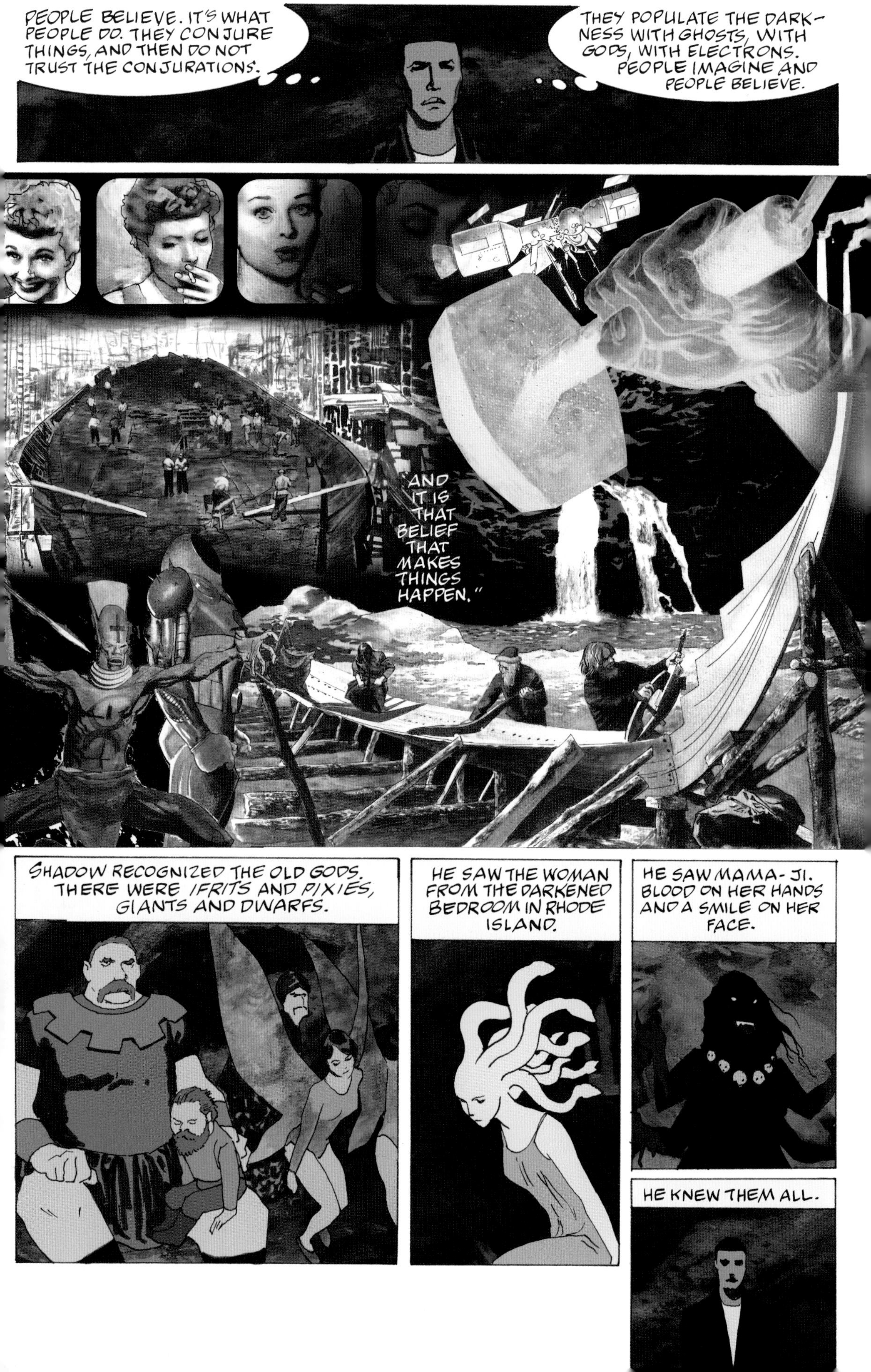

PEOPLE BELIEVE. IT'S WHAT PEOPLE DO. THEY CONJURE THINGS, AND THEN DO NOT TRUST THE CONJURATIONS.
THEY POPULATE THE DARKNESS WITH GHOSTS, WITH GODS, WITH ELECTRONS. PEOPLE IMAGINE AND PEOPLE BELIEVE.
AND IT IS THAT BELIEF THAT MAKES THINGS HAPPEN."
SHADOW RECOGNIZED THE OLD GODS. THERE WERE *IFRITS* AND *PIXIES*, GIANTS AND DWARFS.
HE SAW THE WOMAN FROM THE DARKENED BEDROOM IN RHODE ISLAND.
HE SAW MAMA-JI. BLOOD ON HER HANDS AND A SMILE ON HER FACE.
HE KNEW THEM ALL.

HE RECOGNIZED THE NEW ONES, TOO.

THERE WAS ONE WHO HAD TO BE A RAILROAD BARON. HE HAD THE AIR OF ONE WHO HAS SEEN BETTER DAYS.

THERE WERE THE GREAT GRAY GODS OF THE AIRPLANES.

THERE WERE THE CAR GODS THERE WITH BLOOD ON THEIR BLACK GLOVES AND ON THEIR CHROME TEETH: RECIPIENTS OF HUMAN SACRIFICE UNDREAMED OF SINCE THE AZTECS.

EVEN THEY LOOKED UNCOMFORTABLE.

WORLDS CHANGE.

OTHERS HAD FACES OF SMUDGED PHOSPHORS; THEY GLOWED GENTLY AS IF THEY EXISTED IN THEIR OWN LIGHT.

SHADOW FELT SORRY FOR THEM ALL. TO EACH SIDE, THE OPPOSITION WERE THE DEMONS, THE MONSTERS, THE DAMNED, ALREADY THERE WAS BLOOD ON THE ROCKS.

IT'S NOW OR NEVER.

HE WALKED INTO THE ARENA. HE COULD FEEL EYES ON HIM, AND THINGS THAT WERE NOT EYES. HE SHIVERED.

YOU ARE DOING JUST FINE.

DAMN RIGHT. I CAME BACK FROM THE DEAD THIS MORNING. AFTER THAT, EVERYTHING ELSE SHOULD BE A PIECE OF CAKE.

YOU KNOW, THIS IS NOT A WAR. THIS WAS NEVER INTENDED TO BE A WAR. AND IF ANY OF YOU THINK THIS IS A WAR YOU ARE DELUDING YOURSELVES.

HE HEARD GRUMBLING NOISES FROM BOTH SIDES.

FROM ONE SIDE OF THE ARENA...

WE ARE FIGHTING FOR OUR SURVIVAL.

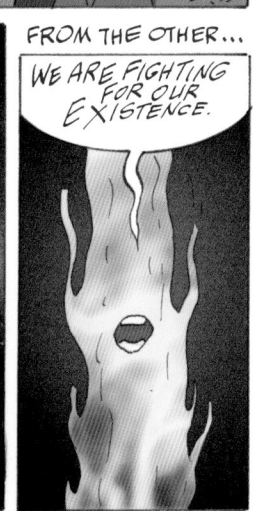

FROM THE OTHER...

WE ARE FIGHTING FOR OUR EXISTENCE.

THIS IS A BAD LAND FOR GODS. YOU'VE PROBABLY ALL LEARNED THAT IN YOUR OWN WAY.

THE OLD GODS ARE IGNORED. THE NEW GODS ARE AS QUICKLY TAKEN UP AS THEY ARE ABANDONED, CAST ASIDE FOR THE NEXT BIG THING.

EITHER YOU'VE BEEN FORGOTTEN, OR YOU'RE SCARED YOU'RE GOING TO BE RENDERED OBSOLETE, OR MAYBE YOU'RE JUST TIRED OF EXISTING ON THE WHIM OF PEOPLE.

THE GRUMBLES WERE FEWER NOW.

THERE WAS A GOD WHO CAME HERE FROM A FAR LAND AND WHOSE POWER AND INFLUENCE WANED AS BELIEF IN HIM FADED. HE WAS A GOD WHO TOOK HIS POWER FROM SACRIFICE AND FROM DEATH. AND ESPECIALLY FROM WAR.

NOW, HE WAS OLD. HE MADE HIS LIVING AS A GRIFTER, WORKING WITH ANOTHER GOD, A GOD OF CHAOS AND DECEIT. TOGETHER THEY TOOK PEOPLE FOR ALL THEY'D GOT.

THEY PUT A PLAN INTO MOTION TO CREATE A RESERVE OF POWER THEY COULD BOTH TAP INTO. SOMETHING THAT WOULD MAKE THEM STRONGER THAN THEY HAD EVER BEEN.

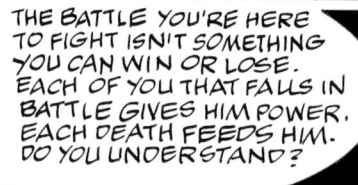

THE GAME THEY PLAYED WAS CALLED...

"LET'S YOU AND HIM FIGHT."

YOU SEE?

THE BATTLE YOU'RE HERE TO FIGHT ISN'T SOMETHING YOU CAN WIN OR LOSE. EACH OF YOU THAT FALLS IN BATTLE GIVES HIM POWER. EACH DEATH FEEDS HIM. DO YOU UNDERSTAND?

OKAY. BUT ODIN. HE DIED. AT THE PEACE TALKS, THE MOTHER-FUCKERS KILLED HIM. HE DIED. I KNOW DEATH. NOBODY GOIN' TO FOOL ME ABOUT DEATH.

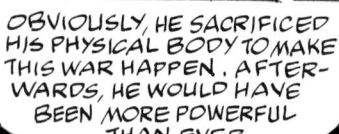

OBVIOUSLY, HE SACRIFICED HIS PHYSICAL BODY TO MAKE THIS WAR HAPPEN. AFTERWARDS, HE WOULD HAVE BEEN MORE POWERFUL THAN EVER.

WHO ARE YOU?

I AM..   I WAS..   I AM HIS SON.

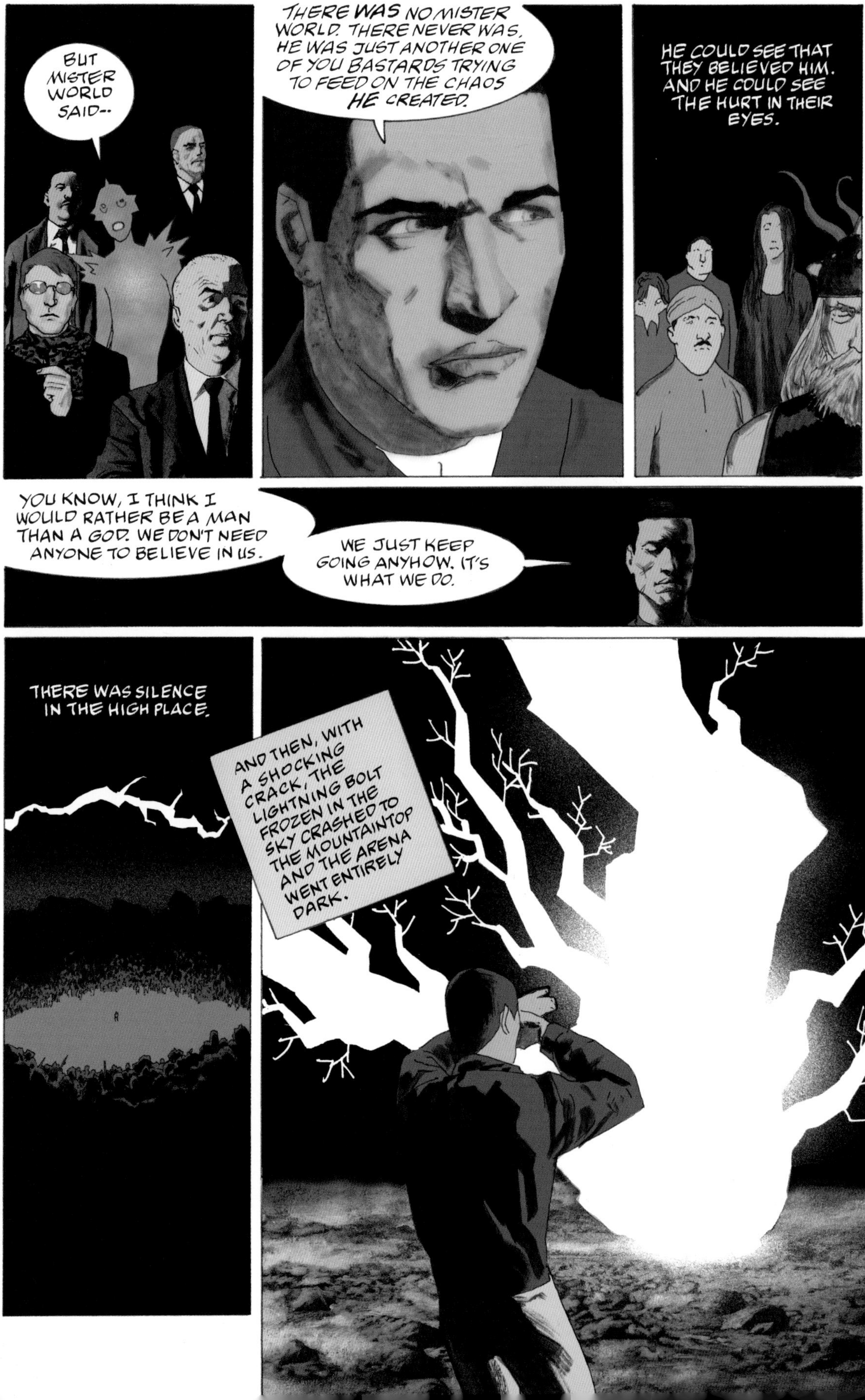
BUT MISTER WORLD SAID--
THERE WAS NO MISTER WORLD. THERE NEVER WAS. HE WAS JUST ANOTHER ONE OF YOU BASTARDS TRYING TO FEED ON THE CHAOS HE CREATED.
HE COULD SEE THAT THEY BELIEVED HIM. AND HE COULD SEE THE HURT IN THEIR EYES.
YOU KNOW, I THINK I WOULD RATHER BE A MAN THAN A GOD. WE DON'T NEED ANYONE TO BELIEVE IN US.
WE JUST KEEP GOING ANYHOW. IT'S WHAT WE DO.
THERE WAS SILENCE IN THE HIGH PLACE.
AND THEN, WITH A SHOCKING CRACK, THE LIGHTNING BOLT FROZEN IN THE SKY CRASHED TO THE MOUNTAINTOP AND THE ARENA WENT ENTIRELY DARK.

THEY GLOWED, MANY OF THOSE PRESENCES, IN THE DARKNESS. SHADOW WONDERED IF THEY WERE GOING TO ARGUE, ATTACK, OR TRY TO KILL HIM. HE WAITED FOR THEIR RESPONSE.

THEN HE REALIZED THE LIGHTS WERE LEAVING... FIRST BY SCORES... THEN BY HUNDREDS.

A SPIDER THE SIZE OF A ROTTWEILER SCUTTLED HEAVILY TOWARD HIM, SHADOW HELD HIS GROUND THOUGH HE FELT SLIGHTLY SICK.

THAT WAS A GOOD JOB. PROUD OF YOU, KID.

THANK YOU, MR. NANCY.

WE SHOULD GET YOU BACK. TOO LONG IN THIS PLACE IS GOIN' TO MESS YOU UP.

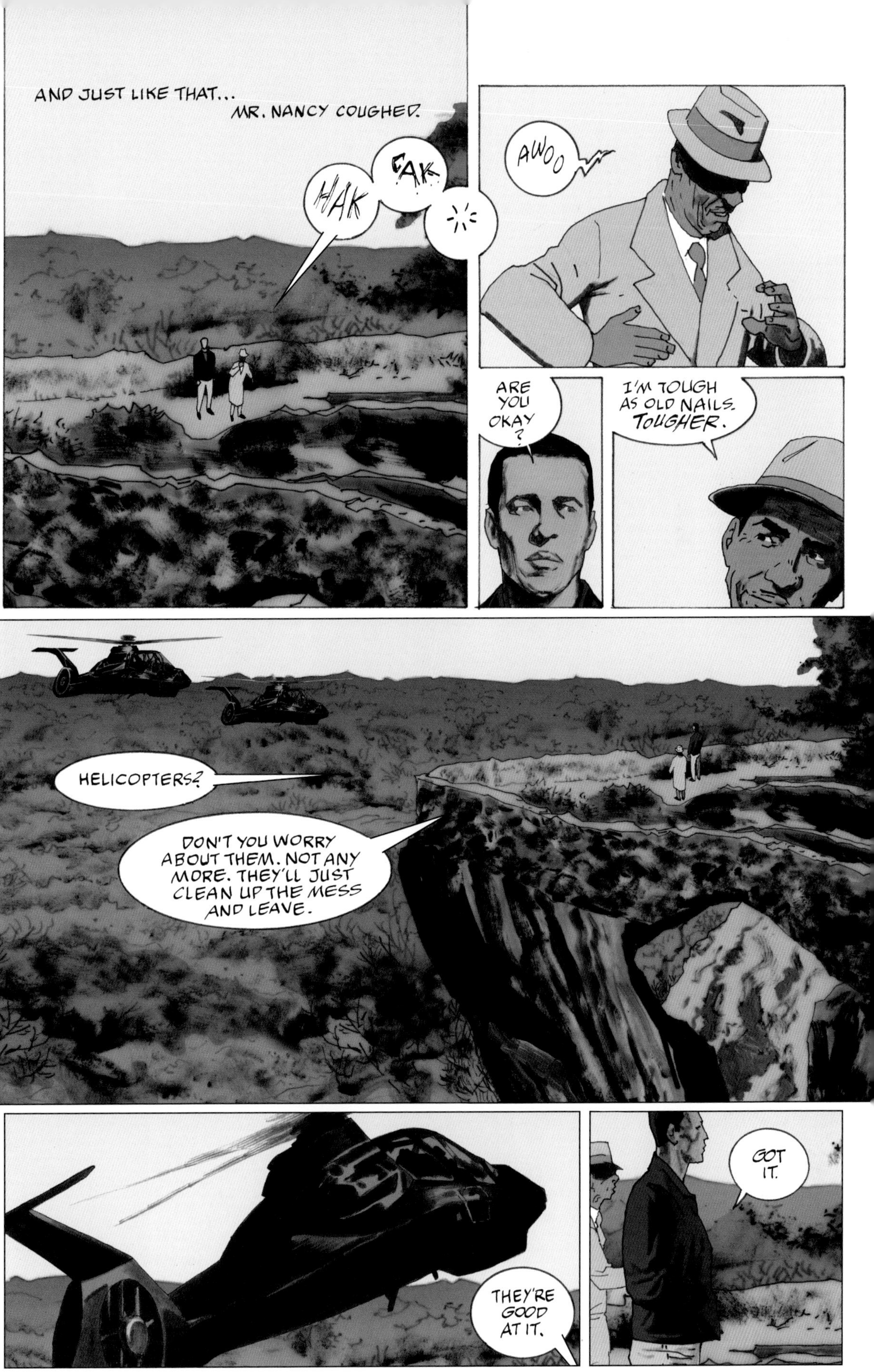
AND JUST LIKE THAT... MR. NANCY COUGHED.
HAK
CAK
AWOO
ARE YOU OKAY?
I'M TOUGH AS OLD NAILS. TOUGHER.
HELICOPTERS?
DON'T YOU WORRY ABOUT THEM. NOT ANY MORE. THEY'LL JUST CLEAN UP THE MESS AND LEAVE.
THEY'RE GOOD AT IT.
GOT IT.

SHADOW KNEW THERE WAS ONE PART OF THE MESS HE WANTED TO SEE FOR HIMSELF, BEFORE IT WAS CLEANED UP.

HE FOUND HER IN A SIDE-CAVERN. SHE WAS ON HER SIDE, WHERE LOKI MUST HAVE DROPPED HER AFTER PULLING THE SPEAR OUT OF THEM BOTH.

LAURA.

HELLO, PUPPY.

WHAT HAPPENED HERE?

NOTHING. JUST STUFF. DID THEY WIN?

I DON'T KNOW, BUT I STOPPED THE BATTLE THEY WERE ABOUT TO START.

MY CLEVER PUPPY.

THAT MAN, MISTER WORLD. I DIDN'T LIKE HIM AT ALL.

HE'S DEAD. YOU KILLED HIM, HON.

GOOD.

HER EYES CLOSED. SHADOW'S HAND FOUND HER COLD HAND.

IN TIME, SHE OPENED HER EYES AGAIN.

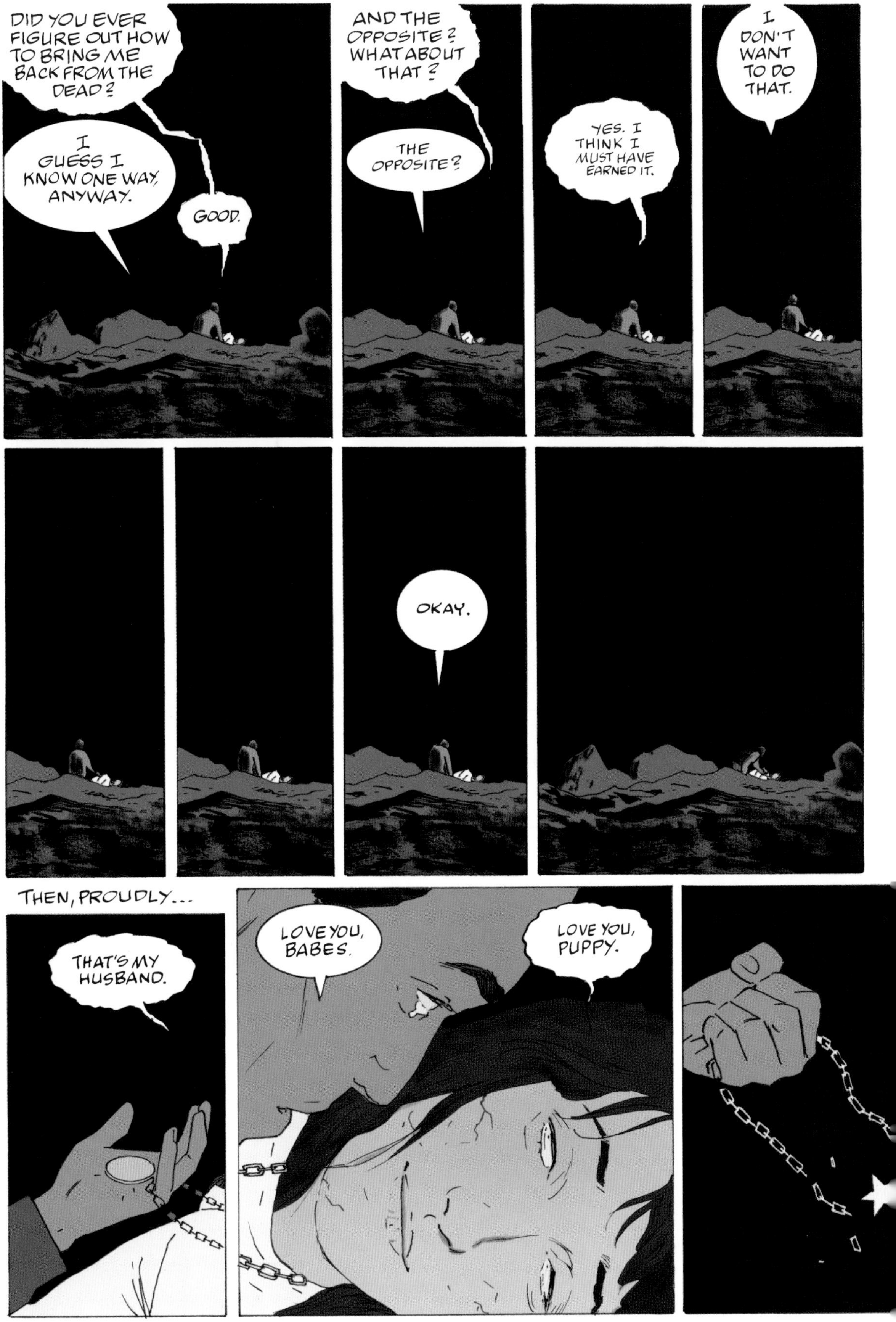
DID YOU EVER FIGURE OUT HOW TO BRING ME BACK FROM THE DEAD?
I GUESS I KNOW ONE WAY, ANYWAY.
GOOD.
AND THE OPPOSITE? WHAT ABOUT THAT?
THE OPPOSITE?
YES. I THINK I MUST HAVE EARNED IT.
I DON'T WANT TO DO THAT.
OKAY.
THEN, PROUDLY...
THAT'S MY HUSBAND.
LOVE YOU, BABES.
LOVE YOU, PUPPY.

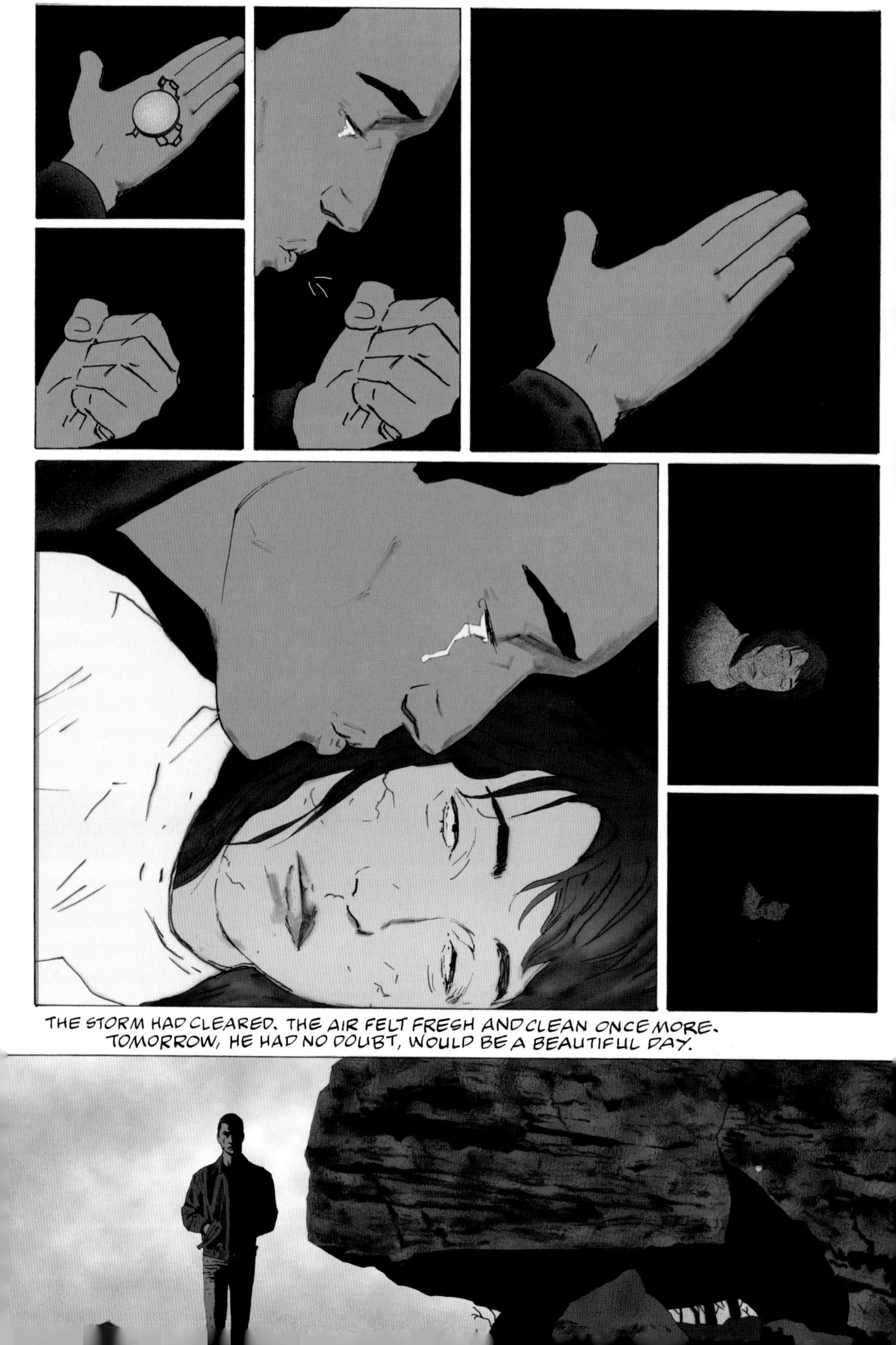
THE STORM HAD CLEARED. THE AIR FELT FRESH AND CLEAN ONCE MORE.
TOMORROW, HE HAD NO DOUBT, WOULD BE A BEAUTIFUL DAY.

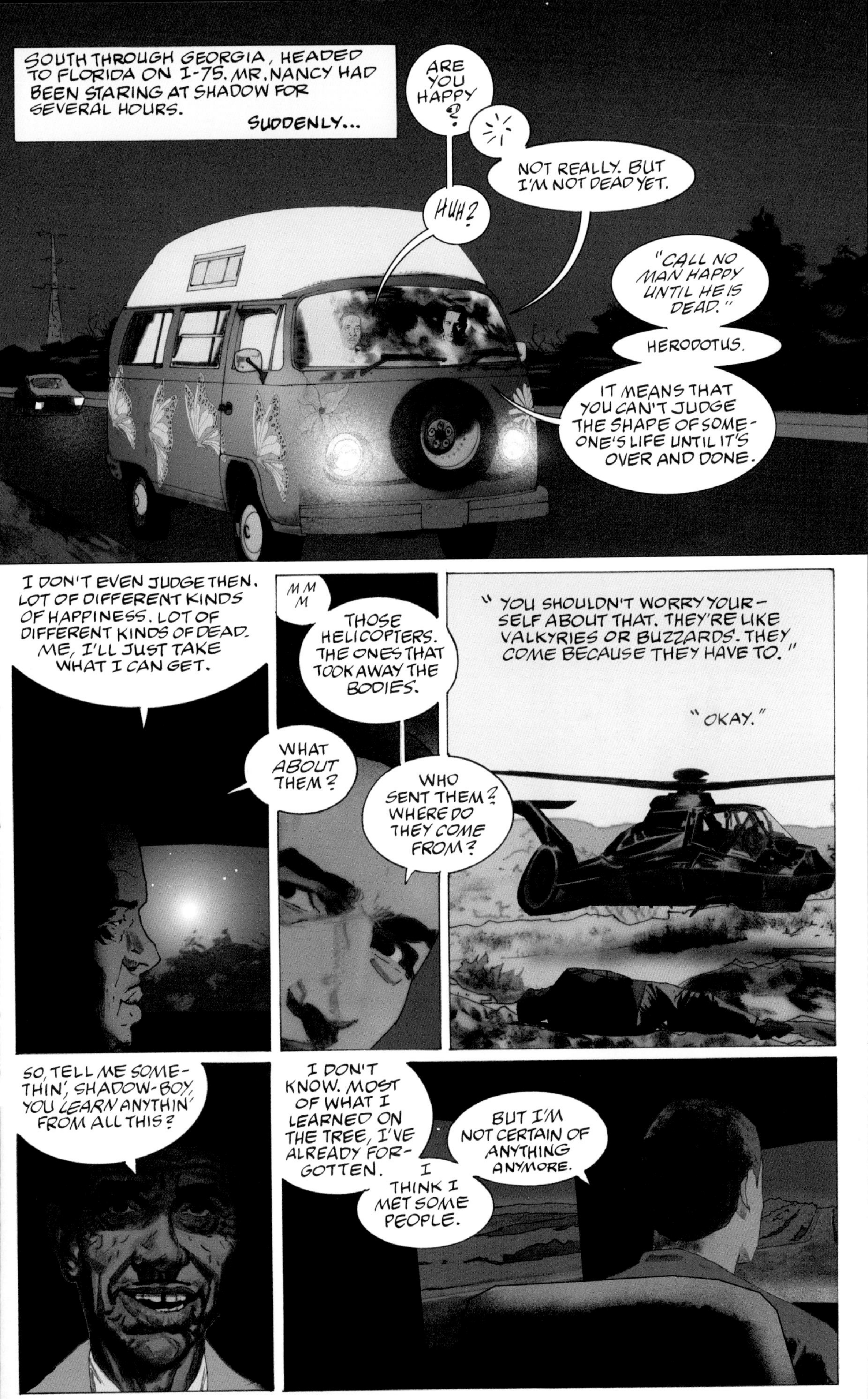
SOUTH THROUGH GEORGIA, HEADED TO FLORIDA ON I-75. MR. NANCY HAD BEEN STARING AT SHADOW FOR SEVERAL HOURS.
SUDDENLY...
ARE YOU HAPPY?
HUH?
NOT REALLY. BUT I'M NOT DEAD YET.
"CALL NO MAN HAPPY UNTIL HE IS DEAD."
HERODOTUS.
IT MEANS THAT YOU CAN'T JUDGE THE SHAPE OF SOMEONE'S LIFE UNTIL IT'S OVER AND DONE.
I DON'T EVEN JUDGE THEN. LOT OF DIFFERENT KINDS OF HAPPINESS. LOT OF DIFFERENT KINDS OF DEAD. ME, I'LL JUST TAKE WHAT I CAN GET.
MMM
THOSE HELICOPTERS. THE ONES THAT TOOK AWAY THE BODIES.
WHAT ABOUT THEM?
WHO SENT THEM? WHERE DO THEY COME FROM?
"YOU SHOULDN'T WORRY YOURSELF ABOUT THAT. THEY'RE LIKE VALKYRIES OR BUZZARDS. THEY COME BECAUSE THEY HAVE TO."
"OKAY."
SO, TELL ME SOMETHIN', SHADOW-BOY. YOU LEARN ANYTHIN' FROM ALL THIS?
I DON'T KNOW. MOST OF WHAT I LEARNED ON THE TREE, I'VE ALREADY FORGOTTEN.
I THINK I MET SOME PEOPLE.
BUT I'M NOT CERTAIN OF ANYTHING ANYMORE.

IT'S LIKE ONE OF THOSE DREAMS THAT CHANGES YOU. YOU KEEP SOME OF THE DREAM FOREVER, AND YOU KNOW THINGS DOWN DEEP INSIDE YOURSELF BECAUSE IT HAPPENED TO YOU.

YEAH. YOU'RE NOT SO DUMB.

BUT WHEN YOU GO LOOKING FOR DETAILS THEY KIND OF JUST SLIP OUT OF YOUR HEAD.

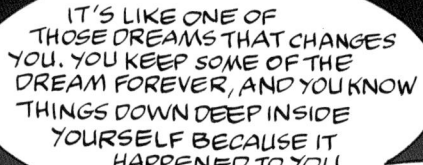

FLORIDA. SHADOW SAW HIS FIRST PALM TREE AS THEY CROSSED THE BORDER AND HE WONDERED...

DO THEY PLANT IT THERE ON PURPOSE JUST SO THAT YOU KNOW YOU'RE IN FLORIDA NOW?

MR. NANCY BEGAN TO SNORE AND HIS BREATH WAS RASPING. SHADOW WONDERED IF HE HAD BEEN INJURED IN THE FIGHT.

?

IT WAS LATE BY THE TIME THEY PULLED UP OUTSIDE A SMALL WOODEN HOUSE IN FORT PIERCE. NANCY INVITED HIM TO...

STAY THE NIGHT.

I CAN GET A ROOM IN A MOTEL, NO PROBLEM.

YOU COULD DO THAT, BUT I'D BE HURT REAL BAD. SO YOU'D BETTER STAY HERE.

THE HOUSE SMELLED MUSTY AND DAMP AND A LITTLE SWEET, AS IF IT WERE HAUNTED BY THE GHOSTS OF LONG-DEAD COOKIES.

SHADOW AGREED, RELUCTANTLY, TO WALK WITH MR. NANCY TO THE BAR AT THE END OF THE ROAD FOR JUST ONE DRINK.

DID YOU SEE CZERNABOG?

HE WAS GONE WHEN I CAME OUT OF THE CAVE.

HEADED HOME. HE'LL BE WAITING FOR YOU THERE, YOU KNOW.

YES.

IT WASN'T MUCH OF A BAR, BUT IT WAS OPEN.

I'LL BUY THE FIRST BEERS,,

ONE BEER.

SHADOW BOUGHT THE SECOND ROUND OF BEERS, THEN STARED IN HORROR AS MR. NANCY TALKED THE BARMAN INTO TURNING ON THE KARAOKE MACHINE...

...THEN IN FASCINATED EMBARRASSMENT AS THE OLD MAN BELTED HIS WAY THROUGH...

WHAT'S NEW PUSSY CAT?

...AND A MOVING, TUNEFUL VERSION OF...

...THE WAY YOU LOOK TO- NIGHT...

BY THE END, THE PEOPLE WERE CHEERING AND APPLAUDING HIM.

WHEN HE CAME BACK TO THE TABLE HE WAS LOOKING BRIGHTER.

YOUR TURN.

A.B SOLUTELY NOT.

BUT MR. NANCY ORDERED MORE BEERS AND HANDED SHADOW A PRINTOUT OF SONGS.

PICK A SONG YOU KNOW THE WORDS TO.

THEN HE WAS PUSHING SHADOW ONTO THE TINY MAKESHIFT STAGE.

JUST SING PLEASE DON'T LET ME BE MISUNDERSTOOD.

THIS ISN'T FUNNY.

THEN THE BACKING MUSIC STARTED AND HE CROAKED OUT THE INITIAL...

BABY ...

NOBODY IN THE BAR THREW ANYTHING IN HIS GENERAL DIRECTION. IT FELT GOOD.

..SOMETIMES I FEEL A LITTLE MAD ...

DON'T YOU KNOW THAT NO ONE ALIVE CAN ALWAYS BE AN ANGEL ...

AND HE WAS STILL SINGING IT AS THEY WALKED HOME, STUMBLING AND HAPPY. HE SANG TO THE CRABS AND THE SPIDERS AND THE PALMETTO BUGS AND THE LIZARDS, AND THE FLORIDA NIGHT.

I'M JUST A SOUL WHOSE INTENTIONS ARE GOOD ...

" OH, LORD, PLEASE DON'T LET ME BE MISUNDERSTOOD."

MR. NANCY SHOWED HIM TO THE COUCH.

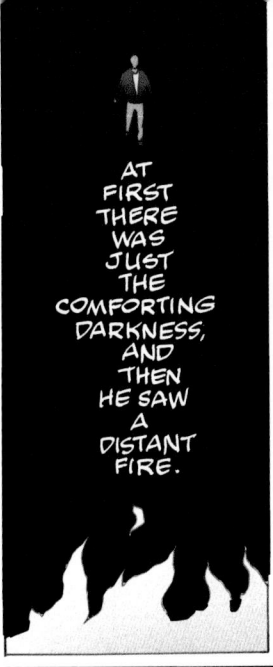

AT FIRST THERE WAS JUST THE COMFORTING DARKNESS, AND THEN HE SAW A DISTANT FIRE.

YOU DID WELL.

I DON'T KNOW WHAT I DID.

YOU MADE PEACE. YOU TOOK OUR WORDS AND MADE THEM YOUR OWN.

" THEY NEVER UNDERSTOOD THAT *THEY* WERE HERE -- AND THE PEOPLE WHO WORSHIPPED THEM WERE HERE-- BECAUSE IT SUITS US THAT THEY WERE HERE.

" BUT WE CAN CHANGE OUR MINDS.

AND PERHAPS WE WILL. "

ARE YOU A GOD?

SHADOW THOUGHT FOR A MOMENT, THAT THE CREATURE WAS AMUSED.

" I AM THE LAND. "

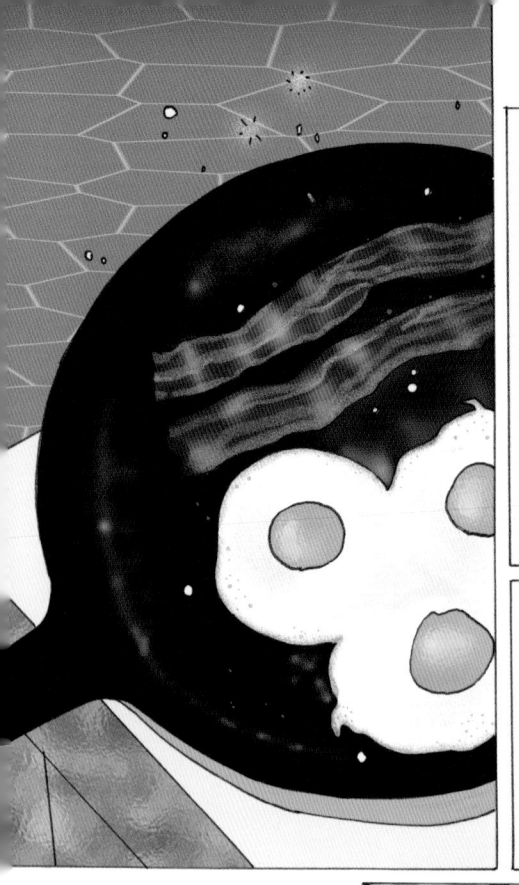

MY HEAD HURTS.

YOU GET A GOOD BREAKFAST IN YOU YOU'LL FEEL LIKE A NEW MAN.

I'D RATHER FEEL LIKE THE SAME MAN, ONLY WITH A DIFFERENT HEAD.

EAT.

HOW DO YOU FEEL NOW?

LIKE I'VE GOT A HEADACHE, ONLY NOW, I THINK I'M GOING TO THROW UP.

COME WITH ME.

IT'S AN ANCIENT AFRICAN HERBAL REMEDY. IT'S MADE OF GROUND WILLOW BARK--THINGS LIKE THAT.

LIKE ASPIRIN?

YUP. JUST LIKE THAT. HERE.

NICE TRUNK.

MY SON SENT IT TO ME. HE'S A GOOD BOY. I DON'T SEE HIM AS MUCH AS I'D LIKE.

I MISS WEDNESDAY. DESPITE EVERYTHING HE DID, I KEEP EXPECTING TO SEE HIM.

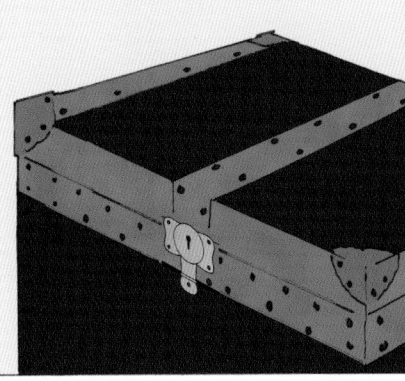

HE KEPT STARING AT THE PIRATE TRUNK, TRYING TO FIGURE OUT WHAT IT REMINDED HIM OF.

YOU WILL LOSE MANY THINGS. DO NOT LOSE THIS.

WHO SAID THAT?

YOU MISS HIM? AFTER WHAT HE PUT YOU THROUGH? PUT US ALL THROUGH?

YES, I GUESS I DO. DO YOU THINK HE'LL BE BACK?

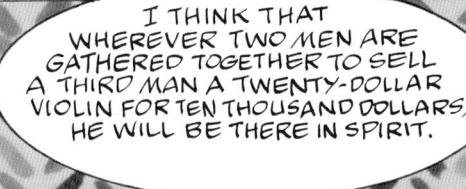

I THINK THAT WHEREVER TWO MEN ARE GATHERED TOGETHER TO SELL A THIRD MAN A TWENTY-DOLLAR VIOLIN FOR TEN THOUSAND DOLLARS, HE WILL BE THERE IN SPIRIT.

SHADOW STARED AT THE OLD TRUNK SOME MORE, WILLING HIMSELF TO REMEMBER.

IF I DON'T GO TO SEE CZERNOBOG WHAT WOULD HAPPEN?

MAYBE HE'LL FIND YOU. BUT ONE WAY OR ANOTHER, YOU'LL SEE HIM.

SHADOW NODDED. SOMETHING STARTED TO FALL INTO PLACE.

HEY. IS THERE A GOD WITH AN ELEPHANT'S HEAD?

GANESH? HE'S A HINDU GOD. HE REMOVES OBSTACLES AND MAKES JOURNEYS EASIER.

"...IT'S IN THE TRUNK."

IT'S IN THE TRUNK!

I KNEW IT WAS IMPORTANT, BUT I DIDN'T KNOW WHY.

IT'S IN THE TRUNK.

I GOT TO GO.

WHY THE HURRY?

BECAUSE...

...THE ICE IS MELTING.

CHAPTER EIGHT

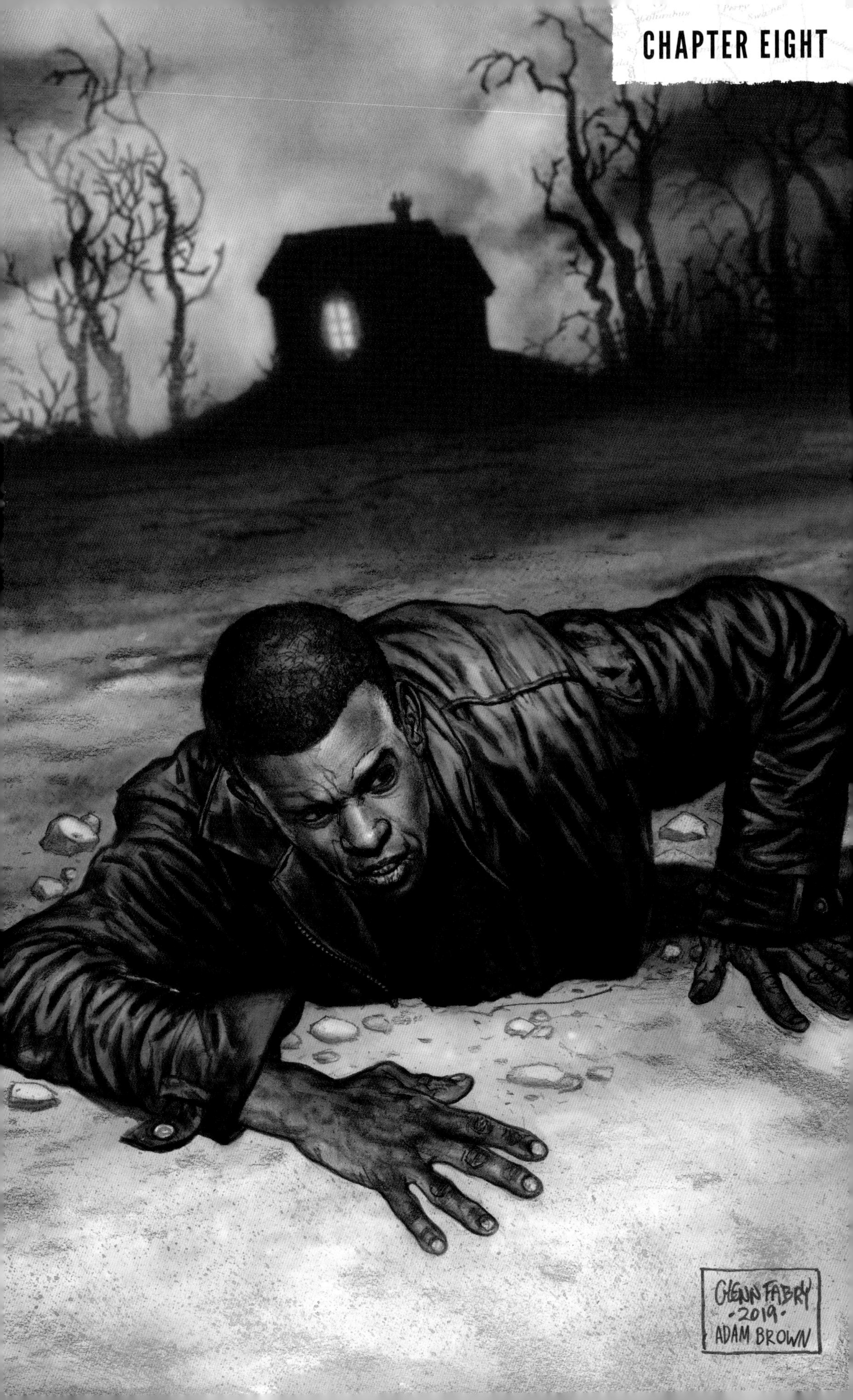
GLENN FABRY
·2019·
ADAM BROWN

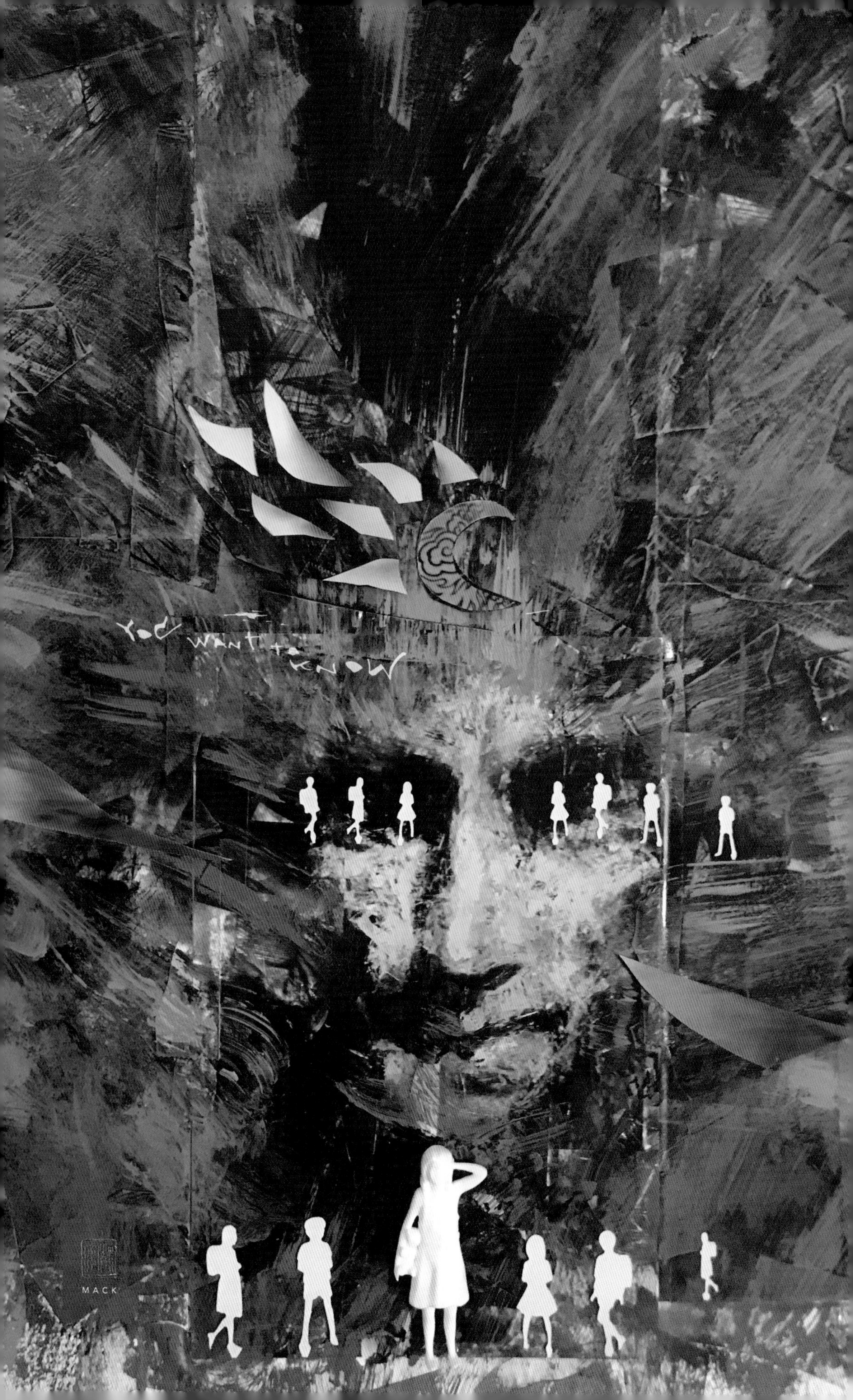
YOU WANT TO KNOW
MACK

26

LAKESIDE. 8:30 a.m.

THERE WERE NO MORE FISHING-HUTS ON THE FROZEN LAKE. THE WATER BENEATH THE ICE WAS DARK AND THE DARKNESS SHOWED THROUGH.

THE ICY LAKE WAS BLEAK AND EMPTY.

THIN ICE

ALMOST EMPTY.
THERE WAS ONE CAR REMAINING ON THE ICE, THE SORT OF CAR THAT PEOPLE ABANDON IN PARKING LOTS. IT WAS THE SYMBOL OF A WAGER, WAITING FOR THE ICE TO BECOME ROTTEN ENOUGH, AND SOFT ENOUGH, TO ALLOW THE LAKE TO TAKE IT FOREVER.

SHADOW WALKED OUT ONTO A WOODEN JETTY AND STEPPED ONTO THE ICE. THE LAYER OF WATER ON THE ICE, DEEPER THAN IT APPEARED, SEEPED INSIDE HIS BOOTS, NUMBING HIS FEET.

HE FELT STRANGELY DISTANT AS HE TRUDGED ACROSS THE FROZEN LAKE. THERE WAS A FEELING OF INEVITABILITY NOW.

THIS IS SUICIDE. CAN'T YOU JUST LET IT GO?

NO. I HAVE TO KNOW.

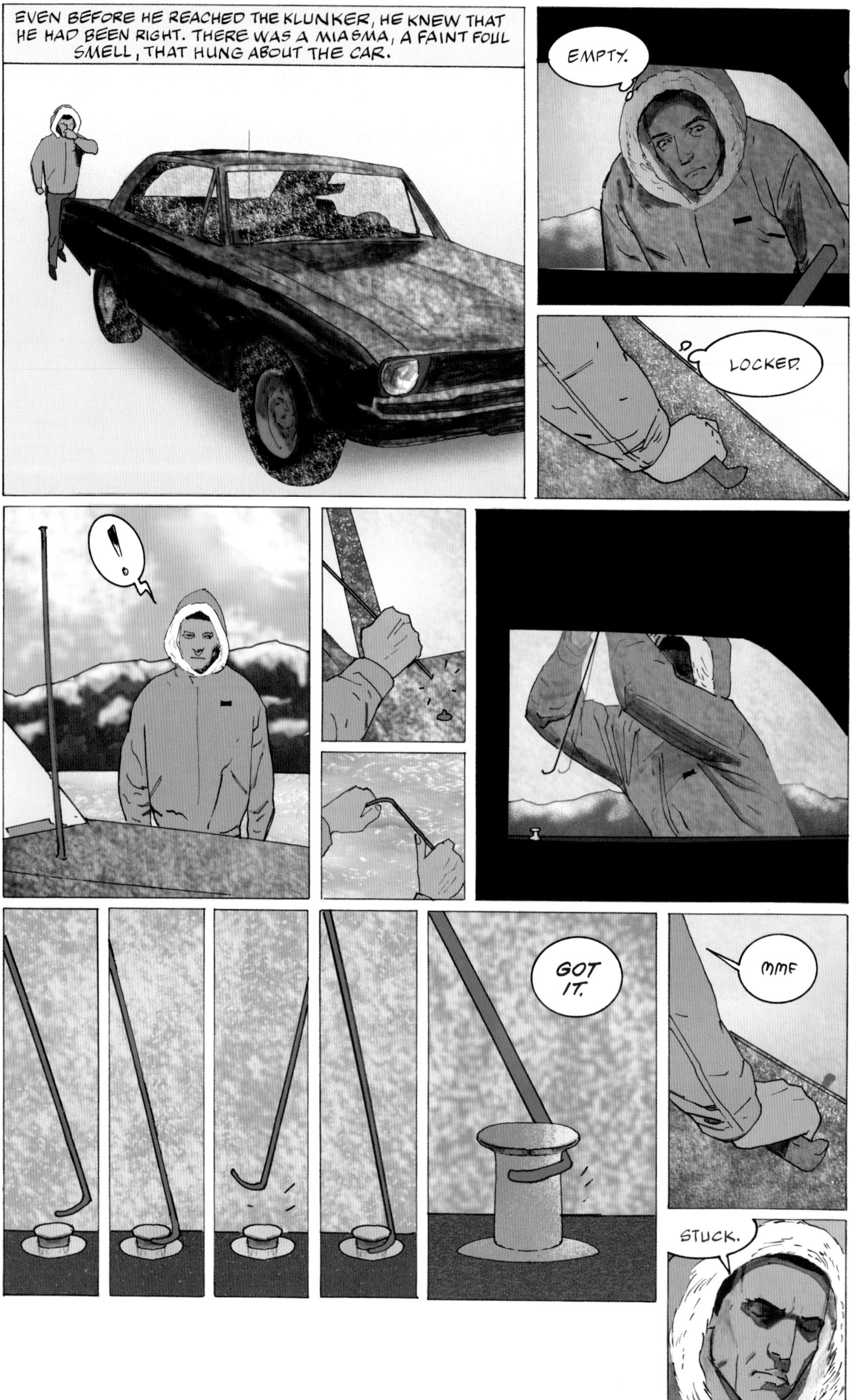
EVEN BEFORE HE REACHED THE KLUNKER, HE KNEW THAT HE HAD BEEN RIGHT. THERE WAS A MIASMA, A FAINT FOUL SMELL, THAT HUNG ABOUT THE CAR.
EMPTY.
LOCKED.
!
GOT IT.
MMF
STUCK.

HE TUGGED HARDER, SLIDING ON THE ICE, AND SUDDENLY...

MMF

HUF

THE MIASMA WAS WORSE INSIDE THE CAR, A STENCH OF ROT AND ILLNESS. HE FELT SICK.

IT'S IN THE TRUNK.

POP

THUNK

THE SMELL WAS BAD, BUT IT COULD HAVE BEEN MUCH WORSE. THE COLD HAD PRESERVED HER, KEPT HER AS FRESH AS IF SHE HAD BEEN IN A FREEZER.

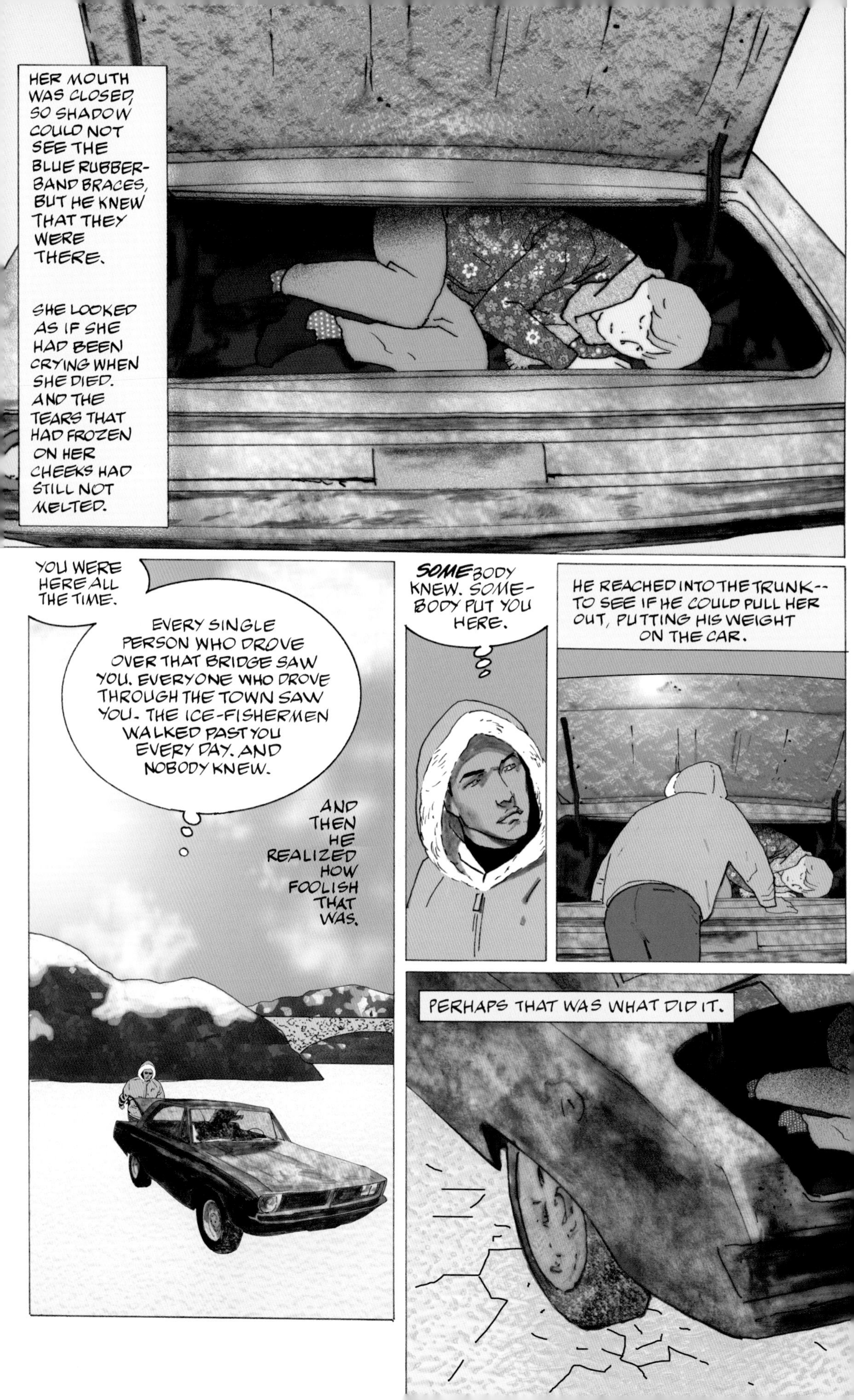
HER MOUTH WAS CLOSED, SO SHADOW COULD NOT SEE THE BLUE RUBBER-BAND BRACES, BUT HE KNEW THAT THEY WERE THERE.
SHE LOOKED AS IF SHE HAD BEEN CRYING WHEN SHE DIED. AND THE TEARS THAT HAD FROZEN ON HER CHEEKS HAD STILL NOT MELTED.
YOU WERE HERE ALL THE TIME.
EVERY SINGLE PERSON WHO DROVE OVER THAT BRIDGE SAW YOU. EVERYONE WHO DROVE THROUGH THE TOWN SAW YOU. THE ICE-FISHERMEN WALKED PAST YOU EVERY DAY. AND NOBODY KNEW.
AND THEN HE REALIZED HOW FOOLISH THAT WAS.
SOMEBODY KNEW. SOMEBODY PUT YOU HERE.
HE REACHED INTO THE TRUNK-- TO SEE IF HE COULD PULL HER OUT, PUTTING HIS WEIGHT ON THE CAR.
PERHAPS THAT WAS WHAT DID IT.

IT WAS TEN PAST NINE IN THE MORNING, ON MARCH THE TWENTY-THIRD.

HE TOOK A DEEP BREATH BEFORE HE WENT UNDER, CLOSING HIS EYES.

HE TUMBLED DOWNWARD. INTO THE MURKY ICE-WATER, DOWN INTO THE DARKNESS AND THE COLD, WEIGHED DOWN BY HIS BOOTS, TRAPPED AND SWATHED IN HIS COAT.

HE TRIED TO PUSH AWAY FROM THE CAR, BUT IT WAS PULLING HIM WITH IT, AND THEN THERE WAS A BANG HE COULD FEEL WITH HIS WHOLE BODY AS IT SETTLED ON THE LAKE BOTTOM.

HIS LEFT FOOT WAS TWISTED AND TRAPPED BENEATH THE CAR. HE BEGAN TO PANIC, THEN...

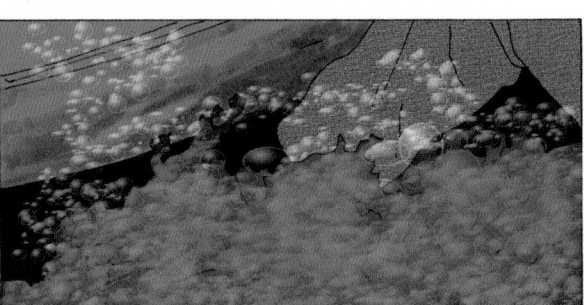

...AND HE OPENED HIS EYES.

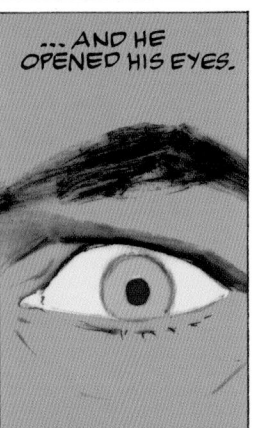

EVEN IN THE MURKY DARK, HE COULD SEE EVERYTHING--ALL THE CLUNKERS OF BYGONE YEARS-- AND EACH ONE, HE KNEW, WITHOUT ANY QUESTION, HAD A DEAD CHILD IN THE TRUNK. THIS WAS WHERE THEY RESTED = LEMMI HAUTULA AND JESSIE LOVAT, SANDY OLSEN AND JO MING AND SARAH LINDQUIST AND ALL THE REST OF THEM.

DOWN WHERE IT WAS SILENT AND COLD.

THE PRESSURE IN HIS LUNGS WAS BECOMING UNBEARABLE.

SOON.

SOON I'LL HAVE TO BREATHE.

OR I'LL CHOKE.

HE PUT BOTH HANDS AROUND THE BUMPER OF THE KLUNKER AND PUSHED WITH EVERYTHING HE HAD.

IT'S ONLY THE SHELL OF A CAR.

THEY TOOK OUT THE ENGINE. THAT'S THE HEAVIEST PART OF THE CAR.

YOU CAN DO IT.

JUST. KEEP. PUSHING.

NOTHING HAPPENED.

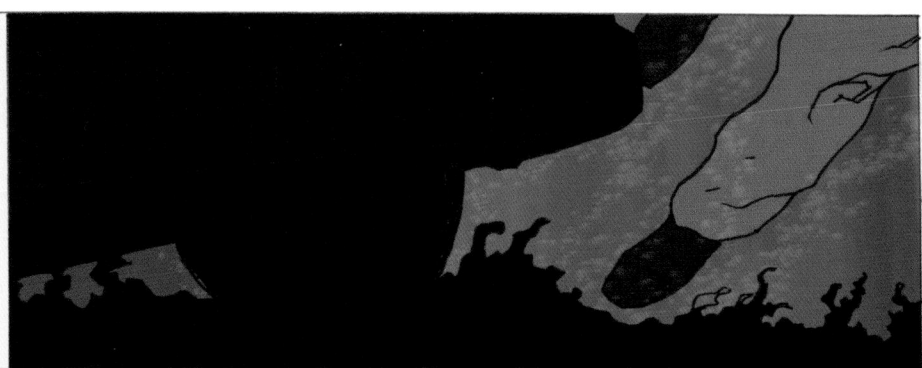

AGONIZINGLY SLOWLY, THE CAR SLIPPED FORWARD IN THE MUD, AND SHADOW PULLED HIS FOOT FROM THE MUD BENEATH THE CAR AND KICKED.

HE DIDN'T MOVE.

THE COAT-- IT'S THE COAT. IT'S STUCK OR CAUGHT ON SOMETHING.

HE FUMBLED WITH NUMB FINGERS AT THE FROZEN ZIPPER...

...PULLED BOTH HANDS ON EITHER SIDE OF THE ZIPPER, FELT THE COAT GIVE AND REND...

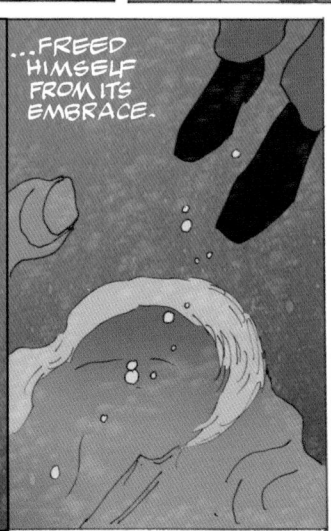

...FREED HIMSELF FROM ITS EMBRACE.

THERE WAS A RUSHING SENSATION BUT NO SENSE OF UP OR DOWN. HE WAS CERTAIN THAT HE WAS GOING TO HAVE TO INHALE, TO BREATHE IN THE COLD WATER, TO DIE.

AND THEN HIS HEAD HIT SOMETHING SOLID.

1 ce

HE HAMMERED AT IT WITH BOTH FISTS, BUT THERE WAS NOTHING TO PUSH AGAINST. THERE WAS NOTHING LEFT BUT COLD.

THIS IS RIDICULOUS.

SOMEWHERE.

PUSH THE ICE *UP.* FIND SOME AIR. THERE'S AIR...

BUT HE WAS JUST FLOATING AND FREEZING AND HE COULD NO LONGER MOVE A MUSCLE, NOT IF HIS LIFE DEPENDED ON IT, WHICH IT DID.

THE COLD BECAME BEARABLE...BECAME WARM.

I'M DYING.

THERE WAS A DEEP FURY THIS TIME, AND HE TOOK THE PAIN AND ANGER AND REACHED WITH IT, FORCED MUSCLES TO MOVE THAT WERE RESIGNED NEVER TO MOVE AGAIN.

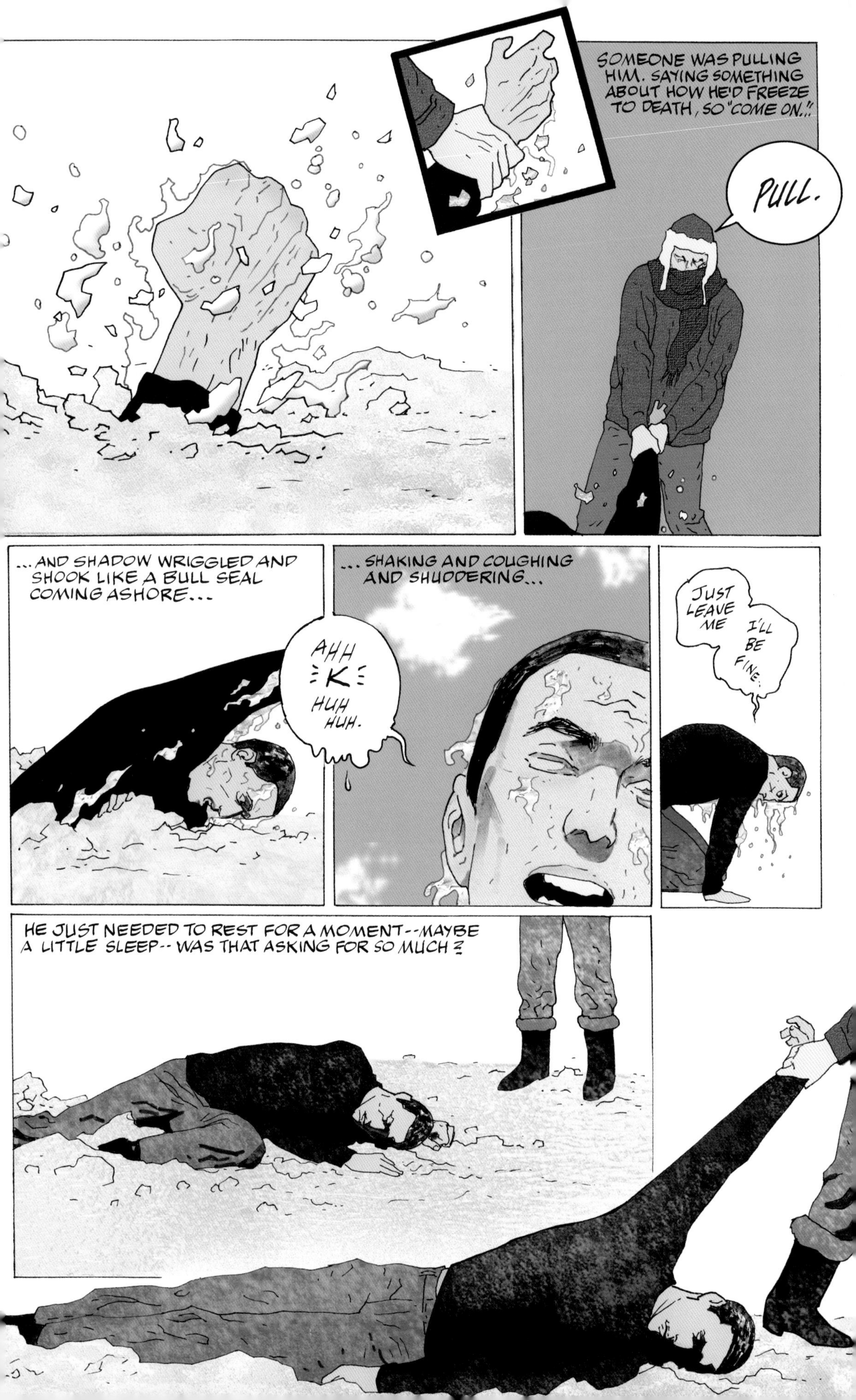
SOMEONE WAS PULLING HIM. SAYING SOMETHING ABOUT HOW HE'D FREEZE TO DEATH, SO "COME ON."
PULL.
...AND SHADOW WRIGGLED AND SHOOK LIKE A BULL SEAL COMING ASHORE...
AHH K HUH HUH.
...SHAKING AND COUGHING AND SHUDDERING...
JUST LEAVE ME
I'LL BE FINE.
HE JUST NEEDED TO REST FOR A MOMENT--MAYBE A LITTLE SLEEP-- WAS THAT ASKING FOR SO MUCH?

THE BUFFALO MAN WAS THERE, AND A WOMAN WITH THE HEAD OF A CONDOR, AND THERE WAS WHISKEY JACK, LOOKING AT HIM SADLY.

HE DID NOT BELIEVE THAT HE HAD FALLEN ASLEEP, BUT HE WAS STANDING ON A VAST PLAIN.

THEY TURNED AND WALKED SLOWLY AWAY FROM SHADOW. HE FELT A SENSE OF LOSS, WANTED TO CALL OUT TO THEM.

BUT EVERYTHING WAS BECOMING FORMLESS AND DEVOID OF SHAPE.

THE PLAINS WERE FADING, AND EVERY-THING BECAME VOID.

THE PAIN WAS INTENSE: IT WAS AS IF EVERY CELL IN HIS BODY, EVERY NERVE, WAS MELTING AND ADVERTISING ITS PRESENCE BY BURNING HIM AND HURTING HIM.

EASY NOW, MIKE. EASY THERE...

"WHAT? WHAT'S HAPPENING?"

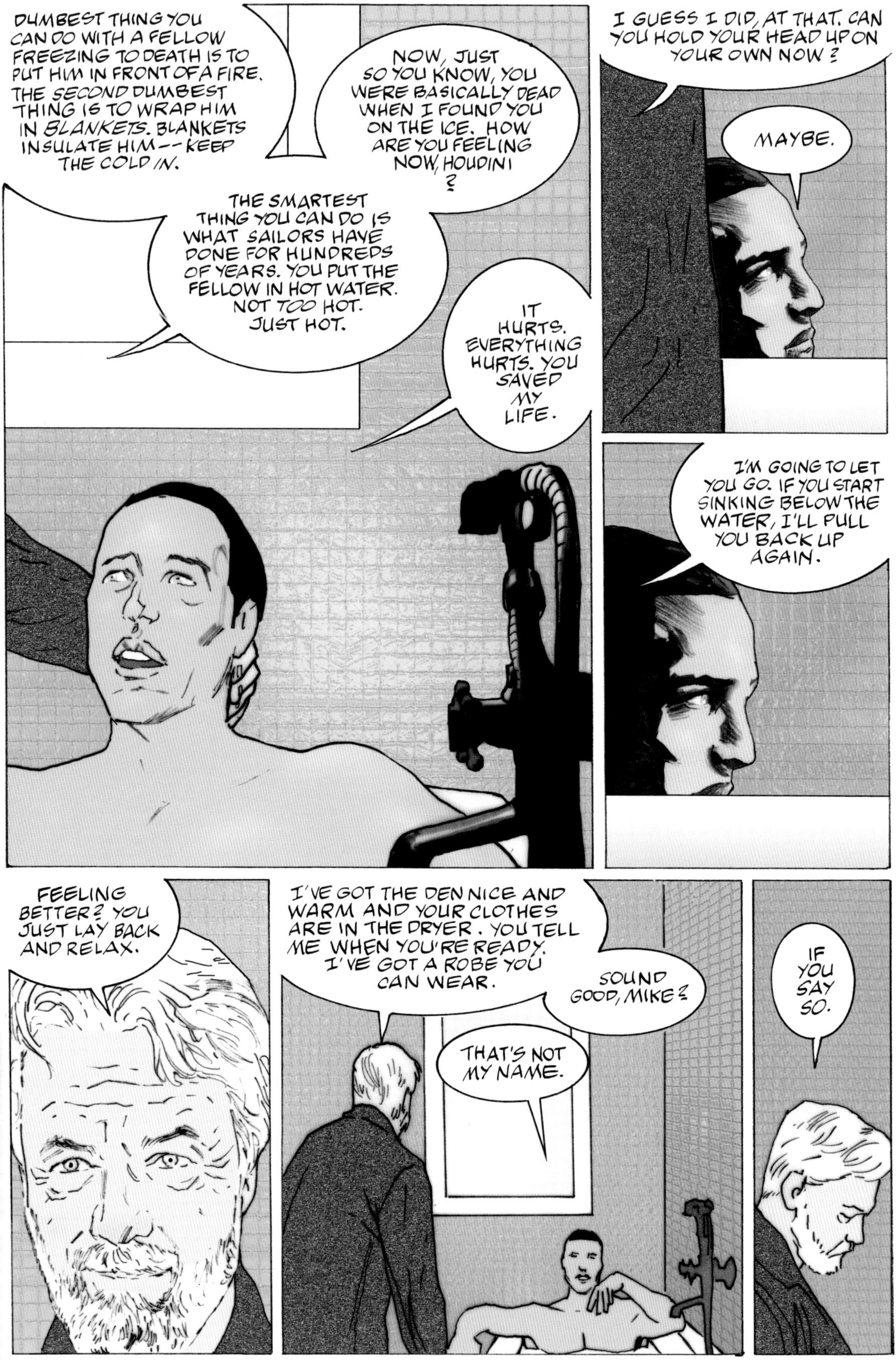
DUMBEST THING YOU CAN DO WITH A FELLOW FREEZING TO DEATH IS TO PUT HIM IN FRONT OF A FIRE. THE *SECOND* DUMBEST THING IS TO WRAP HIM IN *BLANKETS*. BLANKETS INSULATE HIM-- KEEP THE COLD *IN*.
NOW, JUST SO YOU KNOW, YOU WERE BASICALLY DEAD WHEN I FOUND YOU ON THE ICE. HOW ARE YOU FEELING NOW, HOUDINI?
THE SMARTEST THING YOU CAN DO IS WHAT SAILORS HAVE DONE FOR HUNDREDS OF YEARS. YOU PUT THE FELLOW IN HOT WATER. NOT *TOO* HOT. JUST HOT.
IT HURTS. EVERYTHING HURTS. YOU SAVED MY LIFE.
I GUESS I DID, AT THAT. CAN YOU HOLD YOUR HEAD UP ON YOUR OWN NOW?
MAYBE.
I'M GOING TO LET YOU GO. IF YOU START SINKING BELOW THE WATER, I'LL PULL YOU BACK UP AGAIN.
FEELING BETTER? YOU JUST LAY BACK AND RELAX.
I'VE GOT THE DEN NICE AND WARM AND YOUR CLOTHES ARE IN THE DRYER. YOU TELL ME WHEN YOU'RE READY. I'VE GOT A ROBE YOU CAN WEAR.
SOUND GOOD, MIKE?
THAT'S NOT MY NAME.
IF YOU SAY SO.

SHADOW HAD NO REAL SENSE OF TIME : HE LAY IN THE BATH UNTIL THE BURNING STOPPED AND HIS TOES AND FINGERS FLEXED WITHOUT REAL DISCOMFORT.

HINZELMAN HELPED SHADOW TO HIS FEET AND INTO A TERRYCLOTH ROBE TOO SMALL FOR HIM. LEANING ON THE OLD MAN, HE WENT THROUGH TO THE DEN.

THE OLD MAN LEFT THE ROOM AND RETURNED WITH A STEAMING MUG.

COFFEE WITH A SPLASH OF SCHNAPPS. THAT'S WHAT WE DID IN THE OLD DAYS.

THANKS. I THOUGHT I WAS DEAD.

YOU WERE LUCKY. I WAS UP ON THE BRIDGE -- I'D PRETTY-MUCH FIGURED THAT TODAY WAS GOING TO BE THE BIG DAY. I SAW BOTH THE CAR AND YOU GO DOWN, SO I WENT OUT ON THE ICE. GAVE ME THE HEEBIE-JEEBIES.

YOU DID A GOOD THING.

THE OLD MAN BEAMED ALL OVER HIS GOBLIN FACE.

SOMEWHERE IN THIS HOUSE, SHADOW HEARD A DOOR CLOSE.

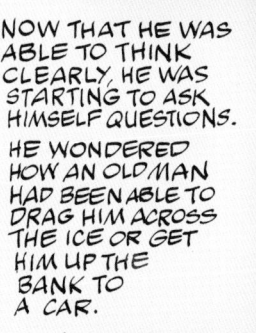

NOW THAT HE WAS ABLE TO THINK CLEARLY, HE WAS STARTING TO ASK HIMSELF QUESTIONS.

HE WONDERED HOW AN OLD MAN HAD BEEN ABLE TO DRAG HIM ACROSS THE ICE OR GET HIM UP THE BANK TO A CAR.

DO YOU WANT TO KNOW WHAT I WAS DOING OUT ON THE ICE?

NONE OF MY BUSINESS.

YOU KNOW WHAT I DON'T UNDERSTAND... I DON'T UNDERSTAND WHY YOU SAVED MY LIFE.

WELL...THE WAY I WAS BROUGHT UP, IF YOU SEE ANOTHER FELLOW IN TROUBLE...

NO, THAT'S NOT WHAT I MEAN.

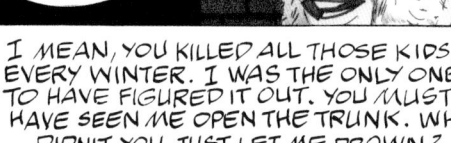

I MEAN, YOU KILLED ALL THOSE KIDS. EVERY WINTER. I WAS THE ONLY ONE TO HAVE FIGURED IT OUT. YOU MUST HAVE SEEN ME OPEN THE TRUNK. WHY DIDN'T YOU JUST LET ME DROWN?

THAT'S A GOOD QUESTION. I GUESS IT'S BECAUSE I OWED A CERTAIN PARTY A DEBT AND I'M GOOD FOR MY DEBTS.

WEDNESDAY?

THAT'S THE FELLOW.

THERE WAS A REASON HE HID ME IN LAKESIDE, WASN'T THERE? THERE WAS A REASON NOBODY SHOULD HAVE BEEN ABLE TO FIND ME HERE.

THIS IS MY HOME...

"IT'S A GOOD TOWN."

HOW LONG HAVE YOU BEEN HERE?

LONG ENOUGH.

AND YOU MADE THE LAKE?

YES. I MADE THE LAKE. I FIGURED THAT THIS COUNTRY IS HELL ON MY KIND OF FOLK. IT EATS US. I DIDN'T WANT TO BE EATEN. SO I MADE A DEAL. I GAVE THEM A LAKE, AND I GAVE THEM PROSPERITY.

AND ALL IT COST THEM WAS ONE CHILD EVERY WINTER.

GOOD KIDS. THEY WERE ALL GOOD KIDS. I'D ONLY PICK ONES I LIKED. EXCEPT FOR CHARLIE NELLIGAN. HE WAS A BAD SEED, THAT ONE. HE WAS, WHAT, 1924? 1925? YEAH, THAT WAS THE DEAL.

THE PEOPLE OF THE TOWN, MABEL, MARGUERITE, CHAD MULLIGAN. DO THEY KNOW?

AND THAT'S YOUR DOING?

THEY KNOW THAT THEY LIVE IN A GOOD PLACE. WHILE EVERY OTHER TOWN IN THIS PART OF THE STATE IS CRUMBLING INTO NOTHING. THEY KNOW THAT.

THIS TOWN. I CARE FOR IT. YOU UNDERSTAND THAT? NOBODY COMES HERE THAT I DON'T WANT TO COME HERE.

THAT WAS WHY YOUR FATHER SENT YOU HERE. HE DIDN'T WANT YOU OUT THERE IN THE WORLD ATTRACTING ATTENTION.

THAT'S ALL.

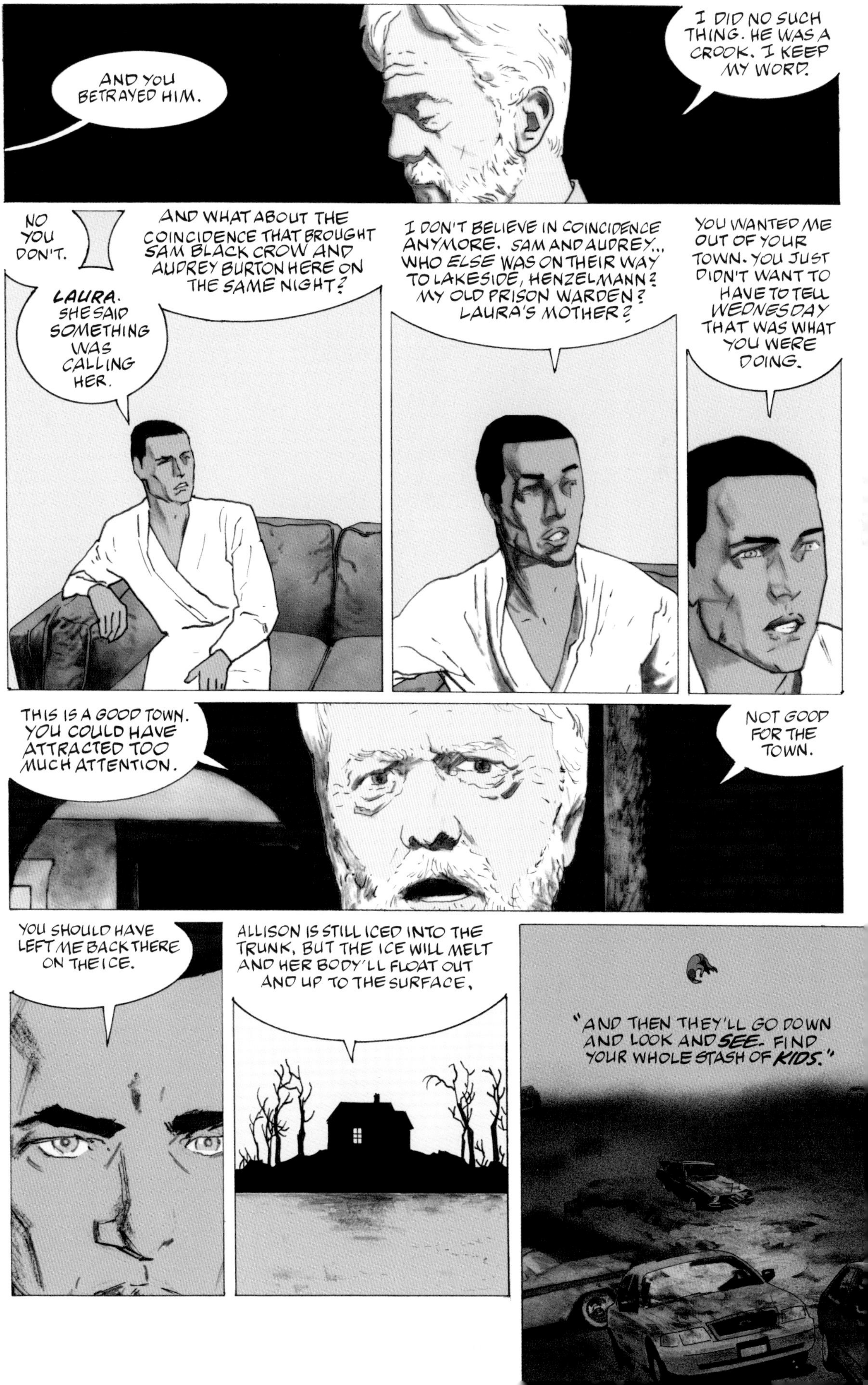
AND YOU BETRAYED HIM.
I DID NO SUCH THING. HE WAS A CROOK. I KEEP MY WORD.
NO YOU DON'T.
LAURA. SHE SAID SOMETHING WAS CALLING HER.
AND WHAT ABOUT THE COINCIDENCE THAT BROUGHT SAM BLACK CROW AND AUDREY BURTON HERE ON THE SAME NIGHT?
I DON'T BELIEVE IN COINCIDENCE ANYMORE. SAM AND AUDREY... WHO ELSE WAS ON THEIR WAY TO LAKESIDE, HENZELMANN? MY OLD PRISON WARDEN? LAURA'S MOTHER?
YOU WANTED ME OUT OF YOUR TOWN. YOU JUST DIDN'T WANT TO HAVE TO TELL WEDNESDAY THAT WAS WHAT YOU WERE DOING.
THIS IS A GOOD TOWN. YOU COULD HAVE ATTRACTED TOO MUCH ATTENTION.
NOT GOOD FOR THE TOWN.
YOU SHOULD HAVE LEFT ME BACK THERE ON THE ICE.
ALLISON IS STILL ICED INTO THE TRUNK, BUT THE ICE WILL MELT AND HER BODY'LL FLOAT OUT AND UP TO THE SURFACE,
"AND THEN THEY'LL GO DOWN AND LOOK AND SEE. FIND YOUR WHOLE STASH OF KIDS."

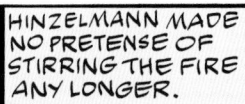
HINZELMANN MADE NO PRETENSE OF STIRRING THE FIRE ANY LONGER.

SHADOW WAS AWARE HE WAS STILL VERY TIRED AND SCARCE ABLE TO DEFEND HIMSELF.

YOU WANT TO KILL ME? GO AHEAD. I'M A DEAD MAN ANYWAY. BUT IF YOU THINK NO ONE'S GOING TO COME LOOKING FOR ME, YOU'RE LIVING IN A DREAM-WORLD. IT'S OVER, HINZELMANN.

ONE WAY OR ANOTHER, IT'S DONE.

I LOVE THIS TOWN.

I REALLY LIKE BEING A CRANKY OLD MAN, AND TELLING MY STORIES AND DRIVING TESSIE AND ICE-FISHING.

I COULD KILL YOU. I'VE DONE IT BEFORE. YOU'RE NOT THE FIRST ONE TO FIGURE IT OUT.

CHAD MULLIGAN'S FATHER--HE FIGURED IT OUT. I FIXED HIM. I CAN FIX YOU.

MAYBE. BUT FOR HOW LONG? ANOTHER YEAR? A DECADE? THEY HAVE COMPUTERS. THEY PICK UP ON PATTERNS. EVERY YEAR A KID VANISHES. THEY'LL COME SNIFFING ABOUT.

TELL ME-- HOW OLD ARE YOU?

THEY WERE GIVING THEIR CHILDREN TO ME BEFORE THE ROMANS CAME TO THE BLACK FOREST.

I WAS A GOD.

MAYBE IT'S TIME TO MOVE ON.

MAYBE IT IS, AT THAT.

BUT WHAT MAKES YOU THINK I CAN, EVEN IF I WANT TO? YOU READY TO KILL ME, SHADOW? SO I CAN LEAVE?

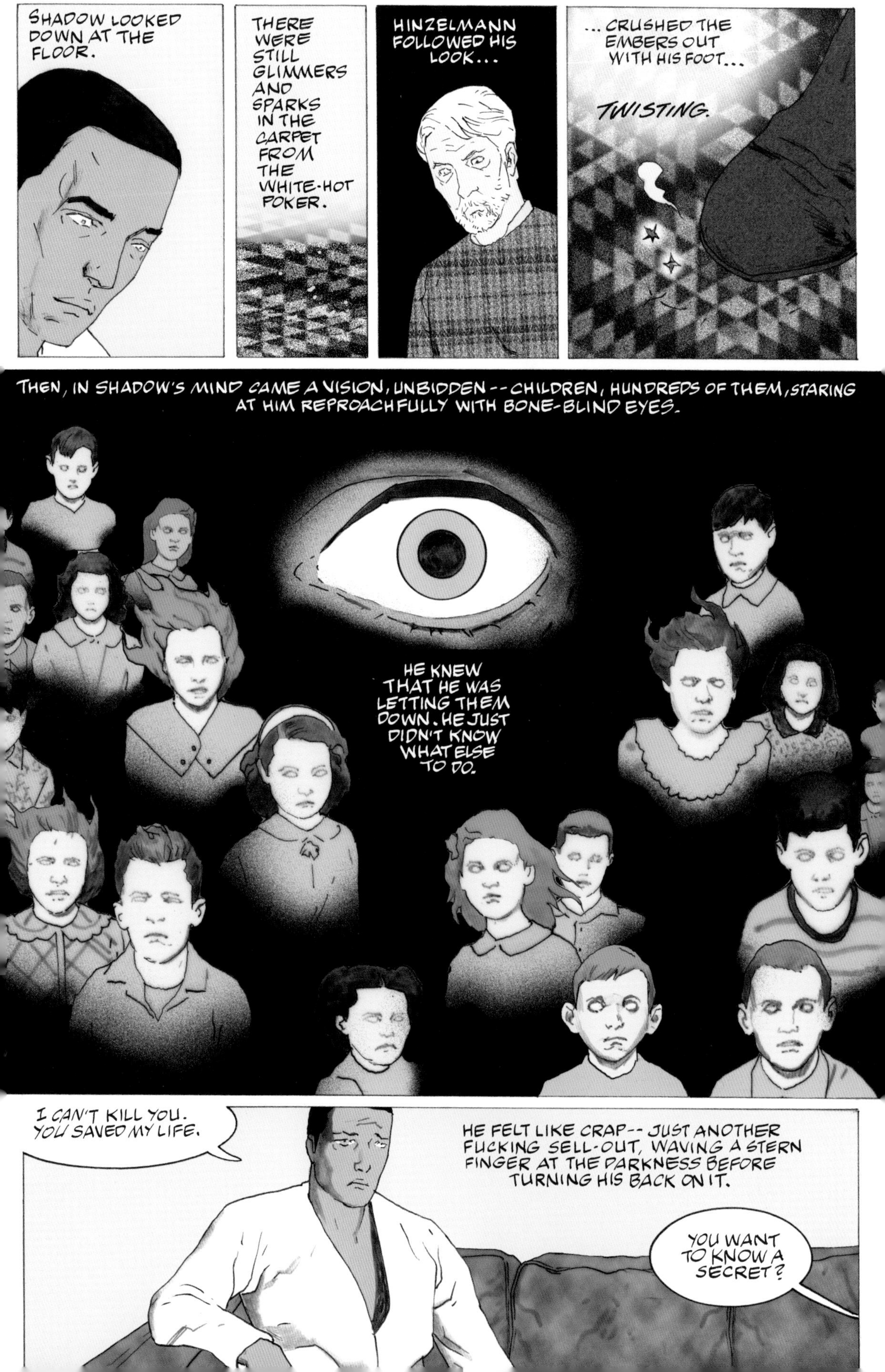
SHADOW LOOKED DOWN AT THE FLOOR.
THERE WERE STILL GLIMMERS AND SPARKS IN THE CARPET FROM THE WHITE-HOT POKER.
HINZELMANN FOLLOWED HIS LOOK...
...CRUSHED THE EMBERS OUT WITH HIS FOOT...
TWISTING.
THEN, IN SHADOW'S MIND CAME A VISION, UNBIDDEN--CHILDREN, HUNDREDS OF THEM, STARING AT HIM REPROACHFULLY WITH BONE-BLIND EYES.
HE KNEW THAT HE WAS LETTING THEM DOWN. HE JUST DIDN'T KNOW WHAT ELSE TO DO.
I CAN'T KILL YOU. YOU SAVED MY LIFE.
HE FELT LIKE CRAP--JUST ANOTHER FUCKING SELL-OUT, WAVING A STERN FINGER AT THE DARKNESS BEFORE TURNING HIS BACK ON IT.
YOU WANT TO KNOW A SECRET?

I'M READY TO BE DONE WITH SECRETS, BUT... SURE.

WATCH THIS.

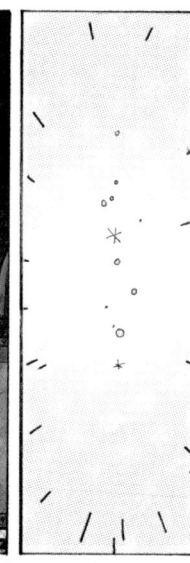

WHERE HINZELMANN HAD BEEN STANDING STOOD A MALE CHILD, NO MORE THAN FIVE YEARS OLD.

HE WAS PIERCED WITH TWO SWORDS. BLOOD FLOWED THROUGH THE WOUNDS WITHOUT STOPPING.

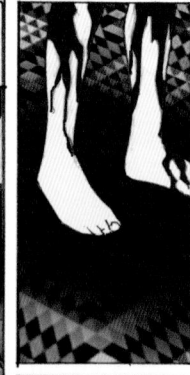

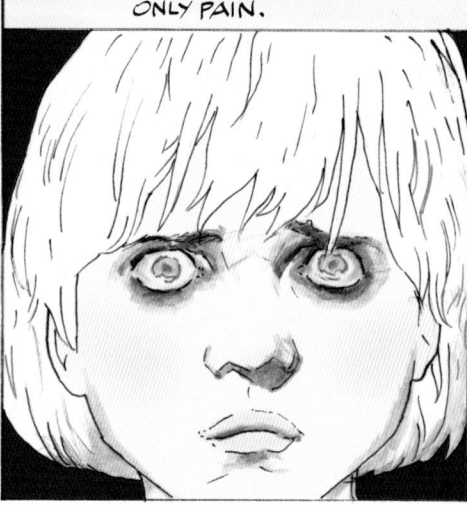

THE LITTLE BOY STARED UP AT SHADOW WITH EYES THAT HELD ONLY PAIN.

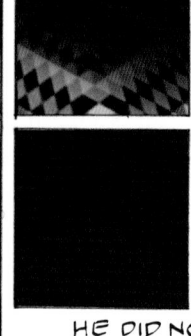

HE DID NOT HAVE TO BE TOLD. HE KNEW.

OF COURSE. THAT'S AS GOOD A WAY AS ANY OTHER OF MAKING A TRIBAL GOD.

YOU TAKE A BABY AND YOU BRING IT UP IN DARKNESS AND YOU FEED IT WELL AS THE YEARS PASS. THEN, FIVE YEARS ON, WHEN THE NIGHT IS AT ITS LONGEST, YOU DRAG THE TERRIFIED CHILD OUT OF ITS HUT AND INTO THE CIRCLE OF BONFIRES.

YOU PIERCE IT WITH BLADES OF IRON AND SMOKE THE SMALL BODY OVER CHARCOAL FIRES UNTIL IT IS PROPERLY DRIED.

THEN YOU WRAP IT IN FURS AND CARRY IT WITH YOU FROM ENCAMPMENT TO ENCAMPMENT, DEEP IN THE BLACK FOREST, SACRIFICING ANIMALS AND CHILDREN TO IT, MAKING IT THE LUCK OF THE TRIBE.

SHADOW WONDERED WHICH OF THE PEOPLE WHO HAD COME TO WISCONSIN A HUNDRED AND FIFTY YEARS AGO HAD CROSSED THE ATLANTIC WITH HINZELMANN IN HIS HEAD.

AND THEN THE BLOODY CHILD WAS GONE, AND THERE WAS ONLY AN OLD MAN WITH A GOBLIN SMILE.

HINZELMANN?

!?

OVER TO TELL YOU THE KLUNKER WENT THROUGH THE ICE IN CASE YOU MISSED IT.

HEY, CHAD.

HEY, PAL. THEY SENT ME A NOTE SAID YOU'D DIED IN CUSTODY.

HEH! SEEMS LIKE I'M DYING ALL OVER THE PLACE.

YOU'VE GOT TO ARREST HIM, CHAD. HE THREATENED TO *KILL* ME.

NO, HE DIDN'T. I'VE BEEN HERE FOR THE LAST TEN MINUTES, HINZELMANN. I HEARD EVERYTHING YOU SAID.

ABOUT THE LAKE.

ABOUT MY OLD MAN.

PUT THAT DOWN, HINZELMANN, *SLOWLY*, HANDS IN THE AIR. TURN AND FACE THE WALL.

THERE WAS AN EXPLOSION OF FEAR ON THE OLD MAN'S FACE...

...AND SHADOW WOULD HAVE FELT SORRY FOR HIM...

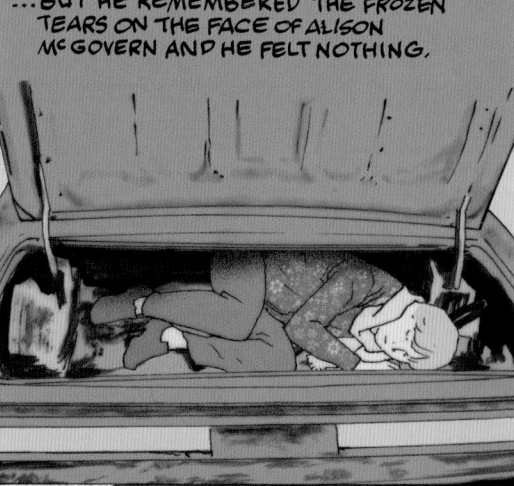

...BUT HE REMEMBERED THE FROZEN TEARS ON THE FACE OF ALISON McGOVERN AND HE FELT NOTHING.

HUNH

THE NOISE OF THE SHOT, IN THE CLOSE QUARTERS OF THE OLD MAN'S ROOM WAS DEAFENING.

ONE SHOT TO THE HEAD, AND THAT WAS ALL.

BETTER GET YOUR CLOTHES ON.

BY THE TIME HE GOT BACK TO THE DEN, MULLIGAN HAD ALREADY HAULED SEVERAL SMOLDERING LOGS OUT OF THE FIREPLACE.

IT'S A BAD DAY FOR A COP WHEN HE HAS TO COMMIT ARSON, JUST TO COVER UP A MURDER.

IT WASN'T MURDER. IT WAS SELF-DEFENSE.

I KNOW WHAT IT WAS.

SORRY, HINZELMANN.

LET'S GET OUT OF HERE.

HOW MUCH DID YOU HEAR IN THERE?

ENOUGH.

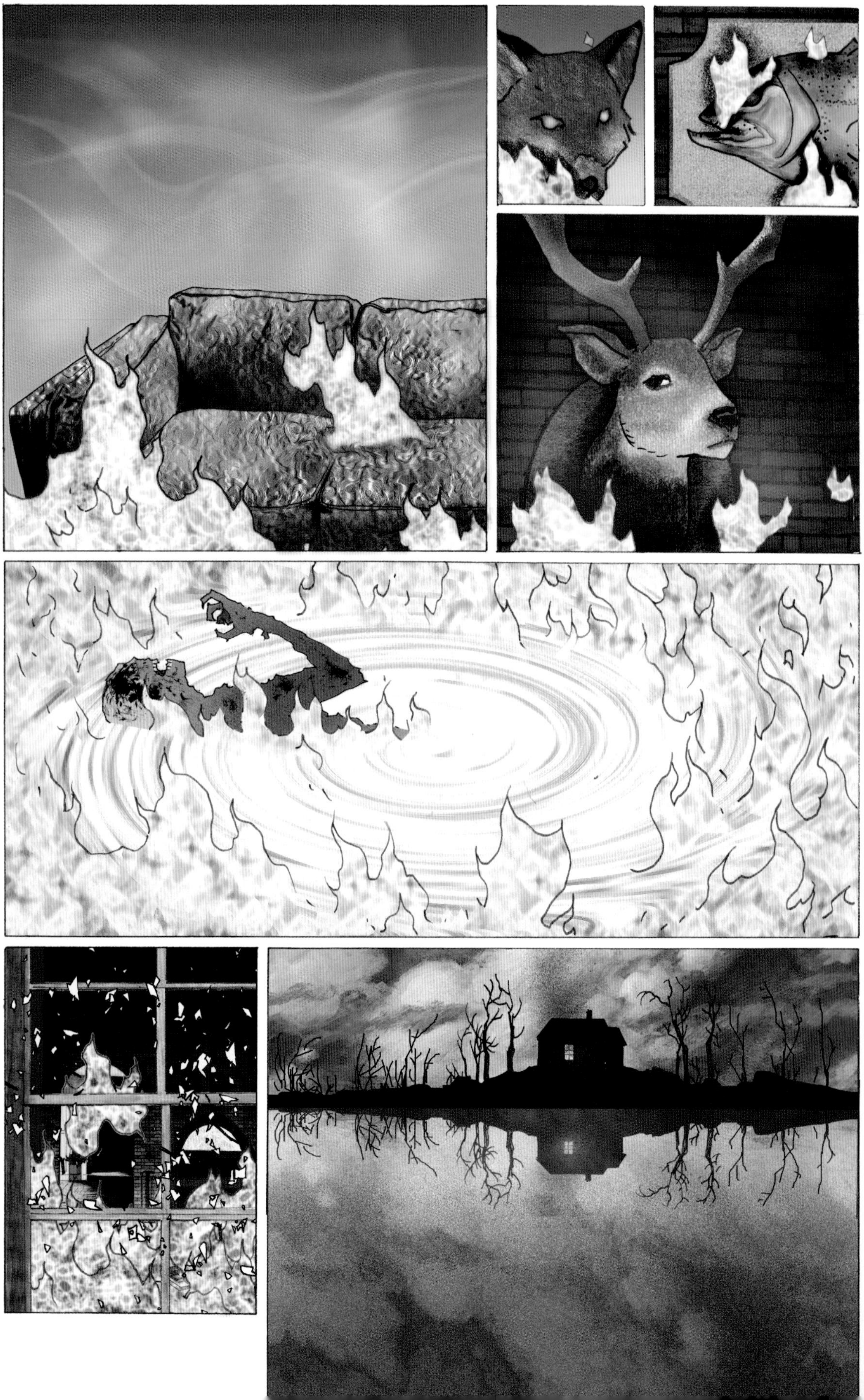

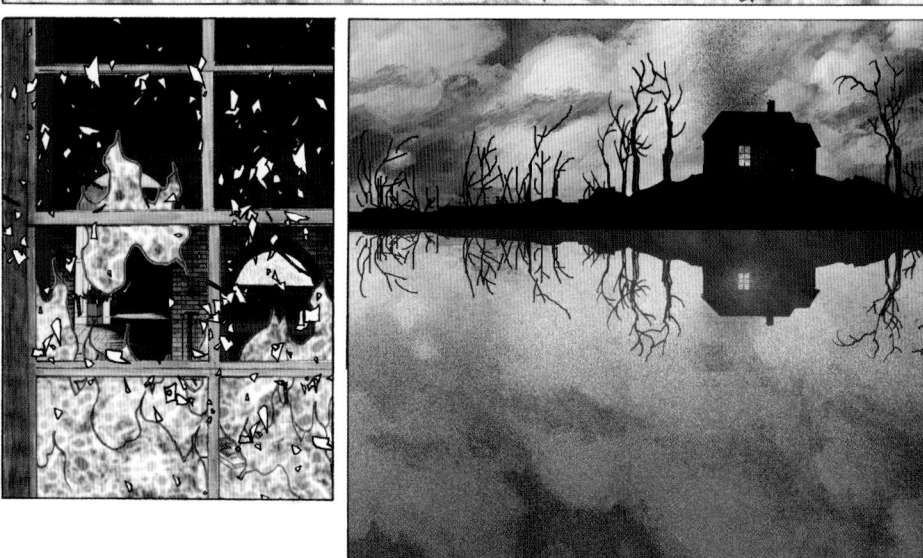

CHAPTER NINE

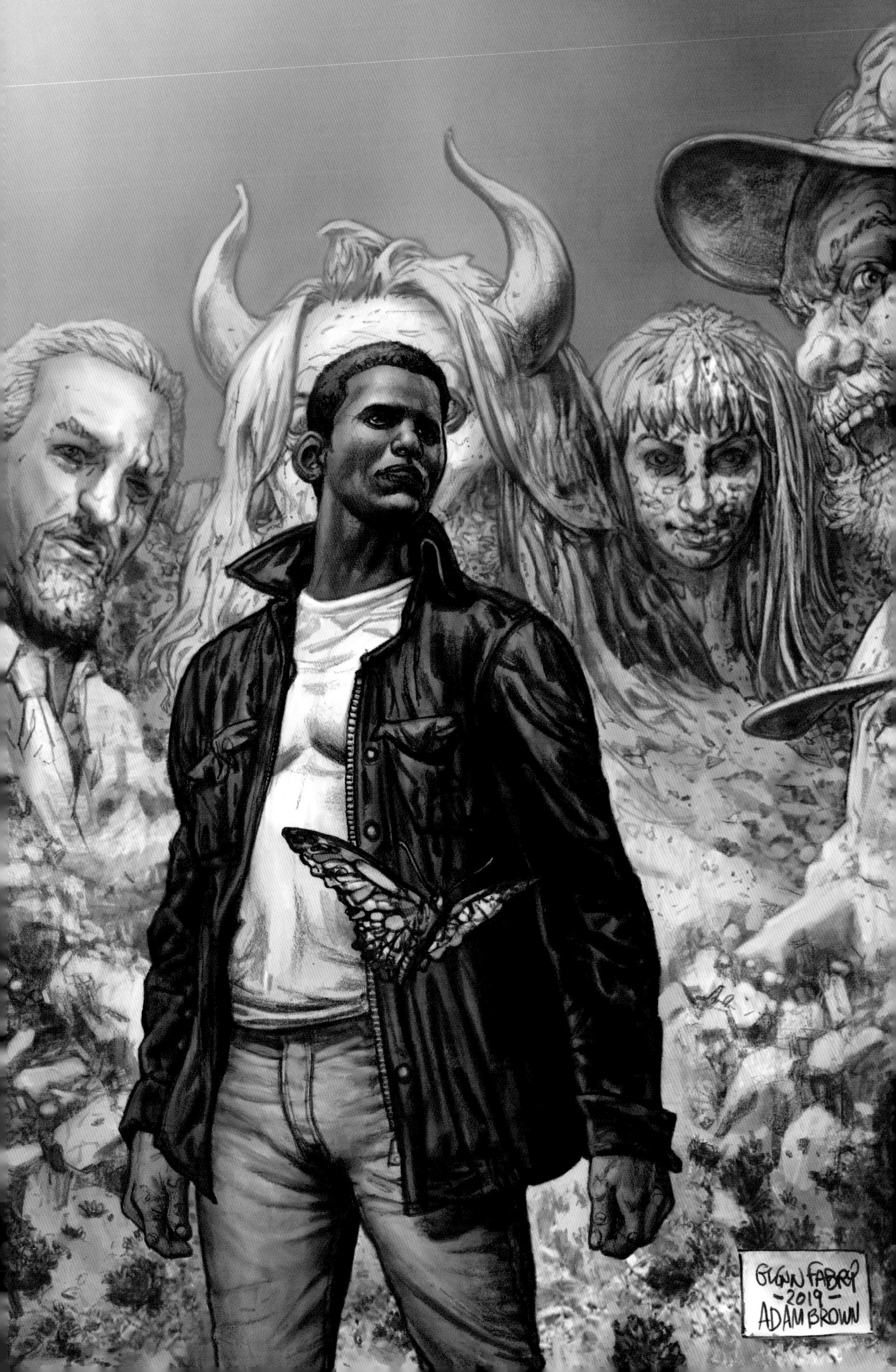
GLENN FABRY
-2019-
ADAM BROWN

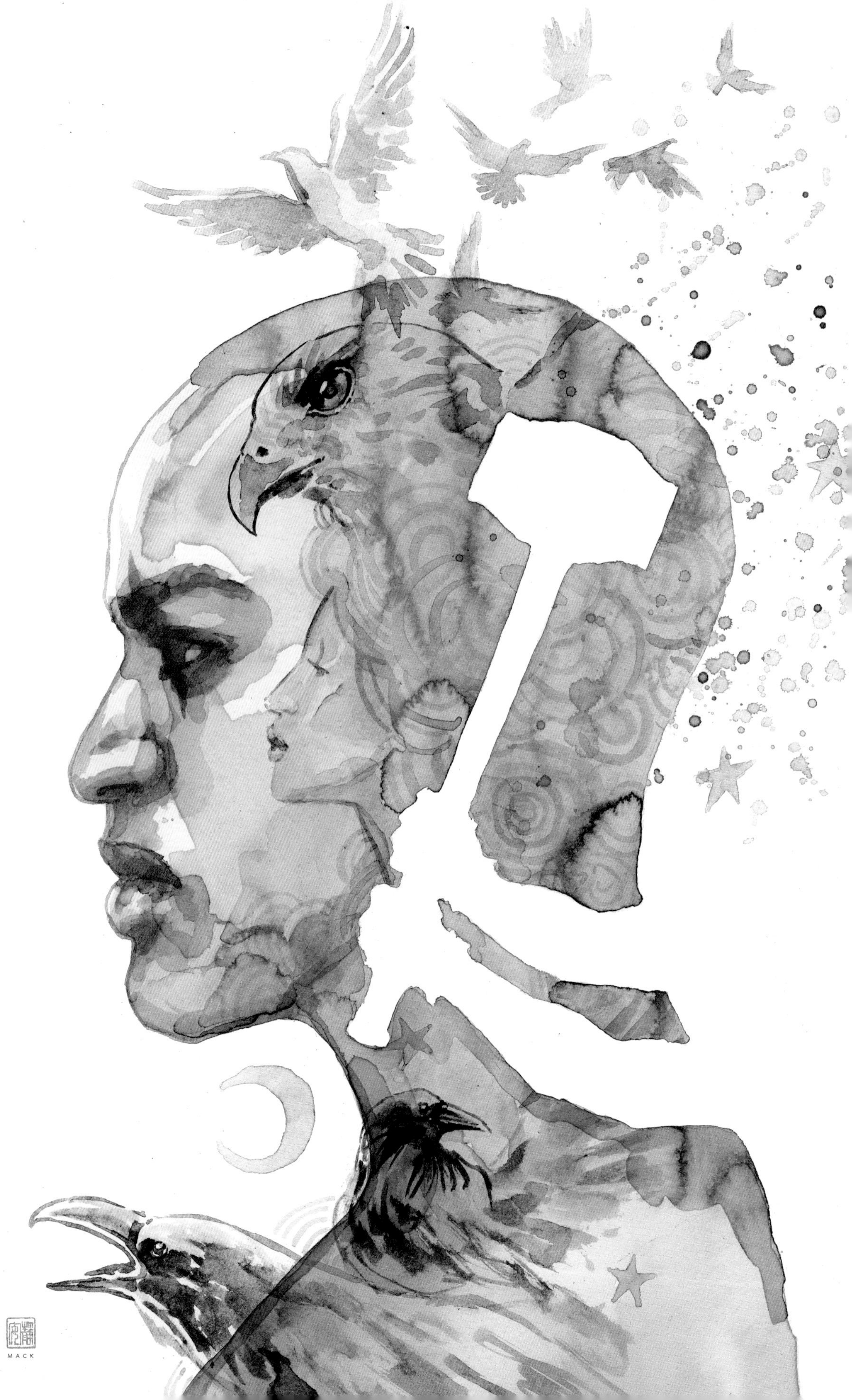
MACK

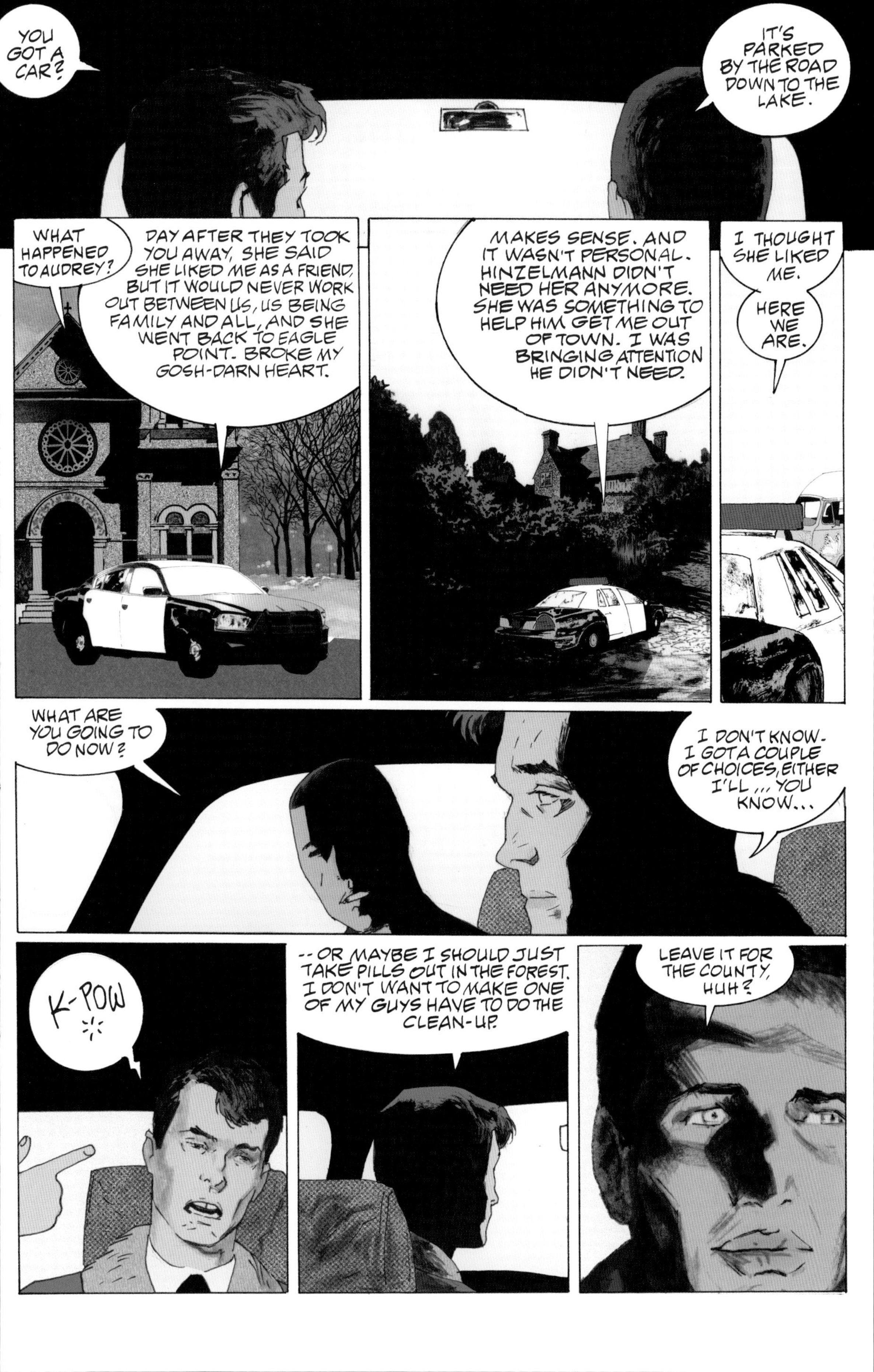
YOU GOT A CAR?
IT'S PARKED BY THE ROAD DOWN TO THE LAKE.
WHAT HAPPENED TO AUDREY?
DAY AFTER THEY TOOK YOU AWAY, SHE SAID SHE LIKED ME AS A FRIEND, BUT IT WOULD NEVER WORK OUT BETWEEN US, US BEING FAMILY AND ALL, AND SHE WENT BACK TO EAGLE POINT. BROKE MY GOSH-DARN HEART.
MAKES SENSE. AND IT WASN'T PERSONAL. HINZELMANN DIDN'T NEED HER ANYMORE. SHE WAS SOMETHING TO HELP HIM GET ME OUT OF TOWN. I WAS BRINGING ATTENTION HE DIDN'T NEED.
I THOUGHT SHE LIKED ME.
HERE WE ARE.
WHAT ARE YOU GOING TO DO NOW?
I DON'T KNOW. I GOT A COUPLE OF CHOICES, EITHER I'LL ... YOU KNOW...
K-POW
--OR MAYBE I SHOULD JUST TAKE PILLS OUT IN THE FOREST. I DON'T WANT TO MAKE ONE OF MY GUYS HAVE TO DO THE CLEAN-UP.
LEAVE IT FOR THE COUNTY, HUH?

YOU DIDN'T KILL HINZELMANN, CHAD. HE DIED A LONG TIME AGO, A LONG WAY FROM HERE.

THANK YOU FOR SAYING THAT, MIKE. BUT I KILLED HIM. I SHOT A MAN IN COLD BLOOD, AND I COVERED IT UP. AND IF YOU ASK ME WHY I DID IT, I'M DARNED IF I COULD TELL YOU.

CHAD, I DON'T THINK YOU HAD A LOT OF CHOICE ABOUT WHAT HAPPENED BACK THERE.

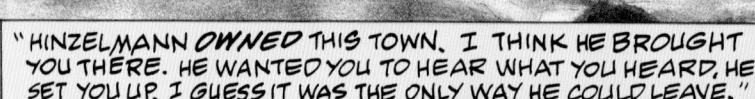

"HINZELMANN *OWNED* THIS TOWN. I THINK HE BROUGHT YOU THERE. HE WANTED YOU TO HEAR WHAT YOU HEARD. HE SET YOU UP. I GUESS IT WAS THE ONLY WAY HE COULD LEAVE."

SHADOW COULD SEE THAT THE POLICE CHIEF HAD BARELY HEARD ANYTHING THAT HE HAD SAID.

HE CLOSED HIS EYES, REMEMBERING THE PLACE IN HIS HEAD THAT HE HAD GONE WHEN WEDNESDAY HAD TOLD HIM TO MAKE SNOW.

CHAD ...

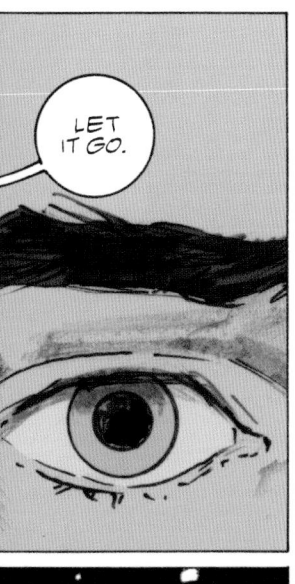

LET IT GO.

THERE WAS A CLOUD IN THE MAN'S MIND, A DARK OPPRESSIVE CLOUD THAT SHADOW COULD ALMOST SEE.

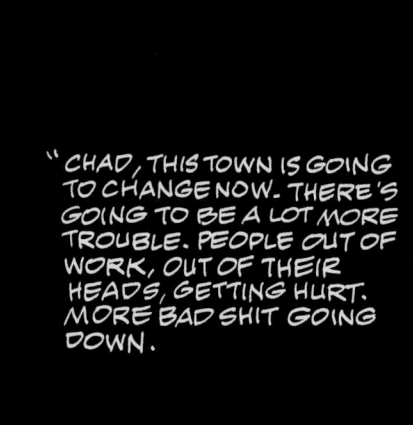

" CHAD, THIS TOWN IS GOING TO CHANGE NOW. THERE'S GOING TO BE A LOT MORE TROUBLE. PEOPLE OUT OF WORK, OUT OF THEIR HEADS, GETTING HURT. MORE BAD SHIT GOING DOWN.

" THEY ARE GOING TO NEED A POLICE CHIEF WITH EXPERIENCE.

" THE TOWN NEEDS YOU.

" MARGUERITE NEEDS YOU."

SOMETHING SHIFTED IN THE STORM CLOUD THAT FILLED THE MAN'S HEAD.

SHADOW PUSHED THEN. "SHE'S WAITING FOR YOU."

MARGIE?

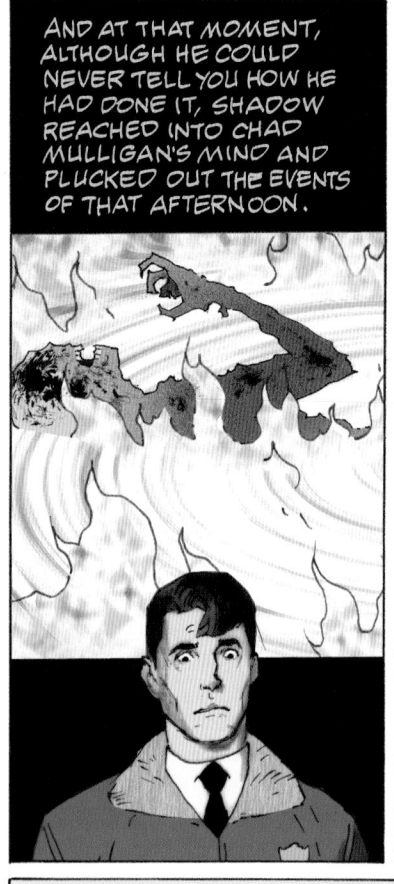

AND AT THAT MOMENT, ALTHOUGH HE COULD NEVER TELL YOU HOW HE HAD DONE IT, SHADOW REACHED INTO CHAD MULLIGAN'S MIND AND PLUCKED OUT THE EVENTS OF THAT AFTERNOON.

GO SEE MARGIE.

IT'S BEEN GOOD SEEING YOU, CHAD, TAKE CARE OF YOURSELF.

SURE.

A MESSAGE CRACKLED OVER THE POLICE RADIO AND CHAD DROVE AWAY.

SHADOW WAS LEFT STARING AT THE GRAY FLATNESS OF THE LAKE AT THE CENTER OF THE TOWN.

ALL THOSE CHILDREN.

SOON, ALLISON WOULD FLOAT TO THE SURFACE.

HE DROVE SOUTH, HEADING FOR HIGHWAY 51. HE WAS ON HIS WAY TO KEEP HIS FINAL APPOINTMENT. BUT BEFORE THAT, HE THOUGHT, THERE WAS ONE MORE STOP TO MAKE. HE HAD ONE LAST GOODBYE.

MADISON.

BEST OF EVERYTHING, SAMANTHA BLACK CROW LIKED CLOSING UP THE COFFEE HOUSE AT NIGHT.

SHE WOULD DO THE FINAL ROUNDS. CUPS AND PLATES WERE RETURNED TO THE KITCHEN, SCATTERED NEWSPAPERS WERE COLLECTED TOGETHER AND PILED NEATLY BY THE FRONT DOOR, ALL READY FOR RECYCLING.

FINALLY, SHE WOULD WIPE AWAY THE LAST OF THE CRUMBS.

SHE ENJOYED BEING ALONE...

TAP TAP TAP

...USUALLY.

HELLO.

HEYYY, NATALIE.

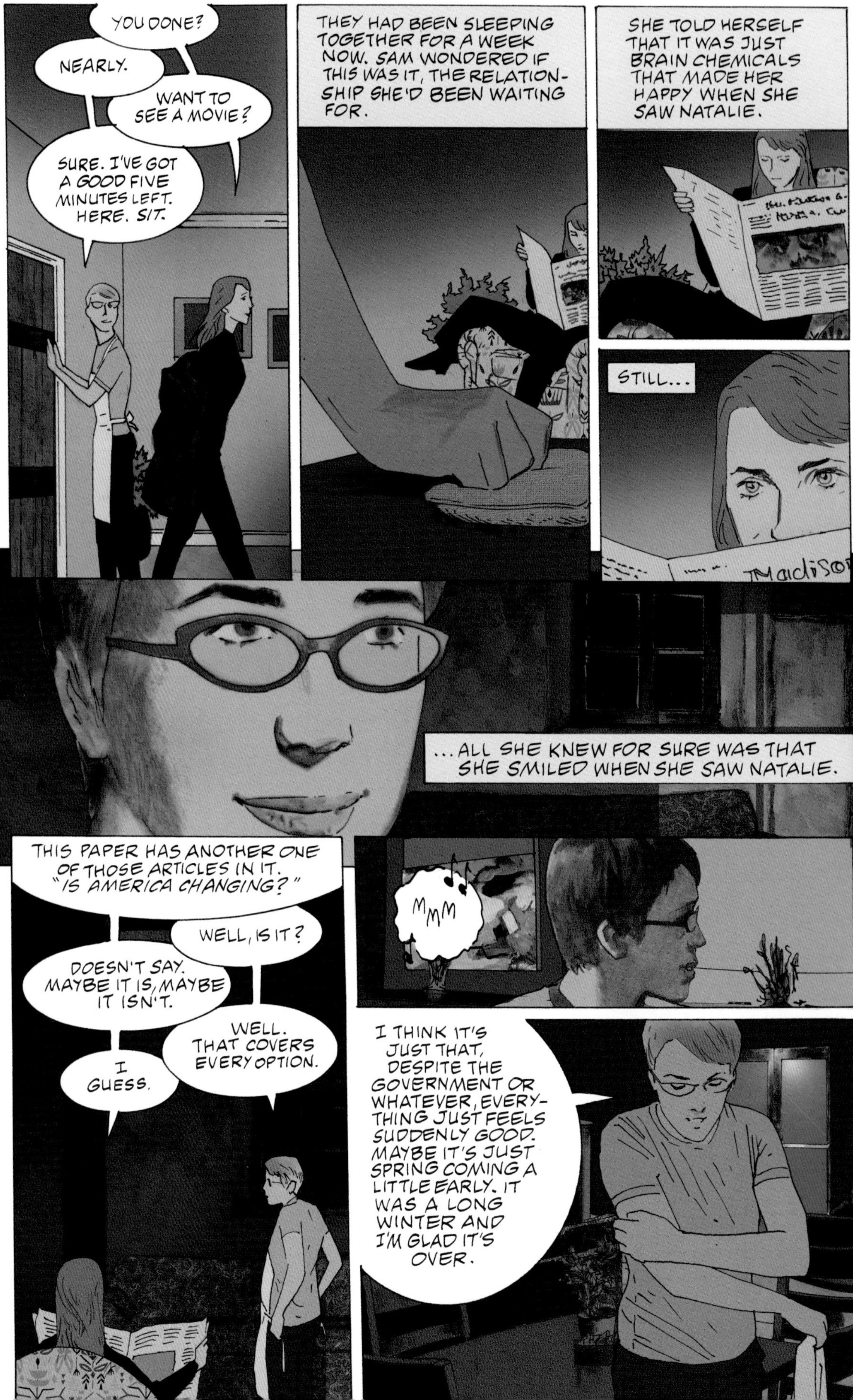
YOU DONE?
NEARLY.
WANT TO SEE A MOVIE?
SURE. I'VE GOT A GOOD FIVE MINUTES LEFT. HERE. SIT.
THEY HAD BEEN SLEEPING TOGETHER FOR A WEEK NOW. SAM WONDERED IF THIS WAS IT, THE RELATIONSHIP SHE'D BEEN WAITING FOR.
SHE TOLD HERSELF THAT IT WAS JUST BRAIN CHEMICALS THAT MADE HER HAPPY WHEN SHE SAW NATALIE.
STILL...
...ALL SHE KNEW FOR SURE WAS THAT SHE SMILED WHEN SHE SAW NATALIE.
THIS PAPER HAS ANOTHER ONE OF THOSE ARTICLES IN IT. "IS AMERICA CHANGING?"
WELL, IS IT?
DOESN'T SAY. MAYBE IT IS, MAYBE IT ISN'T.
WELL. THAT COVERS EVERY OPTION.
I GUESS.
MMM
I THINK IT'S JUST THAT, DESPITE THE GOVERNMENT OR WHATEVER, EVERYTHING JUST FEELS SUDDENLY GOOD. MAYBE IT'S JUST SPRING COMING A LITTLE EARLY. IT WAS A LONG WINTER AND I'M GLAD IT'S OVER.

ME, TOO.

IT SAYS IN THE ARTICLE THAT LOTS OF PEOPLE HAVE BEEN REPORTING WEIRD DREAMS.

I'VE HAD SOME WEIRD DREAMS RECENTLY.

THEY GOT WEIRD ENOUGH THAT I ACTUALLY STARTED KEEPING A DREAM JOURNAL. THEY SEEM TO MEAN SO MUCH WHEN I'M DREAMING THEM.

I WRITE THEM DOWN WHEN I WAKE UP.

AND THEN WHEN I READ THEM, THEY DON'T MEAN ANYTHING AT ALL.

I DID SOME DREAM WORK. TELL ME. I'LL TELL YOU WHAT THEY MEAN.

OKAY.

SOMETIMES I HAVE BEEN DREAMING OF PEOPLE WHO FELL FROM THE SKY.

SOMETIMES I'M UNDERGROUND, TALKING TO A WOMAN WITH A BUFFALO HEAD. AND SOMETIMES I DREAM ABOUT THIS GUY I KISSED IN A BAR.

?

KISSED, HUH? SOMETHING YOU SHOULD HAVE TOLD ME ABOUT?

IT WAS A *FUCK-OFF* KISS.

YOU WERE TELLING HIM TO FUCK *OFF*?

NO -- I WAS TELLING EVERY-ONE *ELSE* THERE TO FUCK OFF. ☀ -- YOU HAD TO *BE* THERE.

HE OWNS MY CAR.

THAT PURPLE THING YOU GOT AT YOUR SISTER'S?

YUP.

WHY DOESN'T HE WANT HIS CAR?

I DON'T KNOW -- MAYBE HE'S IN PRISON. MAYBE HE'S DEAD.

DEAD?

I GUESS. A FEW WEEKS BACK, I WAS CERTAIN HE WAS DEAD. *E.S.P.* OR WHATEVER.

BUT THEN I STARTED TO THINK MAYBE HE WASN'T.

I GUESS MY *E.S.P.* ISN'T THAT HOT.

WHERE DID YOU GET *THOSE* FROM?

WHAT?

THOSE FLOWERS -- THE ONES YOU'RE HOLDING -- SAM, WHERE DID THEY COME FROM?

OH. YOU ARE SO *SWEET.* SHOULD HAVE SAID SOME-THING WHEN YOU GAVE THEM TO ME, SHOULDN'T I? THEY ARE LOVELY.

I DIDN'T GIVE THEM TO YOU.

AND NEITHER SAID ANOTHER WORD UNTIL THEY REACHED THE MOVIE THEATER.

SHADOW HAD PARKED NEAR THE CAPITOL BUILDING. HE PASSED A PAYPHONE, CALLED INFORMATION, AND THEY GAVE HIM THE NUMBER.

NO, SHE'S NOT BACK YET. PROBABLY STILL AT THE COFFEE HOUSE.

HE STOPPED ON THE WAY TO THE COFFEE HOUSE TO BUY FLOWERS...

... FOUND THE COFFEE HOUSE AND STOOD IN A DOORWAY ACROSS THE ROAD, WAITING.

AT 8:10 SAM BLACK CROW WALKED OUT OF THE COFFEE HOUSE IN THE COMPANY OF A SMALLER WOMAN, HOLDING HANDS TIGHTLY, AS IF TO KEEP THE WORLD AT BAY.

A FEW WEEKS BACK, I WAS CERTAIN HE WAS DEAD. E.S.P. OR WHATEVER.

BUT THEN I STARTED TO THINK MAYBE HE WASN'T.

I GUESS MY E.S.P. ISN'T THAT HOT.

HE FELT A PANG, LIKE A MINOR CHORD BEING PLAYED INSIDE HIM. IT HAD BEEN A GOOD KISS, HE REFLECTED, BUT SAM HAD NEVER LOOKED AT HIM THE WAY SHE WAS LOOKING AT THIS GIRL, AND SHE NEVER WOULD.

THEN HE WALKED UP THE HILL BACK TO HIS CAR, AND HE TOOK HIGHWAY 90 SOUTH TO CHICAGO. HE DROVE AT OR SLIGHTLY UNDER THE SPEED LIMIT. IT WAS THE LAST THING HE HAD TO DO.

HE WAS IN NO HURRY.

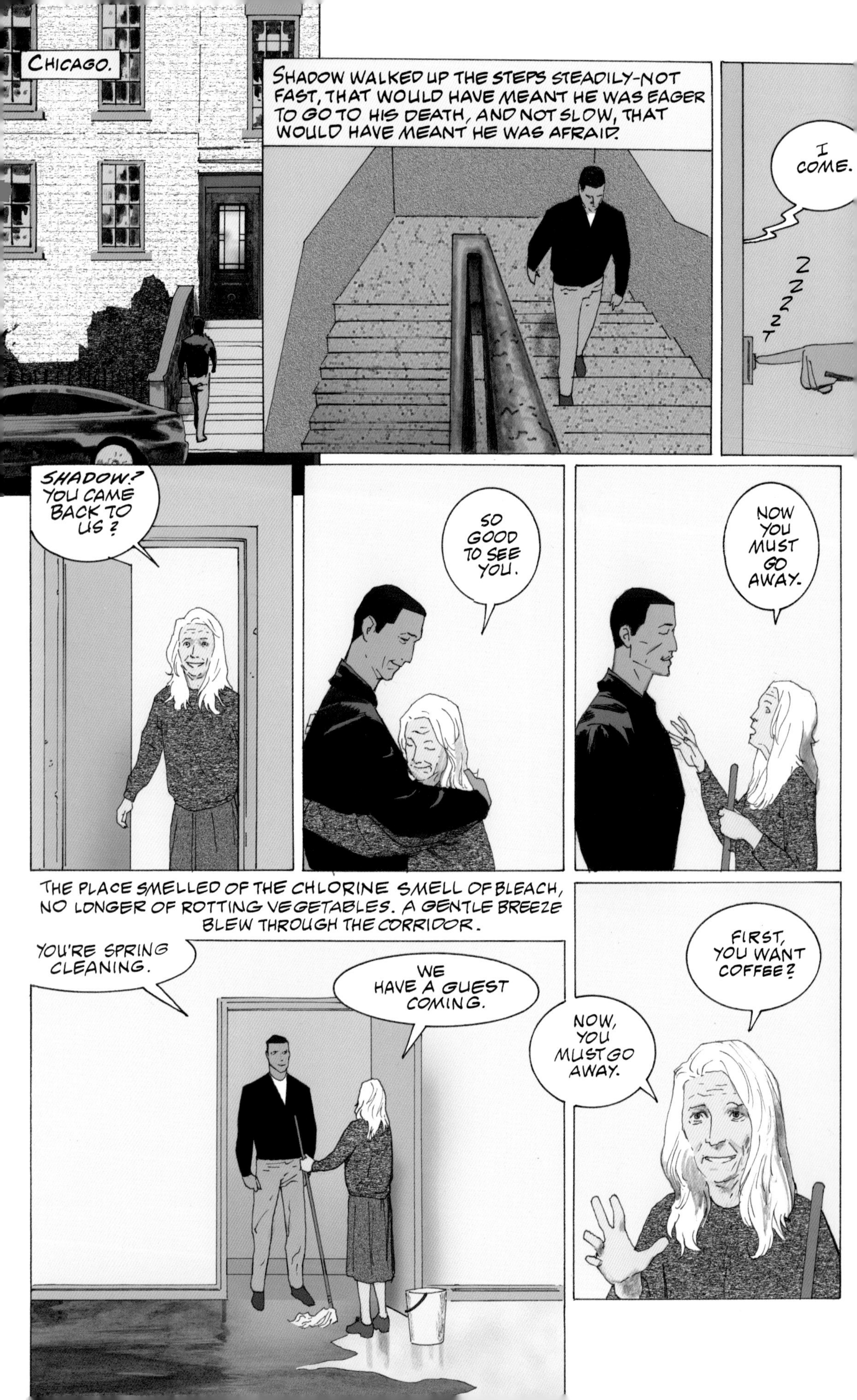

CHICAGO.
SHADOW WALKED UP THE STEPS STEADILY-NOT FAST, THAT WOULD HAVE MEANT HE WAS EAGER TO GO TO HIS DEATH, AND NOT SLOW, THAT WOULD HAVE MEANT HE WAS AFRAID.
I COME.
ZZZZZ
SHADOW? YOU CAME BACK TO US?
SO GOOD TO SEE YOU.
NOW YOU MUST GO AWAY.
THE PLACE SMELLED OF THE CHLORINE SMELL OF BLEACH, NO LONGER OF ROTTING VEGETABLES. A GENTLE BREEZE BLEW THROUGH THE CORRIDOR.
YOU'RE SPRING CLEANING.
WE HAVE A GUEST COMING.
FIRST, YOU WANT COFFEE?
NOW, YOU MUST GO AWAY.

I CAME TO SEE CZERNOBOG. IT'S TIME.

NO, *NO.* YOU *DON'T* WANT TO SEE HIM. NOT A GOOD IDEA.

I KNOW. BUT, YOU KNOW, THE ONLY THING I'VE LEARNED ABOUT DEALING WITH GODS IS THAT IF YOU MAKE A DEAL, YOU KEEP IT. THEY GET TO BREAK ALL THE RULES THEY WANT. WE DON'T.

IS *TRUE.* BUT COME BACK TOMORROW. HE WILL BE GONE THEN.

ZORYA UTRENNYAYA, TO WHO ARE YOU TALKING? THIS MATTRESS I CANNOT TURN ON MY OWN, YOU KNOW.

GOOD MORNING, ZORYA VECHERNYAYA. CAN I HELP?

!

THE MATTRESS. IT NEEDS TO BE TURNED.

WHAT ARE YOU *DOING* HERE?

I'M HERE BECAUSE BACK IN DECEMBER, A YOUNG MAN PLAYED A GAME OF CHECKERS WITH AN OLD GOD AND HE LOST.

I CAN'T.

COME BACK TO-MORROW.

IS YOUR FUNERAL. NOW YOU GO AND SIT DOWN. ZORYA UTRENNYAYA WILL BRING YOU COFFEE. CZERNOBOG WILL BE BACK SOON.

THE SITTING ROOM WAS JUST AS HE REMEMBERED IT. THIS WAS WHERE HE HAD PLAYED CHECKERS WITH CZERNOBOG, WHERE HE HAD WAGERED HIS LIFE TO GET THE OLD MAN TO JOIN THEM ON WEDNESDAY'S LAST DOOMED GRIFT.

THE SAME GRAY CAT SLEPT ON THE ARM OF THE SOFA...

...UNIMPRESSED.

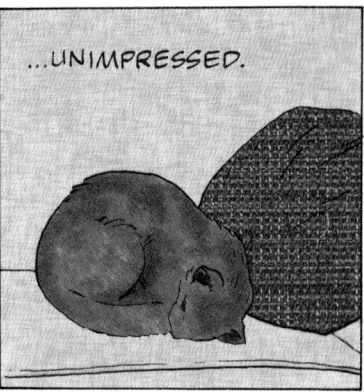

I SAW ZORYA POLUNOCHNAYA AGAIN. SHE CAME TO ME UNDER THE WORLD, AND SHE GAVE ME THE MOON TO LIGHT MY WAY. AND SHE TOOK SOMETHING FROM ME. I DON'T REMEMBER WHAT.

SHE LIKES YOU.

SHE DREAMS SO MUCH. AND SHE GUARDS US ALL. SHE IS SO BRAVE.

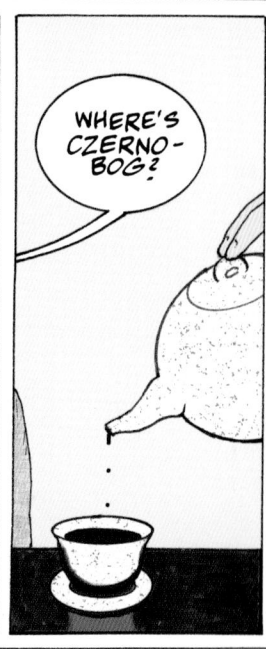

WHERE'S CZERNO- BOG?

HE SAYS THE SPRING CLEANING MAKES HIM UNCOMFORTABLE.

HE GOES OUT TO BUY NEWSPAPER, SIT IN PARK, BUY CIGARETTES.

PERHAPS HE WILL NOT COME BACK TODAY. YOU DO NOT HAVE TO WAIT.

WHY DON'T YOU GO?

COME BACK TOMORROW.

I'LL WAIT.

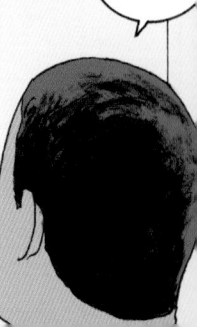

IT WAS ONE LAST THING THAT NEEDED TO HAPPEN, AND IF IT WAS *THE* LAST THING THAT HAPPENED, WELL, HE WAS GOING THERE OF HIS OWN VOLITION. AFTER THIS, THERE WOULD BE NO MORE OBLIGATIONS, NO MORE MYSTERIES, NO MORE GHOSTS.

THE COFFEE WAS AS BLACK AND SWEET AS HE REMEMBERED.

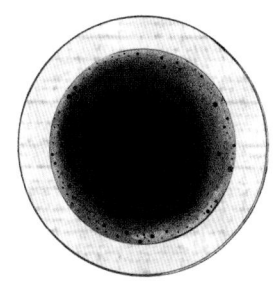

HE HEARD A DEEP MALE VOICE IN THE CORRIDOR.

SHADOW.

I CAME. OUR DEAL. *YOU* CAME THROUGH WITH YOUR PART OF IT. THIS IS MY PART.

IS NOT ...

MAYBE YOU SHOULD GO.

IS NOT A GOOD TIME.

TAKE AS LONG AS YOU NEED. I'M READY.

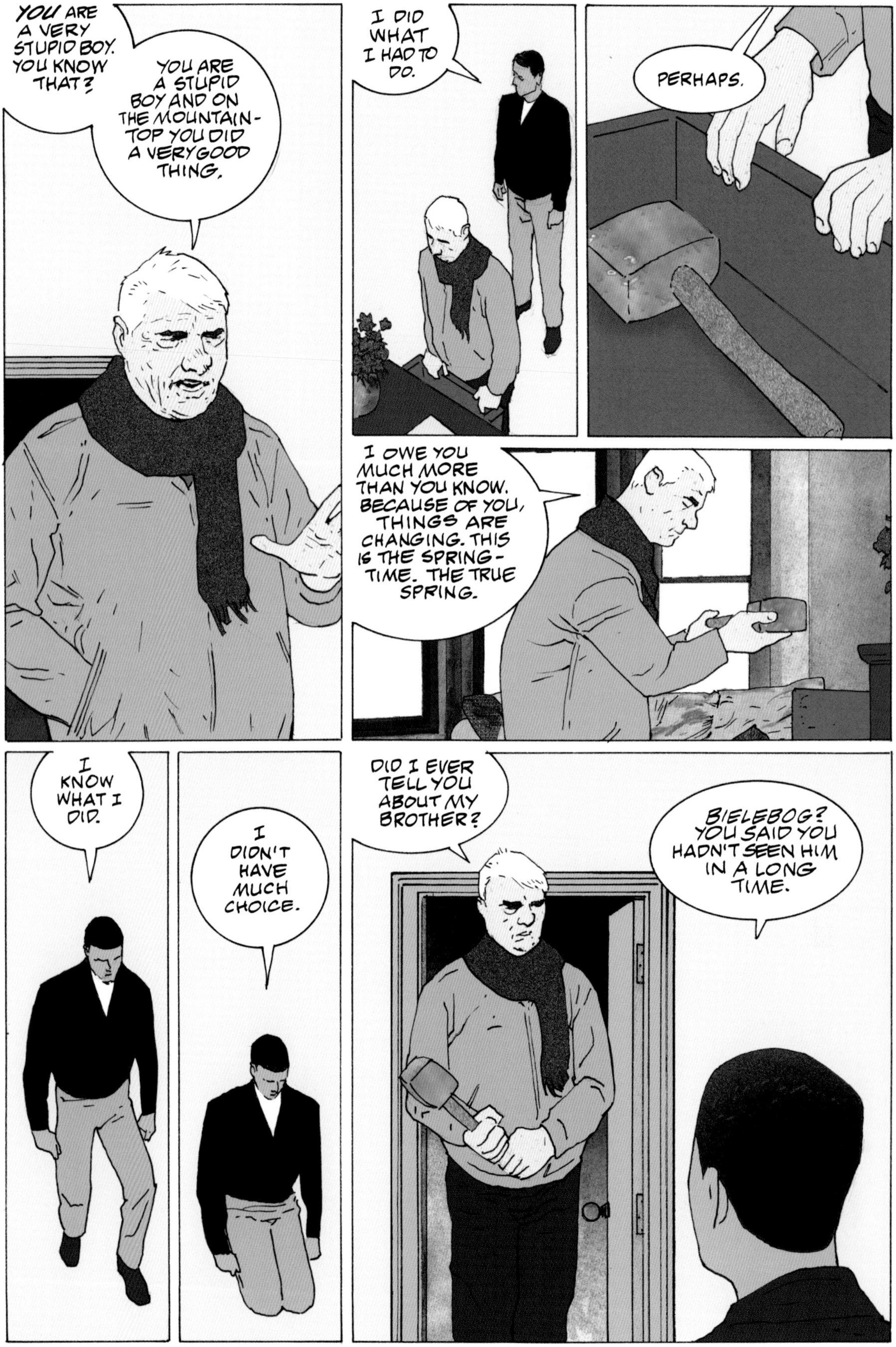

YOU ARE A VERY STUPID BOY. YOU KNOW THAT?
YOU ARE A STUPID BOY AND ON THE MOUNTAIN-TOP YOU DID A VERY GOOD THING.
I DID WHAT I HAD TO DO.
PERHAPS.
I OWE YOU MUCH MORE THAN YOU KNOW. BECAUSE OF YOU, THINGS ARE CHANGING. THIS IS THE SPRING-TIME. THE TRUE SPRING.
I KNOW WHAT I DID.
I DIDN'T HAVE MUCH CHOICE.
DID I EVER TELL YOU ABOUT MY BROTHER?
BIELEBOG? YOU SAID YOU HADN'T SEEN HIM IN A LONG TIME.

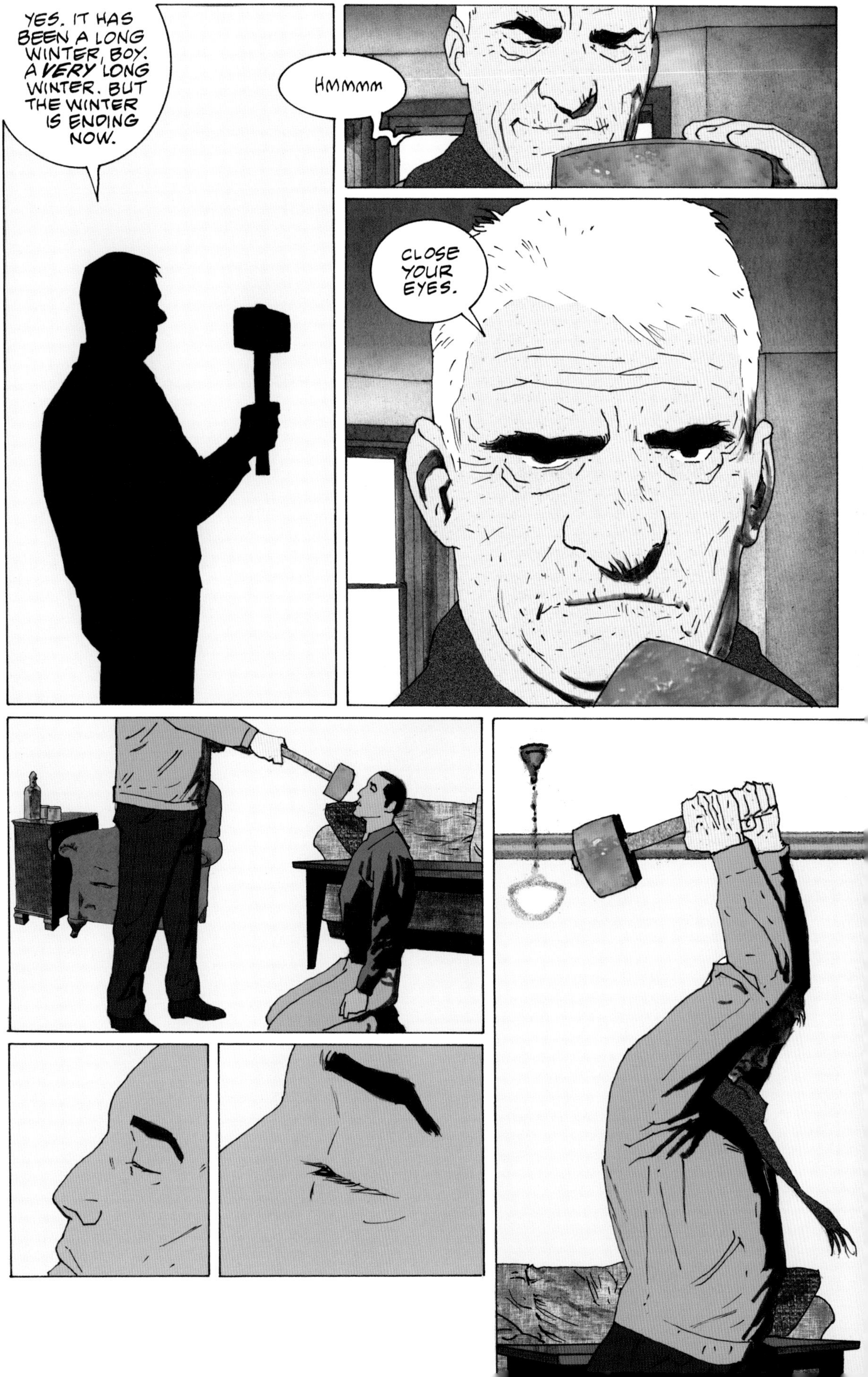

YES. IT HAS BEEN A LONG WINTER, BOY. A *VERY* LONG WINTER. BUT THE WINTER IS ENDING NOW.

HMMMM

CLOSE YOUR EYES.

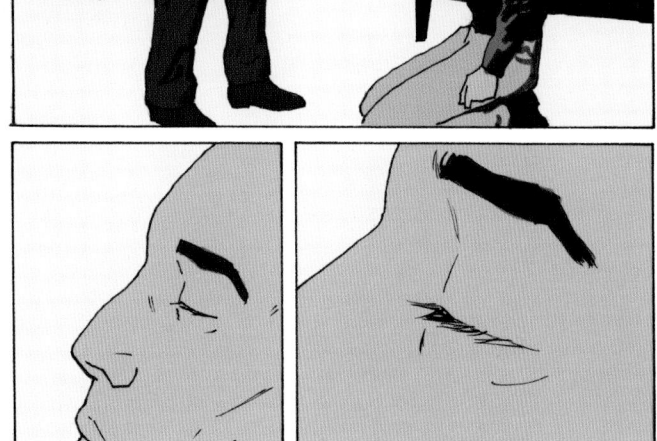

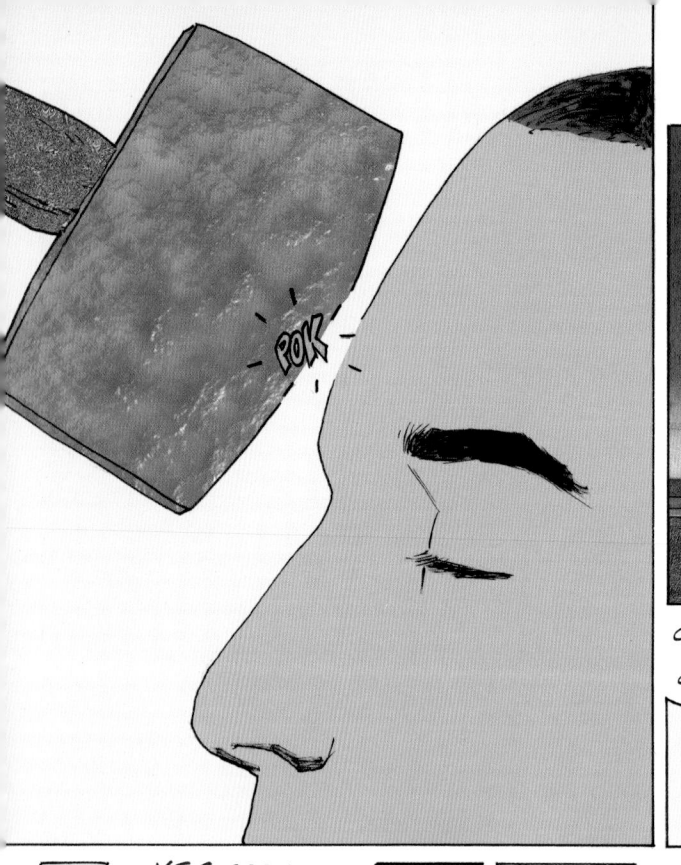

THERE. IS DONE.

CZERNOBOG? *ARE* YOU CZERNOBOG?

YES, FOR TODAY. BY TOMORROW, IT WILL ALL BE BIELEBOG.

BUT TODAY, IS STILL CZERNOBOG.

THEN *WHY?* WHY DIDN'T YOU KILL ME WHEN YOU COULD?

BECAUSE THERE IS BLOOD.

BUT THERE IS ALSO GRATITUDE.

"AND IT HAS BEEN A LONG, LONG WINTER."

THANKS.

YOU'RE WELCOME. NEXT TIME YOU WANT TO PLAY CHECKERS YOU KNOW WHERE TO FIND ME. *THIS* TIME I PLAY WHITE.

THANKS. MAYBE I WILL.

BUT NOT FOR A WHILE.

NEITHER OF THEM SAID GOODBYE.

SHADOW KISSED ZORYA UTRENN-YAYA ON HIS WAY OUT...

... AND HE KISSED ZORYA VECHERNYAYA ON THE BACK OF HER HAND...

... AND HE TOOK THE STAIRS OUT OF THERE TWO AT A TIME.

P O S T S C R I P T

REYKJAVÍK IN ICELAND IS A STRANGE CITY. A VOLCANIC CITY. THE SUN WAS SHINING, AS IT HAD SHONE FOR WEEKS NOW: IT CEASED SHINING FOR AN HOUR OR SO IN THE SMALL HOURS, THEN THE DAY WOULD BEGIN AGAIN.

THE BIG TOURIST HAD WALKED MOST OF REYKJAVIK THAT MORNING, LISTENING TO PEOPLE TALK IN A LANGUAGE THAT HAD CHANGED LITTLE IN A THOUSAND YEARS.

THE UNENDING DAYLIGHT HAD MADE SLEEP ALMOST IMPOSSIBLE, AND HE HAD SAT IN HIS HOTEL ROOM THROUGH THE WHOLE LONG NIGHTLESS NIGHT READING A GUIDE BOOK AND *BLEAK HOUSE*.

SOMETIMES HE SIMPLY STARED OUT THE WINDOW.

FINALLY, THE CLOCK AS WELL AS THE SUN PROCLAIMED IT MORNING.

HE BOUGHT A BAR OF CHOCOLATE AND WALKED THE STREETS, SMILING AT THE PRETTY WOMEN, BECAUSE THEY MADE HIM FEEL PLEASANTLY MALE, AND AT THE OTHER WOMEN BECAUSE HE WAS HAVING A GOOD TIME.

OCCASIONALLY HE WAS REMINDED OF THE VOLCANIC NATURE OF ICELAND: A SULFUROUS QUALITY TO THE AIR.

HE WAS NOT SURE WHEN HE BECAME AWARE THAT HE WAS BEING OBSERVED. HE WOULD TURN FROM TIME TO TIME, BUT SAW NO ONE OUT OF THE ORDINARY.

HE WENT INTO A SMALL RESTAURANT, WHERE HE ATE CLOUDBERRIES AND SMOKED PUFFIN AND ARCTIC CHAR.

EXCUSE ME, YOU ARE AMERICAN?

YES.

THEN, HAPPY FOURTH OF JULY.

HA. YES, RIGHT. INDEPENDENCE DAY.

HE LEFT A TIP ON THE TABLE AND WALKED OUTSIDE. A COOL BREEZE WAS COMING IN OFF THE ATLANTIC.

ONE DAY I WILL HAVE TO GO HOME.

ONE DAY I WILL HAVE TO MAKE A HOME TO GO HOME TO.

HE WONDERED WHETHER HOME WAS A THING THAT HAPPENED TO A PLACE AFTER A WHILE, OR IF IT WAS SOMETHING THAT YOU FOUND IN THE END.

HVERNIG GENGUR?

BLEAK HOUSE

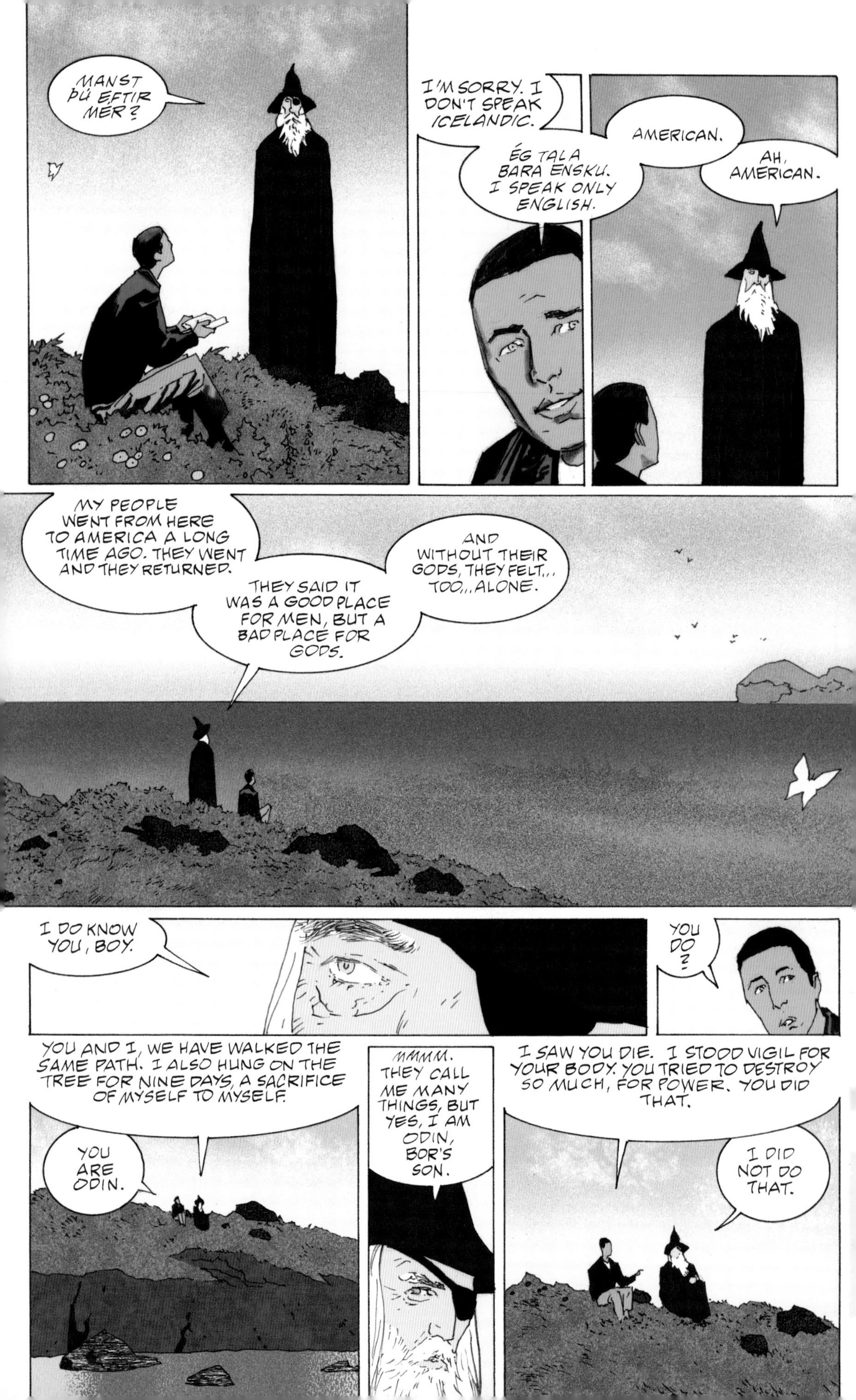
MANST ÞÚ EFTIR MÉR?
I'M SORRY. I DON'T SPEAK ICELANDIC.
ÉG TALA BARA ENSKU. I SPEAK ONLY ENGLISH.
AMERICAN.
AH, AMERICAN.
MY PEOPLE WENT FROM HERE TO AMERICA A LONG TIME AGO. THEY WENT AND THEY RETURNED.
THEY SAID IT WAS A GOOD PLACE FOR MEN, BUT A BAD PLACE FOR GODS.
AND WITHOUT THEIR GODS, THEY FELT... TOO... ALONE.
I DO KNOW YOU, BOY.
YOU DO?
YOU AND I, WE HAVE WALKED THE SAME PATH. I ALSO HUNG ON THE TREE FOR NINE DAYS, A SACRIFICE OF MYSELF TO MYSELF.
YOU ARE ODIN.
MMMM. THEY CALL ME MANY THINGS, BUT YES, I AM ODIN, BOR'S SON.
I SAW YOU DIE. I STOOD VIGIL FOR YOUR BODY. YOU TRIED TO DESTROY SO MUCH, FOR POWER. YOU DID THAT.
I DID NOT DO THAT.

WEDNESDAY DID. HE WAS YOU.

WILL YOU GO BACK--TO AMERICA?

HE WAS ME, YES-- BUT I AM NOT HIM.

NOTHING TO GO BACK FOR.

AND AS HE SAID IT, HE KNEW IT TO BE A LIE.

THINGS WAIT FOR YOU THERE. BUT THEY WILL WAIT UNTIL YOU RETURN.

SHADOW SAID NOTHING. HE HAD HAD ENOUGH OF GODS AND THEIR WAYS TO LAST A LIFETIME. HE WOULD TAKE A BUS TO THE AIRPORT, HE DECIDED. GET A PLANE TO SOMEWHERE HE HAD NEVER BEEN. HE WOULD KEEP MOVING.

HEY, I HAVE SOME-THING FOR YOU. HOLD YOUR HAND OUT.

?

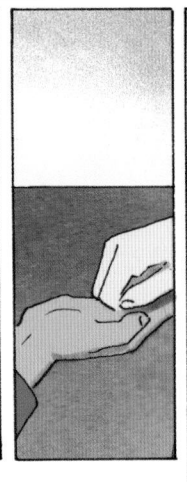

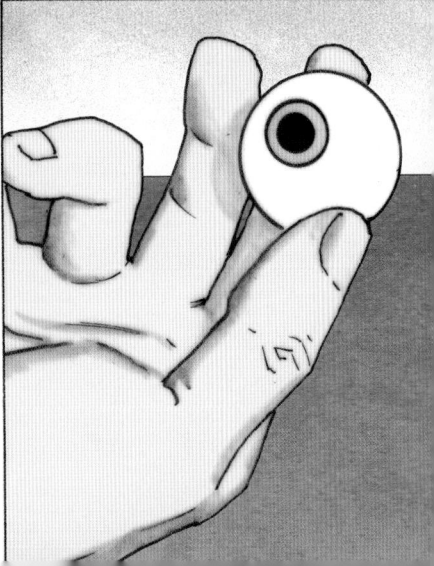

HAHA. YES. HOW DID YOU DO THAT?

MAGIC.

TAKK KÆRLEGA I SHALL TAKE CARE OF THIS.

YOU'RE WELCOME.

AGAIN. MORE. DO AGAIN.

YOU PEOPLE. YOU ARE NEVER SATISFIED. OKAY. THIS IS ONE I LEARNED FROM A GUY WHO'S DEAD NOW.

AND THAT'S ALL THERE IS.

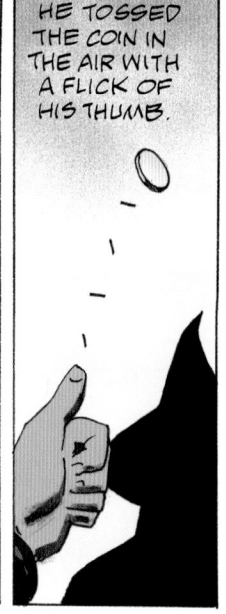

HE TOSSED THE COIN IN THE AIR WITH A FLICK OF HIS THUMB.

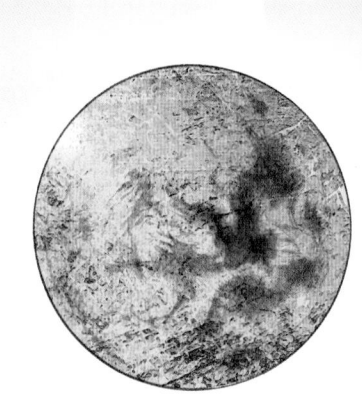

IT SPUN AT THE TOP OF ITS ARC IN THE SUNLIGHT, AND IT GLITTERED AND GLINTED AND HUNG THERE IN THE MID-SUMMER SKY AS IF IT WAS NEVER GOING TO COME DOWN. MAYBE IT NEVER WOULD.

SHADOW DIDN'T WAIT TO SEE. HE WALKED AWAY AND KEPT ON WALKING.

AMERICAN GODS
SKETCHBOOK
NOTES BY **SCOTT HAMPTON**

Oddly enough, though it was a book I'd heard people rave about for years, I hadn't read *American Gods* at the time I started this project. In order to keep it fresh and not spoil the story for myself, I read the book chapter by chapter as the pages came in. So, when the character Hinzelman was introduced I cast myself as this nice old guy who was fond of telling tall tales. Little did I realize that he turns out to be not nearly so nice later on.

I'll step in and play different characters in a pinch. Here I am as Czernobog and Nancy.

Jennifer Lange is not only one of the best colorists in comics, she's also my go-to model for pretty much anybody with great proportions. I cast myself sometimes as characters with garbage posture. Here she's playing Shadow. Our Maltipoo, Chloe, had to be restrained from sitting in her lap.

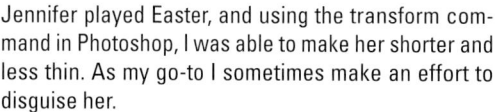

Jennifer played Easter, and using the transform command in Photoshop, I was able to make her shorter and less thin. As my go-to I sometimes make an effort to disguise her.

These are layouts by P. Craig Russell provided to Scott Hamptom to draw from.

MORE TITLES FROM

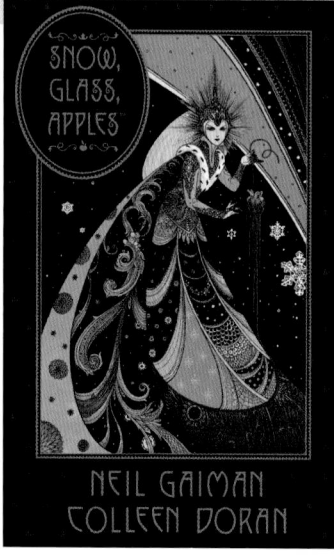